JOURNAL OF
REHEARSALS

JOURNAL OF REHEARSALS

a memoir by

Wallace Fowlie

DUKE UNIVERSITY PRESS   DURHAM N.C.   1977

L.C.C. card no. 77–79809
I.S.B.N. 0–8223–0401–5

Printed in the United States of America
by Heritage Printers, Inc.

to Pauline Hanson

Other books by Wallace Fowlie

MONOGRAPHS

Lautréamont 1973   *Stendhal* 1969   *Jean Cocteau: The History of a Poet's Age* 1966   *Rimbaud: A Critical Study* 1965   *André Gide: His Life and Art* 1965   *Paul Claudel* 1957   *Mallarmé* 1953

LITERARY HISTORY

French Literature: Its History and Its Meaning 1973   *The French Critic* 1968   *Climate of Violence* 1967   *Dionysus in Paris* 1960   *A Guide to Contemporary French Literature* 1957   *Age of Surrealism* 1950   *The Clown's Grail* 1948   (*Love in Literature* 1965)   *Jacob's Night* 1947   *Clowns and Angels* 1943   *Ernest Psichari* 1939   *De Villon à Péguy* 1944   *La Pureté dans l'art* 1941

TRANSLATIONS

Complete Works of Rimbaud 1966   *Don Juan* by Molière 1964   *The Miser* by Molière 1964   *What I Believe* by Mauriac 1963   *Classical French Drama* (5 plays) 1962   *Two Dramas* of Claudel 1960   *French Stories* 1960   *Baudelaire: Flowers of Evil and Other Works* 1964   *A Poet Before the Cross* by Claudel 1958   *Seamarks* by Saint-John Perse 1958   *The Journals of Jean Cocteau* 1955   *Mid-Century French Poets* 1955   *Sixty Poems of Scève* 1949

Contents

Foreword

For more than twenty years my life has been a traveller's, although I have been firmly attached to a teaching post: for twelve years in Vermont (at Bennington College) and fourteen years in North Carolina (at Duke University). My travels have been for a day or two in order to speak at some institution, or for a month's visit to France or Italy. But always I seem to be preparing the next trip, making the plane and the hotel reservations, choosing the appropriate bag, securing cash and traveller's checks. An hour before departure, I am always faced with the most difficult decision of all, one that involves in my particular life the most constant and the most serious moral issue: shall I slip into the overnight bag a book or a notebook?

A book would mean indolence, indulgence, enjoyment. A notebook would mean work, satisfaction of the spirit, reaffirmation of a life principle. The question is quite simple: do I have sufficient stamina during those long unoccupied hours of travelling—in airports and airplanes—to hunt for words and sentences that express my thought and which may be consigned to the opened notebook? Even bare notes and unformed sentences would give me some sense of occupation if not fulfilment. From my earliest years the reading of a book has never failed to stimulate a desire to write about the book, or write further in whatever literary project I had already begun.

At the moment of leaving my apartment, on the occasion of most departures, I solve the dilemma by choosing a volume from the Pléiade series to accompany the notebook. Not, in other words, a volume I plan to reread from cover to cover, but one appropriate for the casual reading of a few pages at a time, which, rather than interrupting whatever writing I am trying to do, may stimulate and feed it. I have used Montaigne in this way, and Pascal. During the most recent trips, I have taken with me Gide's *Journal*, not the first, but the second volume covering the years 1939–49. The portrait of Gide in his seventies commenting on the early war years, as he moved about in southern France, from Vence to Grasse to Nice, and from there to Tunis, where he finished his translation of *Hamlet*, has been for me the most constant model of a man devoted to literature. At a moment in history when Gide felt that all the efforts of culture might be on the verge of disappearing, he steadfastly labored over hard passages in German, reread the first two tragedies of Racine, revised his estimate of Renan, and marvelled over the exquisite beauty of a line of Mallarmé.

Memoirs are, in a simple sense, memories of the past. The act of writing them changes them into what they really were for the writer and therefore into what they may signify for a possible reader. To remember and to recreate is to adapt into a universal pattern an isolated episode or the ephemeral life of a sentiment. Nothing of the past should be denied or rejected, but it is a hopeless task to put all memories into written memoirs. A book, no matter how freely, how casually composed, takes over and imposes its own order on remembered episodes and dreams. The book creates the life in the same way that a nonbeliever might claim prayer creates God.

The writing continues, notebook follows notebook, provided the episodes, returning in words, astound the writer in their newness and significance to him. Even to himself he is different in the recalled passages, and during the time of the writing he is made strangely aware of the character whom his friends and acquaintances take him to be. As notebook follows notebook, he moves beyond that character into an experience not unlike metempsychosis.

It is not unusual for a memory to bring me back to myself in one of the various roles I have played—not characters in plays—but my own self in life, bending to the circumstances of a given moment and place that made me stranger to the same body and mind in other circumstances and other moments. But it is unusual to feel my soul moving into an object and becoming so possessed by it that I become it. That is metempsychosis, I suppose, the "big word" used on the first page of Proust and which Joyce uses at the beginning of *Ulysses* when Molly asks Bloom, "Who's he when he's at home?" Indeed it is a question we ask about our self and which this book of memoirs tries to answer.

The repertory of remembrances is limitless: faces, colors, actions, smells, verses, sounds. When one of them returns—usually in a flash and unpredictably—it brings with it a surrounding scene of action so intensified that it demands of me some acknowledgment of significance I had not acknowledged heretofore. Life is first lived—but superficially—and then it is remembered when meanings begin to accrue and shades deepen.

Memories do not exclude, but a book has to exercise some principle of selection. Here I have been guided by a love for literature, and especially the literature of France, which began early in my life and has never wavered. The teaching of French literature and the attempt to write books about it have been more than a mere vocation. I would call them now a love affair, scandalous and passionate, marked by all the traits that lovers bear: avidity, joy, ecstasy, jealousy. Almost all of the stories I am attempting to record here have been tested in the classroom to occupy moments of respite and relaxation for teacher and students alike. After the passing of a few years—or several years—the stories seem to be remembered more than the lessons themselves.

The writing of this book has revealed to me what I would not otherwise have discovered about myself: a strange concatenation of motifs and effects. At the basis of any such prolonged introspection, there is undoubtedly the taste for self-contemplation, as behind every confession there is the desire to be absolved. To confront the reflections of what we were once is a strange experience. We realize first that our childhood is our entire life because it has all the keys of the future. At the source of our being there is not only our self, but there is the mixture of races, of multiple personalities, of very distant pasts.

I prefer to look upon this book as a notebook, as notes taken on a man's life, as it remains just outside of his peregrinations and barely separable from a mimetic experience that is often hallucinatory.

JOURNAL OF REHEARSALS

I

Dr. Myers   circus   Chaplin   Pearl White

Memories have an insistent way of pairing off in couples. Among my earliest are two which are very different from one another, but which, through the years, have developed a curiously close relationship. They form now a bondage, and one explains the other. Like a marriage of two influences, they have produced me and sharpened much of the temperament which I might claim as being mine.

The first is a memory of sermons, of the rich vibrant sermons I listened to on all the Sundays of my childhood. The weekdays seemed to prepare for this event of eloquence, and the long Sunday morning service itself led up to the sermon as the climax of the week and the morning. I always "felt" the sermon by catching its intensity and power. If it happened that I understood parts of it, I was encouraged in believing that I had increased in knowledge and goodness.

Although I had been born and lived in Brookline, Massachusetts, the church that my mother and I attended was in Boston. Tremont Temple, as it was called, belonged to the Baptist denomination. The main services were held in a large auditorium furnished with two balconies. Nothing ecclesiastical marked the exterior aspects of the church. The fire was in the hearts of the congregation and especially in the words of the preacher, Dr. Cortland Myers. He was without any doubt the first human being, outside the members of my immediate family, who distinguished himself clearly to my childhood, whom I revered and thought of as a separate individual.

The platform or pulpit from which he spoke was massive enough to

[3]

hold the chairs of perhaps twenty deacons. They appeared first, just before the beginning of the service, and mounted the stairs of the pulpit in order of their age and dignity. I carefully watched each one as he sat down in his habitual place. They wore black swallow-tailed coats. In the process of sitting down, the deacons rescued these black tails, like displaced wings, from the seats of their chairs, and dropped them over their legs. The assistant pastor came in alone, just before Dr. Myers, in much the same way that the concertmaster of a large orchestra takes his place after the main body of musicians have been seated. The general aspect of the pulpit was not unlike that of the Boston Symphony Orchestra, which I was to watch a few years later with the same weekly regularity that I displayed for the deacons and pastors of Tremont Temple.

In the front of the pulpit stretched a polished metal bar before which Dr. Myers stood as he preached and on which he leaned in a vast variety of postures. He was a highly dramatic speaker, and the position of his body always bore a close relationship to the rhetorical emphasis and effect. In every sermon there was a climax, approximately five minutes before the end, and that was the unpredictable part. The gestures and intonations during the exposition and early parts of Dr. Myers' sermons were fairly sober and repetitive. But with the crescendo and accumulation of images and ideas and Scripture texts, when his voice mounted to high-pitched frenzy and his arms waved in strenuous accompaniment, there was a long moment of fear and embarrassment on my part. I remember Dr. Myers on one Sunday morning, in an instant of great eloquential heat, tearing off the stiff cuffs of his dress shirt which were deadening the thumps of his hands on the metal bar, and hurling them to the floor. No one laughed. We were used to such demonstrations which only served to support and project his words.

Yet the histrionics of Dr. Myers' sermons do not represent my strongest memory of him. He initiated me into the universe of speech. He taught me the persuasiveness of language so that it became for me, as early as I can remember, the ultimate accomplishment of man's intelligence. Through his sermons he even taught me that beyond speech extends another realm, which is composed of silence and which offers the most total kind of happiness to which man can attain. That doctrine was both shocking and awesome to me. Thereby he denounced his own eloquence. When he told us that the greatest of sermons were nothing compared to the simple prayer of a child and that the heart of God was more surely touched by penitence than by knowledge, I felt that I was beginning to understand something of the mysterious order of the world.

His words, which flowed with such abundance and which were said with such forcefulness and sincerity, were always concerned with the mysteries of God and with the persistent stubbornness of man in not effecting some relationship with God. One of my most distant impressions is that of Dr. Myers not liking man. Of course I am not sure whether this was actually the case; but the antics of men, their tepidness and their waywardness irritated him. The more he talked about them, the more explosive he became, because the discovery of one sin in man led to ten others, and the sum of accusations grew rapidly.

The title of one of his sermons, which I may have heard at the age of ten or eleven, survived in my mind long after all the substance of the sermon disappeared. It was composed of the Hebrew words *El Shaddai*, and followed by their translation, "The God who is enough." I still remember my concentration on the sermon and the enchantment I felt while the elaborate periods, articulated in every tone between *piano* and *fortissimo*, resounded through the vast hall. I came away that morning with a sense of satisfaction. It was more than the satisfaction of having been instructed in morals and religion, because that I had experienced many times previously. As I think back on it today, it must have been the satisfaction that can come from listening to the beauty and eloquence of words without necessarily understanding them.

Complementary with my early memory of speech in the sermons of Dr. Myers, is my first memory of silence, in the clowns of a circus.

I presume that the noise of my first circus was the loudest and most prolonged of any I had yet heard. It rivalled the gaudiness of the circus colors. Yet at intervals throughout the show, there were moments of culminating silence when a particularly awesome feat was being performed. Then everything would stop. All eyes in the gigantic tent would be fixed on one sole acrobat swinging through the air in the top center of the tent toward what resembled certain catastrophe. But he did seize the bar of metal in the correct fraction of time as it swung back toward him, and then succeeded in hurling himself to the position which climaxed all other positions.

At such moments they would even cease beating the drums, and all

[5]

other stunts would be over and the performers out of the way. These became wonderfully pure moments, consecrated by silence, which, I had first realized in a circus, was more exciting than noise.

The first part of the tumblers' routine in the center ring was confused with the activities going on in the other two rings. I readily agreed with the announcement that they were all members of the same family. Their sizes varied from the young lad and small girl, used to decorate lightly the topmost parts of the formation, to the massive gray-haired father who could hold so many on his shoulders. They were all dressed in blue, even the young woman (was she mother or sister?) who never participated in the actual feats, but remained on the side and seemed to direct with graceful gesticulations.

Gradually, as the compositions they formed became more complicated and more breathtaking, the contiguous rings diminished in importance and finally emptied themselves. The family of tumblers, now well under way in their leaps and somersaults, held the center of the circus, and I knew that another silence was being prepared.

I must have been as much interested in what they were thinking as in what they were doing, because I remember watching the expressions on their faces, especially the fleeting expressions which replaced the professional smile at the end of a trick. Before the new combination of positions began forming, in the brief moment of respite when the audience, too, relaxed and turned their eyes away from the tumblers, I could see on their faces an expression of such anxiety and loneliness that they became for me human beings. The lesson I learned from the family of tumblers at this first circus was the vast disparity that may exist between public and private life. The physical prowess of the actors and the applause from the spectators had not been sufficient to insure happiness for them. The fragmentary look of worry which passed over the faces of the boys as well as of the men, and especially its silence and secretiveness, was more significant to me than the cartwheels and the rose formations.

The triumphant smile, which camouflaged the strain and tension of the great moments when they supported themselves and defied the limitations of the human body, was accompanied by silence from the public and the band. In a certain measure, the silence marked their distance from the public. The pyramid they formed with their bodies, when it was finally intact, seemed to exist for and by the homage of silence. But it seemed also to push the lives of the acrobats into another world, to alter their personalities and make them unrecognizable.

[6]

After the disappearance of the blue-costumed tumblers, my attention fixed on the clowns. Thus far I had been only dimly aware of them. They had been moving in and out of the rings and along the fringes of the public, seizing distracted moments with individuals. But now I began realizing that they were the principal performers of the circus, that every distorted gesture they made was central and familiar to all men, that every grimace was a telling and deep reflection. The clowns possessed all the litheness of the blue tumblers, but they had deliberately stripped themselves of all beauty. This became the first real problem of the circus I wanted to analyze and explain.

Whereas the other performers in the circus had all sought to enhance their beauty with makeup and tight-fitting costumes, the clowns had tried to obtain the opposite effect of grotesqueness in their oversized trousers and their false noses. The clowns were not playing themselves, as the tumblers and acrobats were; they were portraying characters different from themselves. Between the real man and the mask of makeup and the ludicrous garb, I realized there must exist a far greater disparity than between the triumphant smile of the tumbler and the brief inward look of personal torment I had spied on. The clown was a character different from the man who played the clown. His makeup was as strong as that of a mask: it would not betray him.

The public laughed because it was not a real man they were watching. The solidity of his mask permitted him to play with abandon and recklessness. Nothing was too humiliating for him to undertake, because in front of the public he was not a man, he was a clown. He had become another being, only faintly reminiscent of man, hardly human, so distorted that it was permissible to laugh.

At first, I tried to laugh with the others and to let myself be carried away by their glee. But they became puppets of themselves in their laughter, uncontrolled in their hilarity. Whatever the explanation, as the mirth became more strident with the increasing antics of the clowns, my despondency and sense of tragedy grew. Their gestures were mechanical and exaggerated, but they seemed to be playing on the brink of a solemn game in which we all participated. They played with danger and fire and death, and still the audience rocked with laughter, unaware that the danger enacted by the clowns was transmitted to us all and that we were therefore mocking ourselves.

The clowns of the circus were the first example of the comic I witnessed, but I sensed, then, and have never ceased wondering at the phenomenon,

[7]

that the comic is one aspect of the tragic, so closely akin to one another that the emotion they elicit may be expressed by tears or laughter. After the silence of the acrobats, when they had formed, with their evenly matched muscles, the perfect human pyramid, came now the still more tragic silence of the clowns.

The white greasepaint, placed in a circle around their mouths, exaggerated the absence of words. I strained to hear something from them and for a long time believed I would. Then I realized that their gestures were words and that their makeup was so eloquent and so permanent that speech would have no place in their performance. I began hearing their silence and understanding it more completely than one can ever understand words. The pantomime of the clowns became comprehensible to me as the eloquential flow of a sermon did when I was unable to follow the details and the meaning of separate sentences.

Especially I learned something of the inexhaustible tenderness and impotence of man when he is caught and held in his drama. The more I watched the heavily lined faces and the red wigs, the greater sadness I saw there. The clown makes no entrance and no exit. He is suddenly before you as though he had been materialized on the spot. You begin to follow his solitary parade, where he exhibits all the heroic gestures of man in a jerky distortion, and you can never tell when or why he disappears from view. He borrows from the time of the main attractions and then effaces himself as if he were the most shy of all the actors . . . . Later in my life, when I was more able to make distinctions, I recognized that the clown depicts the tragic although his act is not tragedy. His improvised handshakes with children of the audience keep him always close to the human, whereas tragedy, which is beyond what can be humanly endured, must be unfolded at a great distance from the public.

The circus was my initiation to life. In the clowns I saw man unashamedly awkward, exalted by the noblest dreams and always tricked in some low way before touching their reality. Thanks to some metaphysical transposition, at which children are often very skillful, I comprehended through the circus the drama and the paradox of man: his greatness and his perpetual weakness, the permanency of his dreams and the fragmentariness of his actions. The tumblers, in the completed pyramids of their bodies which lasted only a second, and the clowns, in the constantly dissolving designs of their antics, represented man's desire for perfection and his incapacity to achieve it.

My thoughts, at first so stirred by the circus, found a new means to irruption in the movies. I might have become a more philosophical and peacefully minded person if films had not existed or if I had in any period of my life resolutely refused to attend them.

The Chaplin films I saw as a boy affected me in much the same way that the circus clowns did, save that in the darkness of a movie house I was able to give way more completely than in a circus tent to the tragedy of those films. On the Saturday afternoons when we watched the Chaplin films, in the midst of screaming children, I descended within myself in order to struggle against the power of man's fate, which I saw each week depicted in the familiar formula of the little man with the cane. With no difficulty, I transposed the formula into my own struggle with the world which, during the films, became clearer and prophetic. All men were in Charlie Chaplin, but especially myself, as he picked himself up after each fight where he was always vanquished and prepared his costume neatly and meticulously for his next encounter with the world.

From saloon to saloon, in the fantastic country of tough miners and crafty speculators, he stalked the girl of his dream who, like the world itself, preferred wealth and brute strength to the innocency of the heart. Like a phantom, his white face peered into all the dens of iniquity without ever reflecting what he saw there. Chaplin was beaten and trampled on, but his heart was never injured and his search never deviated.

This was the weekly miracle I watched. The Chaplin film was the sign of gaiety for all those in the movie house. They laughed from start to finish, from the initial shot of the little figure walking up the road toward the camera, swinging his cane of deceptive lightness, to the ultimate fade-out of the same little figure walking down the road away from the camera, swinging the same cane rescued from so many battles and skirmishes.

I puzzled over why we all laughed at the little man's somersaults and defeats, at his constant willingness to repair the universe, at his innocency growing so blatant that all the opposites of innocency joined forces to obliterate him. But he was never completely obliterated. That helped to reassure me. If the dream of the little man appeared ironic in terms of the world's wickedness, the reverse was true also, and the world's wickedness never succeeded in weakening the resistance of the little man's dream. The world, furious at being denied, waged all the battles, but the heart of one man continued to beat in the midst of the battles.

To elicit such fury became for me the mark of heroism. From Chaplin

I learned a lesson of such significant universality that it would be impossible to measure the debt I feel toward his art. His was a further lesson on silence, one which I apprehended better, having been initiated into the silent self-surrendering of the clowns. But Chaplin's mathematical precisions in tenderness surpassed the clown's more erratic and improvised depictions of terror. Chaplin's heroism was easier to follow because it was more stylized, more "precious." His films were a routine on life in dance form. They were almost ballets when the bully picked him up and held him aloft. His pathos was so poignant during the few seconds when he permitted himself the expense of pathos, that my compassion then for Chaplin the scapegoat flooded all my other feelings during the film.

The jerkiness of his body, so apparent when he tilted from side to side, and the utter gracefulness of his hands as they held, lost, and recaptured only to lose again, the hands of his sweetheart, composed the pattern and the epic of what was in my childhood, and has not ceased to be in my manhood, the intangible dream of the heart. The clowns had sketched all this in fragments. Chaplin fused the parts into a whole and danced before my eyes the drama of the ancient and innocent heart. He was a shadow, and speechless, but I understood, without hearing, what he would never have said.

But there was another type of film appearing at the same time, and which I watched during my ninth year, more frequently than the Chaplin films. It was the "serial," a meager chapter of which was exposed each week. The story moved so slowly that I was able to miss many chapters and still keep up with the plot. During the course of *The Ruby Ring* I fell hopelessly in love with the heroine, Pearl White. Because of Pearl White's blond beauty, sensuality is associated in my mind with danger. Each chapter of *The Ruby Ring* was the heroine's escape from one plot to kill her, into a more terrifying and more fiendish plot. The end of the last reel always showed her being thrown to the lions, or falling through a trapdoor to certain death, or being suspended head down over a pot of burning oil and gradually lowered.

Her beauty was just as awesome to me as the perils each chapter of the serial propelled her through. I was attached to her by the strongest bonds of serfdom, enslaved to her will and her whims. At that age I had never heard of metempsychosis, but I arrived at a belief that I had known her at another age when the roles were reversed, when I was the one endangered

[10]

and she the worshipper. From my seat in the darkened hall, I watched her slender figure move across the screen as if she had come out from my past to be recognized again and loved again desperately. I was the courtly lover, watching from a distance, loving only with my eyes but feeling throughout my body all the passions and stilled terror of love. In my fantasy, Pearl White became so fused with me physically and spiritually, that we were joined in marriage. She was my spouse, more real to me than all the beings I had encountered in my daily life. The screen on which she appeared always the same, entrancingly beautiful and exotic, was the true world of time and space. Only the illusion was true when I was nine years old.

My first love assumed the proportions of a myth, retold each week that I was fortunate enough to attend its representation. Each week a new sacrifice was enacted of a ritualistic sort. My pleasure was mingled with and perhaps generated by the always imminent loss of my spouse. Pearl White was my Eurydice descending each week to the underworld. There in my dreams I tried to follow her and rescue her, and was always obstructed by some demonic fascination I developed for her torturers and her jailers. Her beauty was so enhanced by the threat of torture and death that ever since, any placid beauty of woman has seemed to me less compelling, less desirable. The ritual of Pearl White's serial became my life of love. There was a lyric part at the beginning of each chapter when I loved her indolently and peacefully as she moved about in strange settings. This was my domestic happiness, when she was purely woman. Then the menace began forming about her. The fate of the ruby forced her into a trap of some dire invention, and my feelings altered from lyric anemia to extreme wildness of suspense. My imagination seemed to be willing that she pass through the torture so that I might love her all the more desperately, in passion, and so that I might sing, during the week to come, like Orpheus, of my lost love.

So, after the example of Chaplin, of the homunculus who taught me the cosmic lesson of the heart and the tragic lesson of gaiety, came the example of Pearl White, of the modern Eurydice who taught me the power of my senses and the fervor which rises from love when it is threatened. In the Chaplin films I saw the universe tilt with a single figure who brandished a weightless cane but whose real defense was an incapacity to participate in evil. His only defect might easily seem a virtue: his lack of intelligence about evil and the traps set by the wicked to demolish the pure in heart. But this was the trait of the clown too, who, speechless in a world of wasted harangues, cartwheeled jerkily into his place in the sun. In the Pearl White

[11]

serial I saw another process and another culmination. There, ugliness was matched by beauty and cunning by skill. There, intricate projects and machinations would be foiled by the seductiveness of a girl whose body could entrance the mind of men as utterly as the ruby of fabulous price.

As in Chaplin's art, where the clown had grown to be identical with the hero, so in Pearl White's film I learned to associate the physical beauty of a young woman with mental torture, with the need to inflict pain, with the setting of waterfront dives, with the type of man who would as brutally seize a woman as he would willingly steal a jewel.

Paradoxically enough, the Sunday sermon I heard did not contradict what I saw in the Saturday movie. The drabness of the school week, from Monday to Friday, and the slow-moving classes where my mind was only intermittently gratified, threw into exceptional relief and importance the silent film that culminated the week, and the resounding periods of the Sunday sermon that initiated the new week and helped to elucidate within my own special mentality the ineffableness of the clown and my deep longing for the absent Eurydice.

"Man" was the subject of the sermons, and he appeared readily in my mind in the sentimental traits of Charlie Chaplin, whose timid smile, breaking out when he felt himself on the brink of happiness, disappeared in a flash as if it had never begun, when the bully kicked him away from happiness. A discourse on man was the beginning of each sermon, but its climax dealt with some trap or other set by the spirit of evil in the world to deviate man from the good. This I was able to attach in my mind to the serial chapter, to the temptation of greed and the power of sensuality, in the midst of which Pearl White walked, playing the dual role of the girl enchanted and the girl who cast a spell over the good and the wicked, yes, even over the young spectator who, when she disappeared from view into some pit or some quicksand, was converted into a mythical singer, into a lamenting poet, whose world had suddenly become emptied of the one presence that had filled it.

[12]

II

Edward Devotion School   French class
Claudel's lecture   Mary Garden

Compared with my memories of the Sunday church service and of the circus clowns, those of the Edward Devotion School are vague and scattered. By the very monotony and persistence of school through my eleventh year, it had reduced itself to a dim background against which various nonscholastic events stand out. I do remember from the third grade the memorization of the interminable *Hiawatha*. Stanza after stanza, jingle after jingle we assimilated, parrot-like, until it seemed that hours were consumed each morning by its dulcet reiteration. A "project" on Indians was being worked out at the same time, and in the front of the classroom, on a large table, an entire settlement was constructed: wigwams, doll squaws and their papooses, and especially, a lake, which was really a mirror. I can still see that mirror-lake as it sparkled forth from the banks of white sand we carefully placed around it. For a time I enjoyed the bright shining quality of the artificial lake and resigned myself to the tedium of Longfellow.

Very recently, almost by chance, I walked over the hard-baked crust of the playground where at every recess period during those early years, I prowled about, agonized at never finding a pattern similar to the classroom, in which I could play. No actual scenes came back to my mind, or faces. But an old forgotten feeling of panic rushed over me. This was the site of my exposure where, in the presence of all the children, I was suffocated by my incapacity to improvise gestures and runs, shouts and games. The hard surface of the ground which, when I was a child, stretched out to great distances, and which, when I was a man, seemed but a brief space to cross between one street and another, resurrected the daily thirty-minute agony of wandering about in search of some design or role by which I might exist spasmodically as the others did. Any happiness I have ever had in life has been learned and rehearsed studiously, prepared and meditated on, and thus converted into a scene to reenact from a rigorous memory. My happiness has always been a performance of a part fairly well insured against failure.

To offset the memory of the playground, my mind travelled inside the building to seize upon a triumph in the sixth grade. That was the year of oral themes, when I could choose, prepare and rehearse what I wanted to say. I was constantly memorizing throughout the year, but I memorized easily, and hence lived in a kind of euphoria, in a well-ordered, well-planned security of speech. My longest oral theme, which I had spent a month preparing, was based on the sinking of the *Lusitania*. The event I described had taken place only two years earlier. The report, designed to move both teacher and pupils, carried well, and I was sent from classroom to classroom to repeat the performance.

In my twelfth year, in the seventh grade, French was introduced, and school became a new kind of place for me, where on three days of the week I was instructed in this foreign tongue. During the very first lesson, an accord was established between myself and the strange vowel sounds I heard pronounced by the teacher, and which we ourselves tried to pronounce. It was the discovery in me of a new region, not merely new muscles in my throat and tongue, but an entirely unfamiliar ethos in which my whole being participated. To reproduce the sounds correctly, I knew that I would have to focus and concentrate all my body on them. I remember that first afternoon trying to recapture alone some of the sounds I had heard in the morning, but it was impossible. I was desolate with fear that I had no ability for languages. My ears retained the memory of those sounds, but I was unable to articulate them. They had disappeared from me as dreams might. I remembered their mystery and their seduction, but I could not form them again.

An entire day intervened between the first and the second lesson, but when I heard the vowel sounds again, I forgot the past forty-eight hours' dismay, and made such an effort to imitate the teacher and remember the correct position of my mouth, that I made progress, and in each lesson thereafter, until the sounds became pure and the words into which the sounds fitted became familiar.

The isolated sounds, which I repeated to myself in my solitude as faithfully as a beginner on the piano repeats his scales, provided me with a sensual pleasure unlike any I had known heretofore. A permitted pleasure, it seemed, because it was so essential to what might become a future power in speech. When we began using the first phrases in French, such as opening a door and saying that we were doing so, it was not only a new experience in language for me, but I actually seemed to be opening the door in a new way. I seized upon the opportunity of making French into a ritual by means of which I might correct all my past blunders and come fresh upon the universe to manipulate it anew. French was to be, justifiably, my studied and rehearsed approach to life, the very kind I had been searching for unwittingly.

During those first two years, when I did not know the language, and to some degree ever since, everything about French seemed enchanted to me and quite distinct from all I had learned about life. Each word I learned to say had its mystery and its charm, which were enhanced by the strangeness of the sound and the ever so slight hesitation I always made over its meaning. The music of a word was apprehended a bit prior to its meaning. Music and meaning became dissociated as two separate experiences, and I consented to their dissociation in favor of music. Pleasure in the music of a word liberated me somewhat from the need of understanding it completely. I preferred to be hypnotized by the sound of French rather than stimulated by its meaning. Each word stood alone and was assessed by me for its value in euphony, for the power it possessed as incantation. What it actually stood for was of secondary importance.

This early strong interest in French would not have come about without the grace and charm and mystery of my teacher, Miss Henry. She was very young, and her beauty was that of someone inaccessible and solitary. She seemed detached from the school and unlike all other teachers. But why shouldn't she? She represented something foreign and exotic. She had even lived in France, and when she spoke French I was transported there in my imagination. By the magic of this new speech, the familiar walls and maps and blackboards dissolved, and there spread out before me an unforgettable land like a mirage.

Miss Henry entered our classroom, presided over by Miss Stebbins, with the dramatic authority of an invader who brings a new message of liberation and indoctrination. She was tall and very erect as though the

[15]

uniqueness of her subject had given her great pride. During the first year when she corrected pitilessly every flaw in our accent, she seemed always threatening us with her desertion. We were perhaps not worthy of this study. Miss Henry kept promising us a moment of revelation, a precise moment in time after which we would understand and speak with the correct accent, a moment after which our intense and awkward concentration would be no longer necessary. It was an unpredictable moment, but it would come if we persevered.

I believed, with Miss Henry, that simple grammar would never bring about this moment of conversion. She taught grammar reluctantly, knowing that it was a mechanical operation, of little mystery and therefore of little import. But Miss Stebbins, the homeroom teacher and our instructor in English grammar, who was a small white-haired lady about to retire from teaching, hovered about our French classes and peered into our French notebooks.

Miss Stebbins' classes were the most expertly organized and executed in the school. She dominated us by a reign of terror, but we learned more about English grammar than about any other subject. She gave us only a few seconds in which to begin our answers to her questions, and if there was a pause, she would tap out the half-seconds with her pencil against the top of the desk. The tapping, like the count after the knockout in the ring, usually unnerved us. To hesitate was to lose all and collapse. If we did not know the rule of the past participle or the dependent clause as fluently as we knew our name, it would be wiser to renounce all hope and sink down ignominiously into our chairs.

Miss Stebbins was agonized during the first months of our French course when there was no reference made to grammar. We were being taught to speak by ear, according to the approved direct method. Miss Henry was interested in teaching us the beauty of the French language and not the science of French grammar. She interspersed songs with pronunciation drills, and we heard stories about Paris if our exercises were well performed. So, almost apologetically, after several weeks of direct use of the language, Miss Henry dictated the first notes on grammar and inscribed on the blackboard the first conjugation. This was the lead Miss Stebbins had been waiting for. During our first free study period, to Miss Henry's meager present tense, she added all the other tenses of the verb. These we had learned in English, but in French there were endings that changed with every person and Miss Stebbins triumphantly taught them all to us. And after the verbs came the pronouns, and so on. We had really a second French course with Miss Stebbins, but it was a secret between her and us. She could now, without any pangs of conscience, allow Miss Henry to lavish her time on pronunciation and songs.

I was eager to know French grammar and was therefore grateful to Miss Stebbins, but I worried for two years that Miss Henry would come upon the class one day learning the useless imperfect subjunctive of some irregular verb. I imagined the terrible scene that would break out and could never resolve to which side my sympathies would go. Miss Stebbins represented the best of the traditional type of teacher. She was efficient and inexorable, and her sense of justice was comparable to the mathematical precision of her subject. But Miss Henry was unlike any teacher I had had. Her handwriting—when she wrote the vowels on the blackboard for the first time, I knew that she must have a sense of life different from all the people I had heretofore met—had the same kind of strangeness that her beauty did. It was the opposite of the Palmer system in which we were all instructed, and against which I then began revolting under the protection of this new authority of a foreign language. Learning to express myself in French permitted and even demanded a new set of values: different handwriting, new companions, new readings. My vision of the universe was doubled. I was becoming two boys, and French was the mask and the acknowledgment of the second boy, far more stylized than the first, far more sure of himself and happy with himself because a mask is real and tangible.

Miss Henry was the magician or the artist of this transformation. I was never sure of how clearly she realized what she was doing to me until one day, in the second year, she took me aside after class. She was offering me a white card. It was a ticket, she said, to a French lecture on the following Saturday afternoon at the Copley Plaza. The lecturer was not only a celebrated poet but the French ambassador in Washington. She added that I would be glad one day of having heard him, even if I did not understand all he said.

At the age of thirteen, I had never heard a real lecture in English, to say nothing of one in French. To hear a lecture for the first time, and in French, flattered my juvenile sense of accomplishment and my yearning for the unusual. During the intervening days, I often looked at the card Miss Henry had given me, and memorized the name printed on it: Paul Claudel. He was to be many things for me: my first poet, my first lecturer, my first Frenchman. I imagined a tall heroic-looking man, whose speech would be rhythmic and lucid since it would contain all the words I had learned during two years.

On my way to the Copley Plaza that Saturday, many things became resolved within me. Deep down in my heart I realized that I might not understand all that M. Claudel was going to say, but no one need know that. The fact of studying French had already liberated me because I was making the Boston trip alone for the first time. The Copley Plaza was a golden maze of grandeur. It too accentuated my independence and my new life. I was certainly the only youngster present and I took my seat near the back of the hall where, conscious for the first time of anonymity and lack of any accomplishment in life, I watched the groups of ladies talking and the preparations going on in the front to receive the poet-ambassador. At the circus and at the movies I had not experienced this same feeling of failure and obscurity. I tried to reason with myself and was almost able to formulate the explanation: this was a world more possible of attainment for me than the world of the circus and the movies. The acrobatics of speech and personality in speech went back as far as the earliest Sunday sermons of Dr. Myers. There, faith in God had united the listeners; here, love of France, of poetry perhaps, was bringing all these people together, and I marvelled that they had come to pay homage to Claudel and to his country and language through him.

When the long introductory speech was over, I was surprised to see stand up before us in the midst of great applause the least poetical looking man in the room. He was short and fat, and resembled, from the distance where I sat, a picture of Humpty Dumpty in one of my earliest readers. His head, perfectly round and almost bald, seemed expressionless and impervious to the ovation he was receiving. To accentuate his circular appearance, M. Claudel wore glasses with thick black frames, so pronounced that I believed them a comic accessory, a clown's trick, which he would remove later. But M. Claudel never took off his glasses.

He began speaking quietly and slowly, and although I did not understand what he was saying, I was sure that he was saying very simple things in a very simple way. Soon there was a pause, when the poet had spoken his very flat prosaic opening sentences, and, as if to put at ease the schoolboy who was present, he moved toward a blackboard that had been placed in the front of the hall. He began speaking again, but using even thinner, drier sentences than before, and with them raised his arm to draw a few altogether simple lines on the blackboard. The lines formed a house of oriental character. Then I did catch the words: *maison chinoise*. But I knew that this was no typical hard and fast lecture, that M. Claudel was playing with us, playing the whimsical innocent as if his fame and attainments permitted him such unorthodox fancy. I delighted in the blackboard sketches. They alone were lucid and comprehensible to me. The language, spoken with so little emphasis, passed over my head. So, I first knew Paul Claudel as a blackboard drawer of Chinese houses, and I was grateful to him for those drawings. The other listeners, who must have wanted a lecture on poetry or civilization, were doubtless disappointed by the arch-simplicity of the great man who, unwittingly, amused and held his youngest listener.

But now I was initiated into an adult preoccupation. Paul Claudel's strange lecture before his Boston audience marked the beginning of a new period in French for me. I had understood the words *maison chinoise*, spoken by a celebrated writer, and that instant of participation in the French language changed me from a schoolboy in a recitation class to a being who used the foreign language as if it were his own. Before attending the lecture, I had vaguely wondered whether one day I might be able to read Claudel's poetry, but now when the lecture was over, I felt that a part of my destiny would be to study his poetry and to understand it in French as one, possessor of two languages, might do.

It would be unjust to ascribe to French my one means of escape from the familiar world of home and school. Even before French, I had studied music. The piano itself never appealed strongly to me, and I never became at all proficient in playing. But about the time of Claudel's lecture on Chinese houses, I began to listen seriously to music, and this habit was to combine in a very natural way with my growing love for French. In fact, the permission granted me by my family to go alone to the Copley Plaza to hear the French ambassador, initiated a new period of freedom when I was allowed to attend concerts in Boston. I began discovering the world on my way to and from concerts and lectures. I found the trolley line on Beacon Street more interesting and crowded than the one on Commonwealth Avenue. The four subway stations of Massachusetts, Copley, Boylston and Park were like four different cities. Massachusetts became for me the gateway to Symphony Hall and the Opera House; Copley was the stop for the Boston Public Library with the paintings of Puvis de Chavannes and the dimly visible Abbey pictures describing the legend of King

[19]

Arthur; Boylston, deeper in the city and more mysterious, I used every six months to call on my dentist, the first man to swear familiarly and casually in my presence; Park was the station for Tremont Temple, Boston Common, Jordan Marsh. These were the worlds, varied and inexhaustible in interest, to which now I might go without a guide. For some time music provided the principal excuse for my journeyings back and forth to Boston.

The first concert I attended alone fell at approximately the same time as Claudel's lecture. It was a solemn and imposing program, given by the Harvard Glee Club in the halls of the Boston Art Museum on Huntington Avenue. More than the expert directing of Dr. Archibald Davison, whose agility I admired as he leaped onto the conductor's stand, and almost more than the inspired singing of the students, I was struck by the program itself. It was a booklet, of large format, because all the words of the choral selections were printed in it. Latin hymns and motets, and parts of the mass, as well as Italian and French poems, seemed designed almost as a course in poetry to instruct us and make us as learned as the singing students. Each program was a survey of the history of music. After the rich baroque music of Palestrina came a solemn Bach chorale, and so continued to the lusty jingling Gilbert and Sullivan chorus which invariably ended the evening.

The only sadness that came over me as I listened to the Harvard Glee Club concerts and watched the painted ceilings of John Singer Sargent, was the feeling I might never again hear such programs. And that was indeed true. The combination of well-trained voices and of a leader rigorous in his choice of the best in music occurred only this one time in my experience, at the museum concerts of Mr. Davison. My short trips to Boston and Huntington Avenue were in reality voyages of great distances and time thanks to Monteverdi and Purcell, to Perotinus and Moussorgsky.

I became proud of these concerts because very early I realized how exceptional they were, and I still believe that only through the combined virtues of Boston and Harvard could such music be resurrected and performed. Boston produced a race of people eager to listen to Bach and Palestrina, and Harvard supplied the necessary scholarship and erudition. I smile now at this provincial aloofness I had as a boy.

In the choral concerts I developed my first notion of history. To enjoy music was only one part of my activity. From the carefully arranged programs I began to have some notions about periods in history. Medieval, Renaissance, classical, romantic were terms I learned something about, and especially learned to distinguish. The precept of Boston's culture

[20]

might be stated in these words: to know is to love. I learned such lessons as these: to love plainchant would require some knowledge of the medieval world, of monasticism, of spirituality localized. To love art meant the learning of its intent, of the effect it aimed to produce and of the content with which it was involved. So, plainchant led me to a revised notion of prayer, and the Palestrina masses, to the knowledge that God had been worshipped, and might still be worshipped, in ornately complicated and highly sensual ways.

My adolescence, fully four or five years of the period, was dominated and tormented by my love for opera. By this time, the circus had become a childhood memory, and films I had grown to consider an inferior and "popular" art. But this proud attitude was possible simply because the gaudiness of the circus and the melodramas of the movies were fully present in grand opera. The new genre was a combination of the theatricality that had entranced my childhood and the art of music which the Harvard concerts had taught me to revere. Opera combined for me and released in me fairly basic primitive instincts and willed highbrow tastes.

The San Carlo Company, in its annual and sometimes biannual visits to Boston, introduced me to the Italian repertory. I began with Verdi and Puccini, and with *Faust* and *Carmen* sung in Italian. Each night the same valiant little conductor would take his stand, at 8:30 sharp, usually without any welcoming applause, and start up the band, with seemingly total indifference. He set the pace and kept it up throughout the evening, no matter what happened on the stage. Once, at Carmen's entrance, the steps on which she appeared, collapsed, but the music went grimly on and she sang the "Habañera." She limped more and more noticeably as the performance continued, but the stalwart conductor had trained a stalwart troupe. Once, in the final act of *La Bohème* we saw, even from the second balcony, the bed sink to the floor when Mimi, greatly oversized for a consumptive heroine, lay down on it for her death scene. But the orchestra went on, and the singing too, thanks to the imperturbable conductor.

The Chicago Civic Company came to Boston for two weeks in the spring. During the first year or two, I was guided in my choice by the fame of the singers. Three roles especially I shall not forget: Claudia Muzio as Aïda, Matzenhauer as Kundry, Chaliapin as Boris. At first I put off, and even avoided the French operas, dominated by a personality I had read much about—Mary Garden. The reports on her singing were doubtful and confused. She sang in less familiar opera that seemed to be produced at her request and to serve her particular art. So I resisted Mary Garden for two

[21]

seasons, and then gave in, because, after all, she was singing in French, and my love for the language had been growing.

My first Mary Garden opera was *Louise* by Charpentier. I borrowed the score from the Brookline Public Library and learned it well before the Chicago troupe arrived in Boston. The performance was memorable for me on many counts. Even before the curtain went up, I knew I had been won over to Mary Garden. I knew that I had avoided her thus far, in order to be introduced to opera in its standard and classic forms, and thus to be prepared for her art which would represent both a climax and a deviation personally communicable to me.

When she appeared in the first act, she was Louise singing the words of the French opera, but she was also Mary Garden, in a world of her own, carefully separated from the set on the stage, from the other singers and the orchestra. She acted and sang with such a unique quality of feeling that she existed alone, responsible for the entire work.

She made a visible preparation for every phrase she sang. I was able to "feel" her singing before it was audible. She would raise her right arm slightly outwards as if to lean on some imaginary prop, and then look down at the floor as she drew in her breath. During the singing of the phrase, she brought her hands gradually together, almost as if they helped to shape the words, and, clasping them just above her breast when the climax was reached, raised herself on her toes. This description will sound ridiculous for one who has not seen Mary Garden sing. But her mannerisms were not affected. They came from her intensity of concentration, from her need to encompass the entire work and project it in every phrase. She created the role on the stage, as no opera singer has ever done, because she was beyond all need of conductor and prompter. The work developed behind her, in another light. She was the work symbolically, ritualistically, standing before us all in her always imminent state of vulnerability. She acted and sang as if she were at all times on the verge of being sacrificed, but she was delirious with the idea as if it achieved her and translated her.

Mary Garden caused me to feel the religious aspect of the theater long before I read in books that the origins of the theater were religious practices, that the public enactment of a role has a propitiatory effect. Because of her art, more that of a priestess than of a singer, I watched *Louise* as if it were a mystery play. When Montmartre had become for Louise and Julien the setting for their love, and when she sang to him, "Depuis le jour où je me suis donnée," she entered upon a state of ecstasy so exalted that it isolated her from Julien and from all the rest of us. I marvelled how the intensity of love increased the solitude of the lover. When Mary Garden sang the words, "Ah je suis heureuse! trop heureuse!" she was already announcing her ultimate flight, the rushing out into the dark and the dispersal of all the emotion she kept contained within her as she sang.

When Mary Garden performed *Le Jongleur de Notre Dame*, I paid particular attention to myself and to the audience, to see if the same phenomenon would recur. In this opera she played the part of a young boy dressed in trousers, but the dance before the Virgin's statue when the juggler performs his tricks as an act of adoration, exhibited the same fervor I had watched in *Louise* and *Thaïs*. There was something more important than the literalness of the part Mary Garden played, something more powerful than the happiness of the young girl Louise, than the carnal temptation of the seductress Thaïs, than the juggler's dance of Jean the pure-in-heart. It was, I suppose, the unusual fervor of the singer herself who surpassed any role she portrayed. The assumption of a role permitted her to become uniquely herself. Each of the roles was a personification of Mary Garden, and allowed her publicly to destroy herself. A phoenix rising from her own ashes. Her beauty became resplendent just before the sacrifice was to be consummated.

The longest and most poignant of all her deaths was Mélisande's. Five successive years I returned to hear *Pelléas et Mélisande*, always performed with Mary Garden, supported by Vanni-Marcoux as Golaud and José Mojica as Pelléas. Then, the Chicago company disbanded, and my interest in opera ceased for several years.

The death of Mélisande which I watched each April possessed for me the significance of spring ritual. Each one of the many scenes is clear in my mind, but I remember the action especially in terms of Mélisande's hair. When the first curtain went up, all I could see on the huge stage was the mass of red hair covering not only her face but her body as well. She was crouched by the water, and the brilliant color of her hair was the only sign of life in the forest. Her hair was deployed in great fullness, but it was without motion. The sombre setting of the woods seemed to exist for the contained fires of Mélisande's hair, for her strange loneliness and her waiting. Later, when she appeared at the other fountain by the castle and tossed her ring into the air to see its reflection, her hair was braided and clung to her back. There we saw her childlike face and her mysterious terror at losing the ring in the fountain. Still later, when at the tower window, she combed her hair and sang to Saint Raphaël and Saint Michel, her untied hair falling in great waves of red flame, seemed to

[23]

symbolize, as it did in the forest scene, her detachment from other human beings, her lonely fervor and expectancy. When Pelléas appeared at the foot of the tower and her affection turned to him, she lowered her head and let him wind her hair through his fingers around his neck. In the scene of jealousy, within the castle, when Golaud humiliates Mélisande in front of the old king, Arkel, I could see only her hair being swung back and forth like a pendulum. All her anguish seemed to be in her moving hair, which again loosed, this time through Golaud's brutality, again signified her break with the world, her relapse into a child's solitude.

In the final death scene her hair was not visible. Only her profile and the pallor of her skin could be seen. All movement on the stage was reduced, as life—unprovided now with Mélisande's hair that had been its symbol, its abundancy and its fire—prepared to change into death. Mary Garden was able to make us believe that the mystery of life was about to take on the even deeper mystery of death. The curtain closed and over it the asbestos fell, because no curtain calls were permitted.

Mélisande's red hair filled for my adolescence much more than the simple climate of opera. It marked my season of conscious melancholia. I realize now that Mary Garden replaced Pearl White, the blond heroine of my boyhood. I was still following Eurydice, whose long hair could take many shapes. Music now resolved my loneliness as previously the depiction of sadism had in the cinema serials. But there was still much cruelty in the opera stories and the persistent theme of blond loveliness endangered. I was in love with the same heroine whose beauty caused disaster and who disappeared, as Eurydice did, into a land of perpetual night.

How perfect is the past! Eurydice had become, more than ever, the object of my search, because of the cadence of a foreign tongue and the enchantment of music. How glass-entombed is the pattern of the past! I see its formality, both mythical and insistently real. To recast it, no inventiveness is needed. Only the descent, familiar and forbidding, into a dim region where, always ahead of me, the fires from a reddish head of hair guide my steps.

III

swan boats   Fenway Court   Harvard   Povla Frijsh

I must have been about fifteen years old when I rode on a swan boat for the first time. That ride marked my initial distinct awareness of Boston as a city. The pond in the Public Gardens is small and decorative. It forms an exotic pause between the long streets that lead from the country into the city: Beacon, Commonwealth, and Boylston, and the center of the city —the Common and the Park Street section. When I learned that the swan boats originated from Boston's early enthusiasm for *Lohengrin*, I approached them more reverently. The Public Gardens took on more prestige for me because of this testimony to art, and I took my place in the boat, not so much for the ride as for the association with an opera and an aria I remembered.

The fellow who propelled the boat with foot paddles sat behind the large wooden swan. We moved so slowly along the edge of the pond that I could see every blade of grass and every flower. At first I found the slowness rather ridiculous. The craft was obviously constructed for children! But I have never seen more children than adults on a Boston swan boat. It is too lifeless and slow-moving for a child. But for an adolescent who has dreamed to Wagnerian music and for adults with a meditative turn of mind, no motion is more propitious than the imperceptible progress the swan boat accomplishes around the pond. The real swans and the ducks take no notice of the feeble monster moving among them. I can still enjoy the great physical peace that comes from a swan-boat ride and the slowing up of the world. Everything changes. The buildings become fluid through the trees. They move and collapse slowly in the opposite direction from that of the boat. Boston revolves in a cyclical panorama: the State House on Beacon Hill with its Bulfinch façade, the bronze statue of Washington at the beginning of Commonwealth Avenue, the Statler Hotel confused with the intervening trees proudly bearing on their bark their Latin names.

The charm of a city is in its variousness. From a country district and from a pastoral setting we demand coherence and a unity of tone. But a city—and this is what I learned from the Boston swan boat—is rich in its contrasts, in its sudden juxtapositions of the simple and the ornate, of the quiet and the noisy, of the contemporary skyscraper and the low provincial roof. As we circumvented the little island in the pond, I experienced a feeling of freedom. In whatever direction I might go, once the boat ride was over, I would discover a new setting filled with unknown people. Each street was a land distinct from all other streets. The city became the site of magic for me, the place of endless transformations, and the swan boat was part of the ritual to lead me into the endlessness and the poetry of the city.

Something akin to this magic I had already felt at films and opera. The concept of a performance, of people acting parts not their own lives, had opened up to me the freedom of life. I could never come to the end of my thoughts about the circus or about opera. Each performance, and, for me, each act of watching a performance, had so many meanings and symbols, that I despaired of reaching any one meaning. Here in the boat I myself was performing, and soon, in crossing the gardens and going down one of the many possible avenues beyond the gardens, I would continue to be actor. In Louisburg Square I would be solemn and sedate, settled into the age and peaceful contemplation the house fronts represented. A thin stretch of green would cross my center, as it did on Louisburg Square, and grace me with the decorous and the gently decorative. Then, on the other side of Beacon Hill, where the streets are narrow and populous, I would feel the city coming to me generously in its many lives, in its children playing under the lumpish buildings and chalking on the walls the name of their first love, or if they were not in love, some obscene word to mark their disdain for life without love.

After the swan-boat ride I was possessed of a new intelligence about the city and recognized its real dimensions as those of a magical place where the past consorted with the present, where puritanism endangered promiscuity, where order besieged disorder. The slowness of the operatic boat and the revolving vision of trees and buildings it had provided, had set

[26]

up in me a new mechanism, a new sensitivity with which I approached the city. I became the recorder, slowly engraving on my memory the pictures of people in the street, of Saint-Gaudens' statue of Phillips Brooks, of the Italianate façade of the Boston Public Library, of the Granary Cemetery on Tremont Street where the inscription on Franklin's monument to his mother and father always moved me, of the tower on the New Old South Church and the flower vendor who always stood at its base. I began, after the swan's tempo had transformed me from a blind adolescent to one who had opened his eyes and could see, not only the objective of his errand, but all the much more interesting objects appearing on the way to his objective. The useless haste and stratagems of efficiency against which a puritan like myself has to struggle were first recognized when I stepped off the swan boat and saw, as I turned my steps in the direction of St. Paul's Cathedral, all the many engaging adventures of the eyes and the mind that lay before me.

I had always been impressed with the sonorous three-part names, so dear to the New England past: John Greenleaf Whittier, Henry Wadsworth Longfellow, Oliver Wendell Holmes, which were spoken in the full form as if that gave them more stature and importance. But I was especially impressed when I first heard a woman's name equally endowed with three parts: Isabella Stewart Gardner. As a child I had been taken to her museum (or palace) to see the flower gardens that fill the central courtyard. When I returned, in middle adolescence, it was ostensibly to see the art collection but privately perhaps to learn something of the character of a woman who had made such a collection and borne a tripartite name such as I had associated with the most productive of our New England writers, and who had been responsible for the various stories I had heard.

Mrs. Gardner now belongs to legend. To do penance on Maundy Thursday she would drive to the Church of the Advent, one of the prominent Anglo-Catholic churches of Boston, and, on her knees, wash the steps leading into the church. At one of her receptions I am told she appeared, not erect at some convenient spot where she might welcome each guest, but supine in an open sarcophagus placed behind a grill. The guests filed past and peered through the grill to see their hostess's small red head resting on white fur in an Egyptian coffin. On that evening Mrs. Gardner had preferred to play mummy and become one of her own museum pieces.

It seems that only the history-of-art professors from Harvard were allowed to open the grill and approach the sarcophagus to kiss Mrs. Gardner's hand.

At Fenway Court, the name given to her palace, she created a world of her own by drawing on the art treasures and furnishings of Europe. But her museum is overcrowded. One grows depressed, walking through the various rooms, with the thought that she was a greedy woman, that the collection is booty pilfered, that she bought up everything in sight. Every museum gives me to some degree the uncomfortable impression of plunder, and I owe that impression to Mrs. Gardner's palace that seems the result of Americanized vandalism. Nothing can relieve the museum's effect of bulging rooms and erratically disposed objects because the grand lady's will prevents any change. Her temperament is thus encased, as are all her objects, and immortalized as are the paintings on her walls, looked at yearly by Boston school children and western tourists.

The first painting I looked at seriously and fervently was in her collection. The subject of the painting, *Europa*, was unfamiliar to me. I was unsophisticated in mythology and Venetian art, but I realized that I was undergoing a novel experience in my attraction to the picture. I was unaware of the sensual subject matter and the actual meaning of the drama depicted. I was caught by something very real in the painting itself, by the way in which Titian had placed the half-naked woman on the back of the bull, by the complicity between the color of the sky and the rosy tint of the human flesh, by the movement of the veils on Europa and the tensed muscles of the bull.

I suppose that such a discovery, as was Titian's *Europa*, is always a recognition. The medium of painting was new for me, but the subject of the painting resurrected experiences only half-submerged in my memory. Did Europa recall that mythology of my childhood in which Pearl White, blond and desperate, struggled with beast and man? Did Mary Garden belong to this lineage of women who threaten the world with their extraordinary powers? And did Isabella Stewart Gardner also belong to it, she who, shelved now among the loot, was permitting me to gaze on Europa?

My experience with the Titian painting revealed to me much more clearly than I had understood heretofore the role and the fate of a certain kind of man which perhaps I was: the interpreter who looks at the world since he is unable to act in it. I looked at Europa stretched on the back of the bull Zeus as he crossed the water, with the feeling that I had been left behind on the other bank. It was the same feeling that sprang up in me when the trapeze artist disappeared behind the curtain of the big tent, or when Pearl White was eclipsed in some sombre trap at the end of the serial chapter, or when Mary Garden sang her last notes at her nightly entrance into simulated death.

When I read in a mythology book that Europa gave her name to the continent of Europe, I wanted, with even more insistence than my study of French had induced, to go there. Europe belonged to my prenatal history. I was descended from the Celts, who were all instinctive bards, and from the Scottish soldiers, and from the Normans. Boston puritanism had forged out of those diverse strains a contemporary mask under which the varying lives and instincts of my ancestors continued to be felt. I was learning how to sing, quietly within myself, about all the dark forms who had retreated from before me.

The song, which a real Orpheus might have created, became the French language which I learned, as Mary Garden did her opera roles. I recited French and thus transformed my world. French was no longer a study for me, it was a mode of apprehending. Oh! I studied and read devoutly, but French books were not like other books. They were gateways to a new universe of feeling and understanding.

In the September when I was to begin my freshman year at Harvard, I fell ill with a long serious illness that kept me confined to bed until the following January. So I began Harvard in February, in the second semester, when everyone else was used to the university and its ways. During the months of illness I had tried to prepare for my first French course, a survey of eighteenth- and nineteenth-century literature. Professor André Morize was giving the course, and once, in school, I had introduced him when he gave a lecture there. His course was, appropriately enough, my first at Harvard. The hall was large and filled with two hundred students.

Professor Morize entered dramatically. As he rushed down the center aisle, silence spread over the room. He appeared like a giant among little men. He dropped his books noisily on the desk, and bending forward his shoulders, he buttoned his suit coat, rose up on his toes and began speaking. The directions he gave first about the course and textbooks sounded like a literary essay to me and I wondered how the actual discussion of the eighteenth century could be any better.

When the real lesson did begin, an elaborately drawn picture of the entire century was given, where each figure stood out clearly, where each idea harmonized or battled with all other ideas, where each part was precisely timed and reasonably proportioned. I followed spellbound this Gallic eloquence, and only feared that there would be nothing left to say in all subsequent lessons.

At the beginning of the hour, when his first sentences had compelled the attention of all of us, I thought that perhaps he had recognized me in the front row. But I soon realized he was as aware of all the students in front of him as he was of the eighteenth century in his mind and memory. Then, near the end of the hour, when he was speaking of deism, he suddenly interrupted the flow of his speech, and, looking directly at me, said, "Eh bien, Fowlie, dites-nous ce que c'est que le déisme." There was a silence, and then I answered.

Many times in my life I have felt a deep sense of gratitude for something said or done, but rarely to the same degree as on that occasion when M. Morize, at my first class in college, asked me to define the meaning of deism. To do it, he had to interrupt a carefully organized lecture and sacrifice a moment of attention from his class. It was not a pedagogic device. It was a means, simple and warmhearted, of welcoming me to Harvard, of saying that he knew I had been ill and that he remembered our former meeting.

So, the first words I spoke in a Harvard classroom were French, and they initiated a period of attentiveness to the history of French literature when I dispatched other courses as quickly as I could in order to devote all time possible to my favorite subject. Courses on separate centuries, on stylistics, on nineteenth-century poetry became the center of my life. Many of the courses were given by M. Morize, and his mode of thought, his exceptional combination of learning and sensitivity, his enthusiasm and vigor made of them such illuminating and gradually familiar excursions that I felt myself appropriating a French view of things. New England temporarily became a strange country. I began seeing the world through the eyes of Barrès, Leconte de Lisle, Montesquieu. I pored over histories of literature as a few years before I had pored over French grammars. There I found, more clearly visible and more courageously stated, thoughts on the high seriousness of life, which I had had myself in a disordered adolescent form. I was becoming clear to myself thanks to those many figures of the past who had written in a land and in a tongue different from my own. I was turning toward them because of what they had written, because of the themes in their books and the clear form into

[30]

which they cast them. Many of the actual themes I recognized as having already appeared in my own sphere, in transcendental New England. To follow them in French had the danger and the attraction of an exotic voyage. I was mentally invading France on all sides, taking possession of provinces and cities, stalking heroic and celebrated figures along the Seine and the Loire. Each new book I took up was a new invasion, and yet all the time I myself was being invaded. One day, although I could ascribe no precise date for it, I realized that I was at home in the land of France which I had never seen, that I was familiar with the names of its streets, the aspects of its buildings, and the books which its writers had produced.

This realization grew in me especially during the Harvard classes I attended of Professor Irving Babbitt. It may have been the last year of his teaching. His subject was Rousseau and the Romantic movement, and early in the course I caught myself paying more attention to the foreigner's view of French thought than to the main body of doctrine. At first, the course was shocking to me. I resented Babbitt's stressing of the denuded ideas in Rousseau without explaining the form of the work and the temperament of the writer. I was accustomed to a lesson planned in terms of *le moment, la vie et l'oeuvre.* But Babbitt plunged into his lesson with resolute sentences that might well form a conclusion. He proclaimed them as truth and then spent the rest of the hour ferreting out proofs of his claim. Everything his hand touched on—he always arrived in class with a heavy green bag of books and stacked them in front of him on the desk— or every quotation his memory could summon up, from the writings of Confucius to those of Whitehead, was converted into a direct use to substantiate his hypothesis.

When at last I accepted the fact that Mr. Babbitt was not a teacher but a moralist and a judge, I submitted myself to his persuasiveness, but to such an extent that during my first years of teaching I had to delete Babbittian tendencies and remembrances of a pose natural to him but ludicrous in me.

When Mr. Babbitt removed his hat in the classroom, his white hair illuminated his face and helped to prepare us for the opening sentences, always destined to shock or startle or amuse. I remember watching him attentively, as one does a leading actor on the stage before he actually speaks. His features were composed in an expression that almost never changed throughout the lecture. He was both Buddha and voice. His was the first contemplative face I had ever watched.

When I think back now on his oral sentences or reread those in his books, I realize they were all of the same pattern, all formed in the same kind of period, which was not so much theory or philosophy (as I once believed) as explanation and definition. He was continually defining the romantic temperament or the dualism in this author and the absence of dualism in that author. And we sat spellbound, hearing the verdict. Immobile in his chair, white-faced, white-haired, and seemingly tranquil, he summoned name after name from among the great thinkers of the past to stand at his right hand, and name after name from among the artists of the Western world after Rousseau, to stand at his left hand. At each lecture we saw the familiar litany-like array of saints on one side and sinners on the other, with Babbitt the supreme judge in the center, the reincarnation of a prophet who in the twentieth century curiously found himself in a Harvard professorship.

Romanticism was ever-present in the lessons flowing one into the other. Often the headlines of the morning paper would be quoted to prove the presence of this malady that was in the very air we breathed. The pile of notes in front of him never seemed to diminish. He rarely turned over one of the pages during the hour. The headlines or one key sentence from his evening's reading provided him with abundant material to denounce modern man. His memory for damaging texts was excellent. And then there was always the display of books on his desk, well-worn volumes bristling with bits of white paper. When he would say, "I have only to choose a quotation at random, gentlemen," our eyes would follow his finger as it opened the book at a very precise paper mark. We felt that Mr. Babbitt never chose at random, but that every passage, marked in his books, served the same purpose. Rousseauism was discoverable in every one who had lived since Rousseau.

Among his students, his lectures were celebrated for the number of authors quoted during a single hour. Almost the only question he would ask of his listeners was, "Who wrote that?" If no one recognized the sentence, it was fairly safe to answer, "Aristotle." But the members of the class had appointed a counter who kept the score of authors mentioned by name in the course of fifty minutes. There was a good amount of betting, and great excitement one day, I remember, when, instead of hitting near the average of thirty-five or forty names, Babbitt generously named seventy-five!

He so debased the name of romanticism for me that I had to put in years of effort to reconsider and reevaluate more justly certain authors, to discover in the romantic temperament something more universal and timeless than Babbitt was willing to see. He turned me, for example, against Wagner, who in my imagination became equated with a disease so pernicious that if once again installed in me, it would destroy every fibre of good.

Throughout my life I have been mildly indifferent to nature. But after Babbitt's lessons, I felt morally wrong to look at any part of nature. When walking along the street, I trained my eyes to watch the asphalt under me in order not to look at a tree! I avoided gardens and parks and never went into the country. My teacher had taught me, as Plato had of old, that even if I spoke to the mountains and the rivers and the flowers, they would not answer me. Only man could answer me. The city, protective of the works of man, was a more suitable setting than the countryside. So I became, temporarily at least, a kind of "humanist" whose principal discipline was the relegation of nature to a place of no importance.

Morize and Babbitt differed widely in temperament and in the art of teaching. But they were the two men whose examples caused me to approach the career of teacher with renewed determination. I had always, since the age of twelve, believed I would become a teacher. I realized that the teacher is not the preacher, nor the clown, nor the film star, nor the opera singer, but that his role, far less dramatic than theirs, is of more immediate use. He has the chance of bringing to life and raising to prime importance some art or some thought. Good students do not ask for explanations of art or thought, but for some highlighting and focussing. Morize arranged, with a remarkable sense of order, whatever subject he was treating: the history of a century, the life of an author, a single poem, and even a single paragraph cut out from a long passage of prose. He taught me the principle of organization, the simultaneous arts of reduction and amplification which teaching is. The teacher has first to choose from what might be said, and then infuse into his chosen themes a life which they would never have in any other circumstance. When, over and over again, the best "thought" in the lesson, the truest perception, is discovered at the moment of teaching, due to some accident of climate, or question, or rhythm of words, the honest teacher must acknowledge that what he has to say is of little importance. What counts in a classroom is manner and intensity. The thing said passes into immediate oblivion unless it is said in a particularized way. Morize's lesson was his organization, timing, symmetry. I can no longer remember what he said literally about Voltaire, but I do remember the architectural marvel of his lesson on *Candide*. Babbitt's lesson was his boldness and gruffness, his relentless reiteration of doctrine, his heavy plunge on a victim, his strangulation hold.

All my various idols, at all periods of my life, both performing masters and artists, have been measured and graded by me in terms of their power to "project" their lesson or their art. This is perhaps an appropriate page in my memoirs to write of the artist whom I watched over the longest period of time and whose art combined many of my interests: French, poetry, music and the skill of histrionics. I heard Mme Povla Frijsh for the first time when I was about fifteen. Between that recital at Jordan Hall, Boston, and her 1949 recital in Town Hall, New York, I attended over twenty concerts. For twenty years I heard every Frijsh program I could get to. When she stopped coming to Boston, I did not hear her for a few years, but then in other years I heard two or three concerts annually, provincial as well as metropolitan concerts.

The very beginning of a Frijsh concert was a spectacle in itself, an entire drama of taking possession, of demanding and holding attention. For minutes before the house lights were turned down, I watched the door on the left of the stage, and when it was opened, I looked into the emptiness it revealed for a few seconds. Then Frijsh appeared, as if she had come from a great distance beyond the door, and usually, at the threshold, when she was in partial view of the spectators, tossed a few words to the accompanist back of her, and then, fully facing the stage and slightly raising with both hands the long trailing dress, entered upon what she made us feel was a new world: the ever-so-carefully lighted stage and the precise spot in front of the piano which she flooded with the abundant silk folds of her dress.

Mme Frijsh was a large woman whose body remained immobile while she sang. Only her head moved and her arms. She changed so many times the way of wearing her hair that I kept in my mind a confused composite picture of her. The expression on her face, the toss of her head and the slight gestures of her hands, all supplemented her singing. She recreated the song primarily by her voice, but as she sang, her body and emotions were fully concentrated on the song. Her body was tensed or relaxed, depending upon the poem. Her face was sombre or gay or ironical. The miracle in Frijsh's art was the rapidity with which she could change from mood to mood. After the applause ceased, a few seconds of a complete turning within herself were sufficient for her to capture a new atmosphere and feeling. She waited patiently until the vision had risen up within her, until she was completely within the new song, and only then raised her head. A nod to the accompanist ended the meditation, and she was able to look squarely at the audience with such a changed expression on her face that we knew she securely possessed the song before the opening notes were heard. Frijsh knew there is a great spiritual distance between any two songs, and she had trained herself to cover that distance in a few seconds of such concentration that she also trained her audience to undergo a similar change, to prepare themselves for a new experience. Frijsh was demanding of her audience. Only those who were willing to make a great effort derived satisfaction.

The major prejudice to overcome concerned the voice itself. Frijsh taught me that the first requisite needed to sing an "art song" is not the standard beautiful voice, but the intelligence and sensibility that will permit the singer to understand the poem and the form into which the music has cast it. Frijsh's voice had strong and surprising contrasts. Her *piano* tones, a kind of falsetto singing, underwent through the years a remarkable change. They grew lighter and lighter, until they were of the most tenuous quality, although completely audible. She forged a soft voice as though it were an instrument apart from herself, and when she used it, it offset her natural "throat" voice that had a shrill metallic texture. This hard voice I grew to love because of the precision and strength with which it supported the poem of the song.

Each song excluded all others in its autonomy, and within it, the miracle was the marriage which the singer performed between the words of the poem and the notes of the composition. She performed, not the poem nor the music but the fusion between them, which was a third work. I often thought it was the "phrasing" in Frijsh's singing that explained the unique success of her performance. She had so completely assimilated the song to her vigorous memory, had so formed a personal vision of it, that the actual singing ran little risk of endangering or damaging the song. She achieved the real sense of performance by the fact that her understanding of the song was intact before she began to sing.

The opening song of each program stood apart from all the rest. With it, she imposed dogmatically her voice, in its middle natural quality. Neither of her extremes was revealed in the first song, neither the delicate nor the strident effect. She sang "out," in straightforward, unflinching fashion, to tell us all over again, for the tenth or twentieth time, that yes, this was what her voice was really like.

The first song established the relationship between Frijsh and her listeners. It was often an Italian song from the classical repertory. It was many times the Gluck aria from *La Sémiramide*: "Vieni, che poi sereno," admirably suited to a neutral bare kind of singing. After the long introduction on the piano, during which the expectation of the audience grew to the high degree desired and planned by Frijsh, the first full notes were sung and on them our attention was solidly attached. The art of this first song was its direct resoluteness. The melodic line was repeated over and over again, but always with the same bold courage, with such insistency that it became hypnotic. The quality of the voice was forced upon us. By the end of the song we had forgotten all other kinds of voices. Povla Frijsh won us over by startling and then beating us into submission. Our critical faculties were suspended, and we engaged upon an experience for the next two hours which was much more than that of a mere song recital.

I often heard as a second song on a Frijsh program "The Butterfly" of Schubert. This, or some other song comparable to it, never failed to convince the audience that they were listening to an exceptional singer, and that it were better to cast aside prejudice. The music was sung so softly and delicately that we wondered how the same woman could have performed this brief sigh of delicate sadness and melody as well as the first full-throated and somewhat monotonous Italian aria.

I still remember a song from the first Frijsh concert I attended. That is, I remember from it an experience of complete immersion in a world of lyrical and dramatic intensity. The French words of the poem were printed on the program. The poet's name, Charles Baudelaire, was unfamiliar to me, although the words of his poem, "Le Balcon," I recognized separately and tried to put their meaning together.

This Debussy song opened the second group on the program. During the first group I had become adjusted and subjugated to the singer's voice, to her strange un-American appearance and to the series of moods her songs created. But no one of the first songs had led me to imagine the possibilities of dramatic power Frijsh possessed. The high point of the evening was "Le Balcon" and it was carefully placed after the first intermission. The rich swirling piano accompaniment, almost Wagnerian in character, prepared for the violence and the sweep of the song. The first high piercing note on *Mère* and the following notes that seemed to rush down all the register of her voice, were sufficient to transform me from a listener into a participant. The Baudelaire poem and the Debussy music fused into one experience associated with life in its rhythm, sound,

[36]

amorous story, death of desire and renewal of desire. The final broad notes: "après s'être lavés au fond des mers profondes," quieted and renewed me. Frijsh had projected a cycle of emotions. She had constructed an entire legend of experience, beginning with the ecstatic satisfaction of desire in the opening stanza: "tu te rappelleras la beauté des caresses"; continuing with the dark search for the meaning of human experience: "ô serments, ô parfums"; and ending with the recommencement of desire: "comme montent au ciel les soleils rajeunis."

The next song, by Fauré, was the illustration of its title: "Le Secret." Its simplicity was its ineffableness. Its art was understatement and suggestion. Frijsh sang it as though it were one breath, one turn away from experience toward a questioning of experience. So much was contained and implied in the song's brevity that I felt that I should not try to remember it or understand what had been accomplished by it.

The song "Infidélité" by Reynaldo Hahn I heard at perhaps half of the concerts. Frijsh established in it a mood of loneliness and romantic nostalgia, and then at the very last line: "Rien n'a donc changé que vous," where her voice broke on the penultimate word, there occurred a breaking through of a particularized kind of sadness into a universal vision of sadness, a tearing of a veil beyond which the vision extended to all the sadness of man's solitude and which flooded the heart with an experience of participation.

In the early years of the Frijsh concerts which I attended, the final encore would inevitably be a French folk song, which she would sing seated at the piano and accompanying herself. The song was almost speech directed at us individually. The formal concert was over and this ultimate moment became sacred to me when Frijsh almost assumed the stature of a human being. She began to play the tinkling rudimentary accompaniment as if she were performing the most casual kind of work—at a spinningwheel, for example. Many times the song was "Auprès de ma blonde," which she tossed to us as if it were a balloon. Each verse was a puff which made it pause in the air, and then the refrain would catch it up just before it fell.

This central period of my adolescence was dominated by the varied escapes which forms of art offered me. They had been prepared in the previous years of my childhood by the circus performers, especially by the silent antics of the clowns, and by the films of Pearl White and Charlie Chaplin where I had watched alternately incomprehensible scenes of sadism and innocence. The pantomime of the circus and the films was the rigid formalized pattern for which I had to invent the emotions and the real story. No voice and no words helped me there. So I began generating the words in me. They were my first poems, clumsy, unwritten, submerged to this day within the storehouse of my subsconscious. I applied the process to the first paintings I looked at, especially Titian's *Europa* in Mrs. Gardner's palace.

The Mary Garden operas and the Povla Frijsh songs were my first examples of pantomime that was audible. In the operas the words were not mysterious. They were merely clarifications of a familiar film pattern I followed, with the added sensuousness of sound. But the poems of the Frijsh songs were only partly comprehensible to me. Most of them seemed to be about night ("Le Balcon") and many about the night of the abandoned lover ("Infidélité" and "La Statue de Tsarkoé-Selo"). The night poems were closed off from the ordinary world I inhabited. I longed to enter them familiarly. Each year that I returned to hear Povla Frijsh, I realized that the poems she sang had served as an experience for me. I returned to the darkened hall and saw at a great distance, in a circle of light, the singer-spouse Eurydice. She taught me the wonder and the mysteries of the world I had left, but the price of such learning was high. I had to leave Eurydice in her circle of light, abandon her to her role of singer and priestess of the transposed worlds of poems, without ever coming to her. Poetry was becoming for me a way of knowledge, and I was dazzled by my faith in it. But poetry is a difficult faith exacting great solitude of mind and body.

IV

a Paris *pension de famille*   Eglise de la Madeleine   diction
lessons   Baudelaire's monument   rue de Lappe

In the summer of 1928, I went to France for the first time. I was nineteen and ready for my third year at Harvard. From the age of twelve, when I began studying French, I had been preparing this voyage. During the first years each grammar lesson represented one step in the direction of France, one further assurance that my fate was inevitably tied up with a foreign country. Then, with the reading of French literature, I marked a new progress and a new approach. The enchantment then turned absolute. When the advance was grammatical, my face was turned toward France expectantly. But when I began reading the essays of Montaigne and the letters of Flaubert and the poems of Rimbaud, I lost myself in France without being there. I began looking back at New England from France, although I still walked along the streets of Boston. One day in the subway the names *Massachusetts* and *Copley*, as they flashed by, seemed foreign to me. What had become familiar were the names I had memorized from a Paris metro map: Vavin, Raspail, Opéra, Grenelle, Porte d'Orléans.

I knew of Paris, before seeing it, the names of its streets, its railroad stations and cafés, its theaters, its museums, its churches. I had traced out on its map itineraries that would lead me through the Middle Ages and the Renaissance and the age of Louis XIV. I had learned the peculiarities of each century by studying pictures of architectural modes and by memorizing poems. One bitter cold day, on Boylston Street, the verses that came to mind were not

> The sun that brief December day,
> Rose cheerless over hills of gray . . . ,

but rather,

> Le temps a laissé son manteau
> De vent, de froidure et de pluie.

I remember distinctly translating my feelings about a New England day by means of a poem of Charles d'Orléans. This was no infidelity. The rhythm of the French lines had held me because the words were not so familiar as those in the Whittier poem. It is easier to have a purely esthetic experience of a poem in a foreign language than of a poem in one's native language. Years later I read this testimonial in the essays of Ezra Pound. It applies to all my approaches to France. Every lesson, cast in French, whether it was poetics, history, politics, biography, theology, seemed more clear and more pure. I had devised a second register of memory. There was, first, my instinctive New England past, containing, for example, my annual visits to Walden Pond in order to evoke Thoreau; and there was now, secondly, my deliberately studied French past, containing, for example, my imaginary visits to Port-Royal-des-Champs in order to evoke Pascal. All expeditions in my life have been planned in advance and undertaken for some literary illumination or communion. The most elaborate of all and the most meticulously prepared was my first voyage to Paris.

France was the coming to life of literature for me. It represented the reverse of what had happened in New England. There I had first visited the Old Manse at Concord and then afterwards read the pages of Hawthorne describing it. But in Paris every scene resembled a dream materialization. Nothing was absolutely new. I remembered it all from books.

My first dinner in Paris, in the *pension de famille* where I had a room, at 3, rue Léopold-Robert, had no counterpart in any already lived experience. Yet I had the impression of being familiar with every part of it: the long narrow table and its red and white tablecloth, the alignment of varying types and ages among the *pensionnaires*, the center of the table, just opposite my place, occupied by Mme Yvet who owned the pension and who directed the conversation. Her eye was sharp when the serving girl passed the dishes, and seemed to control the portion of food one helped oneself to. But when the food was once apportioned in a reasonable kind of order and economy, her face relaxed and the sharp eye turned soft. Mme Yvet then engaged on topics of high culture as if she were a school mistress and we were her school children sent from many different countries. The French language had to be reduced to its most elemental form in order to include as many *pensionnaires* as possible. There was first a leading question on some monument, addressed to a newcomer: "Avez-vous vu la Saint Chapelle?" And a conclusive statement always followed: "Elle est magnifique, la Sainte Chapelle!" Each syllable was articulated slowly and loudly as if by raising her voice and shouting, she would be understood better. Food was the second topic. "Aimez-vous les haricots au beurre?" was often asked and permitted a lengthy explanation of the word *au*.

Mme Yvet's pension, my first home in Paris, was the resurrection for me of a Balzac novel. Each dinner was a recapitulation of scenes I remembered reading in *Le Père Goriot*. The setting of the crowded dining room and the atmosphere of paying guests each trying to hide from the others the secret pattern of his existence, forced us all, Americans, Swedes, Germans and French, into diminished Balzacian characters. The conversation, already so stylized and tense, due to Mme Yvet's guidance, sounded as if we were all reading parts from some novel. Mme Yvet turned us into puppets, speaking politely and saying nothing. The stories we told were never about ourselves and the past we referred to was that of monuments or historical figures. I never learned what the little English lady who sat next to me did during the day, although once she did say that she had lived in Paris for twenty years.

On the other side of the table and beside Mme Yvet, sat a thin pale boy of my own age, who had come from the States, knew no French at all, and evidently had no intention of learning it. We usually talked briefly after dinner in his room or in mine, and perhaps because of the pension atmosphere I refrained for a week or two asking him what he was doing in Paris. Then finally in good American fashion I asked him bluntly one evening what his occupation was. I had guessed he must be working because of his great fatigue at night, his increasing pallor, and the voraciousness with which he consumed his food. Had he been seated in my place at table, directly opposite Mme Yvet, he would not have been able to serve himself so abundantly. Each serving dish was held to his left and under the right breast of Mme Yvet, which was sufficiently large to prevent her from seeing over and under it. He would wink at me when the generous mountain of vegetable was transported to his plate, and then, before Mme Yvet could shift into a position from which she might survey his plate, he had devoured half of the mountain. His answer to my question was given directly: "I don't want the others to know, but I am studying ballet."

When he told me that Mme Yvet knew and was guarding his secret from the *pensionnaires,* I felt grateful to her for the protection her secretiveness had maintained. I had never seen a ballet or dancing of any kind at that time, and I wondered about the need of anonymity the ballet student felt about his profession. He described to me the dancing of Nijinsky in the role of the faun, and I felt the boy's convictions when he spoke of those few tense moments in the ballet when Nijinsky's life was realized, projected and transcended. At that moment in my room at Mme Yvet's pension, I placed Nijinsky among the precious clowns of my childhood, and told the American fellow that I expected one day to see him on the stage of an opera house, his face floured for work. This came true. Years later, at performances of the Ballet Theater in New York, I recognized him among the other dancers on the stage of the Metropolitan and sent to him across the footlights a silent mental message of greeting.

On my first Sunday in Paris I attended for the first time in my life a service in a Catholic church. Like most Protestants I was fearful of the Catholic church and certain that I would be awkward, ill at ease, and perhaps, by my ignorance of ceremonial, create among the faithful an ungraceful picture. I had been told in America how every one rose or knelt at the same time during mass, and so I was somewhat surprised and relieved to find that at the Madeleine people behaved individualistically. Some stood, others knelt, and still others sat. But I was more struck by the habit they all had of keeping their eyes open all the time and their heads erect. I wondered what connection there was between the beads they held in their hands and the ceremony being performed at the altar.

Gradually I realized that the postures of the faithful were being controlled by that ceremony at the altar and by the singing of the choir. The ceremony had a focus, and I believed I could place it at the very center of the altar. Three priests, in green vestments, moved deliberately about the center. The words they sang from time to time led into the various chants of the choir, and these seemed to hold the attentiveness of the parishioners. I was outside the circle. I did not know how to come into contact with the center.

This thought led me to a partial understanding of the function of the priest. It must be, I thought, that he stood for us, that his prayers encompassed ours. His movements were stylized and aggrandized because they were more than his own. "Scapegoat" was not exactly the word I was trying to use. But I began thinking of each gesture as propitiatory and sacrificial. My eyes and ears became more actively engaged. To follow the drama, one had to watch it. I was accepting, in some tentative fashion, a new attitude toward prayer by means of which one's mind is caught up in a reenactment of worship. I had been accustomed in the Protestant service to turn inward, to search for the motives of previous acts and to measure present desires. The ceremony of the mass was pulling me out from myself and projecting me toward the pivotal point at the altar.

This was not a new experience for me. Several minutes had passed before I realized that what I felt in watching the priests move about the altar, I had felt long ago at the circus when my eyes, fixed on the movements of the clowns, permitted me or even forced me, to break loose from myself and rush outward and ahead toward the image of man, not myself, but involving me, because he too was tilting and wrestling with the universe. I remembered one of the clowns once throwing above his head a red ball and looking at it as if it were the sum of all mysteries. He was unable to catch it as it fell to the sawdust earth, and he wept over his failure. Near the end of the mass, when there was a moment of great silence, I saw the center priest raise high over his head a small white disc which I felt must be the communion wafer. The image was so similar to that of the clown and the red ball that the moment in the Madeleine was united with my childhood and the first act of adoration I had watched performed publicly, not in a church but in a circus tent. The clown had thrown the red ball into the air, and it had fallen down beyond his reach. It was as if I watched the collapse and dispersal of his dreams. But the priest held to the small wafer with both of his hands. He slowly pulled it down as if toward his heart. No tragi-comic dénouement shattered the silence and the worship.

The unity and interpenetration of feeling among the faithful, which in Protestant services were achieved by the persuasive eloquence of the sermon, were achieved at the Madeleine by this solemn gesture of the priest. A sharp bell sound, in three parts, only deepened the silence. And this also reminded me of the key circus trick, which would be prepared noisily and then executed in silence. Until that moment in the mass, I had been unable to distinguish any words sung either by the priest or by the choir. Then, as if thrown into relief by the silence, three words, sung by a single tenor voice, were totally clear to me: *Ave verum corpus*. A solemn delight filled me as I heard and understood the words. A lecture from a freshman history course at Harvard, when Professor Merriman had explained the doctrine of transubstantiation, came to my mind. I repeated the three words to myself when the choir took up the subsequent and indistinguishable words of the motet, and they joined with the one gesture of the priest that had been clear to me. The words had come to justify and explain the gesture, just as they had in opera, in *Le Jongleur de Notre Dame*, for example, when, as Mary Garden died, she sang, "Enfin, je comprends le latin!"

My experience at this first mass was one of unaccountable familiarity. I had recognized behind the complex and ornate ceremonial the deep simplicity of the mass and had related it to the simple communion service of the Baptist faith when, as a child, I had watched Dr. Myers stand up on the platform each first Sunday of the month and say to the sedate deacons on both sides of him and to us in the congregation, "This is my body. . . ." There had been a silence then, comparable to the silence in the Madeleine when the priest raised the wafer over his head. I was proud thus to recognize Boston in Paris, my first pastor in this lavishly garbed priest, the Tremont Temple moment of quiet in the Madeleine silence, and relieved to experience my childish awe at the communion service in the Elevation of the Host.

Early in the summer I arranged through correspondence to begin a series of diction lessons with Mlle Fayolle-Faylis, former actress and sociétaire de la Comédie-Française. I enjoyed her letters which gave me in elaborate language the tram directions I might follow to reach her house. Even on the envelope she had written *très pressée* as if she were very anxious to begin the lessons and as if the postman would accede to her desires and hasten along the streets to deliver her epistle to my modest *pension de famille*.

I was not disappointed. The vestibule to which the maid led me resembled the setting of dream-fantasies I used to have after reading Balzac. Each decade of the nineteenth century seemed to be represented: portraits, bric-a-brac, satin-covered delicately legged chairs, mementos of the past behind glass. I had begun to feel that my breathing in such a room was obscene when one of the many doors opened, and Mlle Fayolle-Faylis came in. I had not heard any footsteps approaching the door and so assumed that she had been waiting behind it for some time in order to prepare herself for the encounter and enter upon the correct mood. Indeed it was a mood she entered on and histrionically projected.

[44]

She paused at the threshold, drew back slightly, raised her left hand to her breast, and after looking at me for a few seconds with tenderness and solicitude, said her first speech, still from the doorway, "Welcome to my country, dear sir." Then she glided toward me, extending her right hand. Her voice was deep and carefully modulated as if she were speaking a part. I imagined first that she spoke in that manner so that a foreigner might understand, but it soon became apparent that her speech was always recited, that her early training as an actress in the grand style of the Comédie-Française had made of her most ordinary discourse an exercise in shading and tone, in overstatement or understatement. The sentiments she expressed at this first meeting in the museum antechamber were so exaggerated that she forced me into a part also. I heard myself articulating sentences the like of which I had never said before. After all, I too had acquired the French language as an actor learning a role, and I could gild ordinary phrases with artificial locutions.

After this brief scene, Mlle Fayolle-Faylis reopened the door used at her entrance, and we went into another astonishing room. It was much more vast but had the same deathlike atmosphere of innumerable meticulously arranged objets d'art and pieces of furniture. In the center, with considerable space around them, were two chairs side by side, and a music stand placed in front of them. Here pupil and teacher sat, and the text to be learned was spread out on the stand as if it were a score. The free space around us was used in subsequent lessons when the lines had been memorized and I could move about, and then the rigorously arranged furniture became the backdrop as the spoken word assumed all the life in the room.

Mlle Fayolle-Faylis copied out for me some lines of the poet Jean Richepin, and the first lesson began. This must have served as initial lesson for countless predecessors, because even when I was able to emit the correct sound, the lesson would not be altered, and Mademoiselle would tell me how the sound was usually mispronounced. When my articulation of the single words had been verified, we proceeded to the grouping of words and the recitation of single lines. I had never had a teacher so bent on hearing errors in her pupil and so eager to perform herself. She could not resist the text and the temptation to declaim it.

Around her neck was a strand of black cloth. Beneath that hung a necklace of jewels, and still lower than the necklace swung two long silver chains, and at the end of each dangled a pencil—one blue, one red. These were her marking instruments. The score in front of us was gradually being covered with blue and red notations to such an extent that I was scarcely able to decipher the words of the poem I had not yet memorized. The blue marks signified one thing and the red marks another, but I soon lost track of the system and decided to depend wholly on my memory. I grew more fascinated by her search for the correct pencil than by the marking she would make with it.

After a few lessons on the miserable poem of Richepin, I asked for a better text. Since she was determined to convert lyrical poetry into pseudo-drama, I suggested a play of Molière I was interested in working on at that time. So we began *Les Femmes savantes.* By the end of the summer I had memorized the entire play. I moved about the room freely as I recited. The music stand would be put to one side, and Mlle Fayolle-Faylis would glide around the corners of the room to watch and listen from advantageous points.

On certain of the warm summer afternoons passed in this strange salon, when I knew the Molière text well and was relieved of the burden of re-membering it, I experienced a form of jubilation unlike any other. I re-member particularly the recitation of the opening scene between Henriette and Armande. It was a finely orchestrated duet. The two roles, far removed from anything personal in me, enabled me to step out from my own char-acter. The shades were drawn in the salon to keep out the hot afternoon sun, the center of the room was stripped for my actions and along the outskirts I could follow, by the sound of the silver pencils as they knocked against one another, the various poses of my teacher as she moved from chair to table. All the action of the first scene was in the lines themselves, in the rhythmically fabricated alexandrines. This was the first time in my life that I felt the intoxication of the actor. The text had been doubly learned, first as a foreign language and then as a series of dramatic roles. I was therefore twice removed from myself. The sentiments were gener-ated from the manner of reading the alexandrines: they possessed an or-dered and sequential form. This was the opposite experience from that of improvised speech and living. It was the difference between order and chaos, between precision and chance. It admirably illustrated the difference I was discovering between Paris and Boston.

After each lesson on the Molière play, I walked back to my pension, across Paris by various routes, and continued to enjoy in retrospect the sensations of reciting a French text and thereby living outside of life in a beautifully formed and dramatically conceived life. The city itself, on those late afternoons of August, became analogous for me with the pattern of the play I had just ceased reciting. I rehearsed the city as I walked in it. Many of the streets were empty between five and six, and so much of the city appeared motionless that I had the impression of crossing an enchanted land, of looking at buildings and monuments and pavements in which every memory of the past was recorded and immobilized.

The parapets along the Seine and the gray buildings on either side represented some of the achievements of a city and what we call civilization. But for me on those warm afternoons they were not separate from the land of France, from the soil itself and the cultivation of the plains and the hillsides that lay just beyond Paris and extended in all directions. The men who had designed the buildings, those who had constructed them and those who now inhabited them, had all come into the city from the country and had brought with them a knowledge of the earth and the seasons, of labor and the symmetry of furrows. France itself was the common heritage, and it was everywhere. The language of Molière I had memorized had come from the same people who had left the countryside to build and to live in the city. Long before I reached the Place Saint Michel, I could see the towers of Notre Dame. My back was toward the west, but I was walking in the direction of those stone towers that bore the light of the sinking sun.

Never was I able to pass a bookstore without looking at the window display. There is something very special about a French book just off the press. The clear lettering against the white page, the colorful band of paper compressing the volume and mysteriously suggesting with its few words the contents, the compact wholeness of the object, all awakened in me an insistent desire to possess it. If I went into the bookstore and actually handled the new volumes exposed on the center table, the desire grew more powerful. The name of the author at the top of the cover was a symbol for me. Each time I saw the name of Valéry, Cocteau, Suarès, Gide, Mauriac, on the cover of a new book, I felt almost as if I were in the presence of the man himself. To this very day I always have the feeling that I will not understand the opening sentences of a new French book. At some point I shall be revealed: all this supposed familiarity with French has been a fraud. All my reading and note-taking and my actual writing in French have been part of a preposterous dream-fantasy.

I liked to alternate my examination of the book displays with periods of walking along the Seine. The water was imageless, and I could watch it with a relaxed feeling after my concentration on titles and the names of authors. My eyes followed the sluggish river in its stone-lined bed, but my mind was filled with proper names flashing on and off as if they were lights. This setting in which I found myself had been cherished in my memory many years when I had lived far away in New England. Now I was a physical part of the scene. I was walking along the Quai Voltaire, guided by the course of the river beside which Villon had once lived and watching the sun-flamed towers of Notre Dame from which Rabelais' giant had once stolen the bells. But growing into this peace and transforming it was a new agitation of spirit, an ambition that had formed in the bookstalls and now enlivened the poetry of the Seine. The new books not only reflected all the past: the language of Molière and the course of the Seine, they had congealed the thought and the deep fermentations of the present. I was bewildered by the ambition to write and fix thus the words that rose up in my mind only to blot out the beloved scene of the quai and the river and the distant cathedral.

The will to write is a seizure and a frenzy. Everything counts henceforth: every acquaintance, every gesture, every tree, every cup of coffee. It is impossible for a writer to waste time. The vaster his reservoir of memories and impressions, the more rigorously he will choose and synthesize. The real delirium of any experience is its transposition into art. No matter how involved he becomes with people, the writer never lives, he observes life. His personal suffering comes from the terrible truth that he is unable to participate in life without recording it, without stylizing and adjusting it.

On several of the afternoons my walk ended with a visit to the Cimetière Montparnasse which was in close proximity to my pension. I had discovered in it the monument to Baudelaire. Ever since I had come across a poem of Baudelaire printed on the program of my first Povla Frijsh concert, he had been the central poet in my life. His face, which I had scrutinized in many photographs, haunted my mind when I read his poetry. My frequent return to his funeral monument in the Cimetière Montparnasse was a ritual of gratitude.

A thin column of stone rises up from the ground, at the top of which the head of a man, typifying the spirit of evil, rests in the cupped shape of two hands. The features, cast in a malicious grin, are almost hidden under stone locks of hair. Underneath this devil's face, which perhaps represents the traits of a possessed human figure, flat on the ground, extends a large slab of stone supporting the life-sized body of the poet wrapped in funeral cloth. Only his face is revealed. It is the same face of the photographs I had examined: the large forehead, the deep sunk eyes, the tortured sensuous lips. But the mask of death has been placed over the face and softens the expression and the features of suffering.

On one of the afternoons, as I was walking around the monument, I came across the name of the sculptor, carved in an obscure corner of the stone: Charmoy. I committed it to memory as I wondered who Charmoy was and whether he was still living. At dinner that evening I mentioned the monument to Mme Yvet, not so much with the hope that she would know about the sculptor, as simply for the purpose of making conversation. As soon as I had spoken the words "Baudelaire's monument," she asked if I had noticed the name of the artist. I replied it was Charmoy. Her black eyes were ablaze with interest, and all the *pensionnaires*, even the most ignorant of the French language, realized that some unusual revelation was to be made. We learned then that Charmoy had lived for some time at her pension and had occupied the very room I was living in that summer. He had fallen seriously ill after completing the Baudelaire monument and Mme Yvet herself had nursed him until the time of his death. She spoke of his courage, the promise of his work, and the warmth of his spirit.

After dinner, as I walked down the long hall to my room, to Charmoy's room, I felt a new intimacy with Paris. The drabness of the small room had now a meaning for me. An opening line of Baudelaire, "Bientôt nous plongerons dans les froides ténèbres," kept recurring to my mind.

My last evening of that first summer in Paris was spent in an unusual way, and helped to weld it together with the second summer, which came two years later, in 1930.

One of my cabin mates on the June boat crossing had been Alexander, an amiable fellow a few years older than myself and many years older in worldly experience. We had spent long hours on the boat talking about France. I knew books better than he did, but he knew Paris and the people of France with an intimacy I envied. With books, he kept telling me, you can go just so far, but the secret and fervor of life lie just beyond them. Actually he was quite a pedagogue himself, one of the most charming I have ever met, and he had insisted many times while we were together on the boat that he would initiate me to Paris his way. He thought my fate should be above that of the ordinary American lad who spends his first summer living in a drab *pension de famille*, taking courses at the Sorbonne and worrying about his accent. Of course, that was just my plan, but I should say in all honesty that if Alexander had been a bit more dictatorial or a bit more convinced that his summer plans and mores were superior to mine, my life might have been quite different.

At the Gare Saint-Lazare we separated. His cab drove off in the direction of Right Bank luxuries, and my cab toward Left Bank asceticism and diction problems. At various times throughout the summer I heard from him: either written messages on exotic looking cards, or actual visits at my pension. He always showed scorn for my way of life, but scorn mingled with wit. I had resolutely turned down his more involved invitations for jaunts and exploits I felt would have been disastrous for me, but I had promised to have dinner with him my last evening in Paris.

The restaurant we ate at was La Mère Catherine in Montmartre. I do not know which aspect of the dinner I enjoyed the most: the food and wine, chosen by Alec with the elegance of a connoisseur, or the general setting of the Place du Tertre where we ate under the trees strung with lanterns, or my host's jovial mood. I would guess he was exaggerating his festive gaiety in order to punctuate my first Paris summer. And he knew that I realized this. I marvelled at his power of charming everyone who approached our table: the waitress, the little flower girl, the man selling fur rugs, the couple sitting at the next table. For each one he had appropriate words, always spoken with the same bewitching smile. I watched each one succumb to his seduction.

It was late when we finished eating, and I remember his pushing me into a cab at the corner of the Place. We were both feeling the effects of the bottle of Pommard we had consumed, and found it difficult to move about and make any progress at the same time. The direction Alec gave the cab driver surprised me: Place de la Bastille. But this was his evening for directions, and I felt docile.

We crossed a good deal of Paris during that drive. The streets were a maze of wonder, half-familiar, half-unknown. I was recapitulating my entire summer, and Alec was recasting it for me with his stories. Every avenue and square reminded him of some adventure, of some meeting he narrated, always in the sober style of the gentleman.

When we got out of the cab at the Bastille, Alec took me by the arm, headed me down the street, and began explaining the rue de Lappe, which was our destination. It was a small street, composed of *bals musettes*, something he thought I should see. He explained that a *bal musette* was a small bar and dance hall where the poorer people went and was frequented by pimps and prostitutes and other dubious characters. I instinctively thought of the few novels of Francis Carco I had read: *Les Innocents* and *Jésus-la-caille*, and assured Alec I would not be a total stranger to such haunts. As we turned the corner into the rue de Lappe, I knew we were in a tough district, and I was happy to have the support of Alec's arm and the Pommard.

The characters under the gas lamps were dressed like those in a Carco novel. The wheezy sound of the accordion we heard each time a door of one of the *bals musettes* opened, seemed natural to me for such a place. We sauntered into the first dive, which was so crowded that we could make no way beyond the door. We backed out and tried the following one. We managed to get into the next two or three and stayed a little while in each one. I was curious to watch the dancers and the various individuals moving around the tables, but Alec's presence prevented me from flaunting my ignorance of such nocturnal life. Just when I was about to confess my less than elementary knowledge, Alec suddenly and unaccountably saddened. He began treating me like an obnoxious younger brother who was in his way, and soon deposited me at my pension door. I tried to learn in what way I had failed him, but he only smiled and asked my forgiveness.

I had resolved during our first minutes in the first *bal* on the rue de Lappe that on my next visit to Paris I would return alone and observe more carefully the habits of the street and the dance halls. This I was able to do two years later, in the summer of 1930. I had just graduated from Harvard, and although I had had little traffic with the world, I felt I had read about it in my various courses on French literature. So, on my first free evening I returned to the rue de Lappe. I thought nostalgically of Alexander and of his expert guidance. A sense of fear seized me at the beginning of the street. I walked along pausing at the doorway of each *bal* without being able to summon courage to enter. Down the street I went, fearful and cursing my fear and cowardice. Finally only one *bal musette* was left before which I could pass. I remember its name: *Aux trois colonnes*. I opened the door. Not many people were inside. A few couples were dancing to a jerky kind of music provided by a piano and an accordion. I sat down at a table, and deploying the small amount of Harvard nonchalance I had acquired in Cambridge, I took out a small notebook from my pocket and began writing in it.

When the waiter asked me what I wanted, he peered into the notebook and asked me if I was an *homme de lettres*. Flattered, I lied and said yes. Whereupon he suggested that when he brought my drink, he would bring me also the proprietor who liked *hommes de lettres* and knew personally a great many. I assured him I would be delighted to have the *patron* accompany my drink, and with a premonition I was not escaping literature as fully as I had expected when I entered the rue de Lappe, I bent down over my jittery note-taking and tried to feel buoyed up by the ever puffing and swelling accordion music.

When I looked up a few minutes later, the young waiter, smiling but ceremonious as only Latins can be, was ushering to my table a gentleman who might easily have been the president of the Republic. Tall and erect, gray-haired, immaculately dressed, the owner of the *bal musette aux trois colonnes* bore a perfect resemblance to Whistler's *Montesquiou* in the Boston Art Museum. The waiter introduced him as "Monsieur Albert." He bowed low, sat down beside me, and without hesitating, plunged into a very literary conversation.

The authors M. Albert discussed were all contemporary, but he made allusions to older writers in terms of the moderns. In keeping with European civility, he had not asked me a single direct question until many minutes had passed. Then his voice became grave and his head bowed in an obsequious fashion when he asked if I had read Marcel Proust. It so happened that because of my spring course at Harvard I had read through the entire novel of Proust. It was very fresh in my mind as the most profound literary experience I had ever had. When I told him that, he smiled with an expression both of relief and preparedness, and spoke his next words as if he were announcing himself to be of the noblest lineage:

"Moi, Monsieur, je suis Jupien."

The bold scenes in Proust's novel where the character Jupien plays a leading part, flashed through my mind in rapid succession, and henceforth in my life have always been associated with the playing of an accordion and the dancing couples who formed a background for the aristocratic features and cultivated voice of Albert Le Cuziat.

Inwardly I was at first incredulous, but later in the conversation I began feeling assured of the man's truthfulness. I learned how one side of this man's personality went into the creation of the character Jupien and how his name was forged into the name Albertine. I began understanding the personality of Proust as it had been reflected in Albert, whose mannerisms, speech and observations were Proustian, as a few years later I began to understand the character and the mind of Renan in listening to his daughter Noémi, whose subtle and rich conversation recaptured the thinking and the reactions that are called Renanian.

[52]

As Albert continued to talk and as his *bal musette* continued to grow more crowded, I felt more and more succinctly how in Paris the two worlds of creative achievement and daily living are close together, how they merge in a sane relationship, and how this marriage tends to diminish both the unreality of artistic creation and the monotony of everyday living. Perhaps I caught this awareness from the expression in the eyes of the young waiter as he passed by our table. He accepted the strange décor and the varied types of people he was serving as if they all formed one universe and were all bent upon the same search for an absolute, however clearly or vaguely the term might be defined. With the same interest and deference, he would serve a young couple at a corner table who never seemed to relax from an amorous embrace, and M. Albert, who, seated with a charlatan American *homme de lettres*, talked about a French novelist whose name was familar to him, but whose novel he would never read. The waiter served the wordless love scene in the corner and the wordy literary gossip at the table with that innately French knowledge that the two were related and necessary and respectable. He alone, perhaps, in the *bal aux trois colonnes* knew how profound, on one side of him, was the dream and silence of love in the midst of raucous accordion playing, and on the other side of him, was the effect of a sentence, "Moi, monsieur, je suis Jupien."

V

Henriette Psichari, 1932   thesis, 1934, Jacques Maritain
André Gide   Renan's Brittany   Mme Favre
mass, rue Monsieur

On the last day of my summer visit to Paris in 1932, I was visiting bookshops in the section of the Petit Luxembourg. My spirits were low, not only because I was leaving Paris, but because the subject of my doctoral dissertation at Harvard—the poetry of Sainte-Beuve—seemed insignificant compared to my new interest in the contemporary religious writers of France. I had been reading Léon Bloy, Péguy, Maritain, Massis. *Le Voyage du centurion* of Ernest Psichari was on my table at Mme Yvet's pension. Back in Cambridge, I would have to begin some of the actual writing of the thesis for which I had no heart.

Near the Church of the Val-de-Grâce, on the rue Denfert-Rochereau, I noticed a small bookstore I had never visited. Its newness attracted me. The books were well arranged in the window where I saw a new edition of Pascal's *Pensées*. Inside, the furnishings were simple and modern. The new books were placed on the tables and shelves as if they were objets d'art. I remained alone in this peaceful atmosphere for a few minutes. In the back of the store, behind the partition, I heard the rustling of paper and a few quiet steps. The woman who then appeared was startlingly beautiful. She was middle-aged. Her face had the regular classic features we associate with Greek art in its depiction of youth, and they had in this woman been softened and deepened by age. A lock of white hair fell over her forehead, but the rest of her hair was black. She was both young and not young.

[54]

Her expression and her first words had the same combination of timidity and assurance.

As I asked my first question, about the edition of Pascal, I wondered how I might prolong the conversation. It became immediately apparent that this would be no problem. Her answer about the Pascal edition was so elaborate and enthusiastic that twenty other questions occurred to me. We went from book to book on the main table, and each one called forth from this lady bibliographical information, stories about the publisher, the author and critical evaluations on the book itself. I did not know which to admire more: the information or the exuberance with which she imparted it. I kept adding to the little pile of books I was reserving for purchase because the description of each new book made it appear more significant than all the others, and I feared interrupting the flow of words or suppressing the look of excitement and fervor on this lady's face.

Finally she asked, in view, I suppose, of the kinds of books I had chosen, if I was especially interested in religious problems. I realized that the purely impersonal part of the conversation was over, and that if I wished any prolongation of this bookstore scene, it would be up to me to confess. I wanted to justify the time and care she had taken, and so reviewed for her the history of my interest in French, culminating in the present torment of a thesis. She agreed with me that the poetry of Sainte-Beuve would be an unworthy subject and pointed out that my interest in the religious movement in France might offer better subjects. Then she asked the leading question of the afternoon:

"Do you know my brother's books?"

The only answer I could make was a further question: "Who is your brother?"

"Ernest Psichari. I am his sister Henriette."

I knew very little about the Psicharis and tried to recall the main facts. Mme Psichari helped me instantly by saying that she was the granddaughter of Ernest Renan, since her mother was Renan's daughter Noémi. I remembered the passage about Noémi in Renan's *Souvenirs d'enfance et de jeunesse*, the Noémi he had known as a boy, in whose memory he named his daughter. I told Mme Psichari that I possessed one of her brother's books, and asked to see the other volumes. She pointed them out to me on a shelf and then left the room to answer a telephone call.

By that time I was highly excited and needed a few minutes' respite. My chance entrance into the shop had been literally an entrance into a chapter from the history of French literature. Not merely history, but the life of

[55]

letters, life in its most entrancing form, with the beauty of Mme Psichari's face bearing the traits of the Greek mountaineers who were part of her background, with her willingness to talk about herself, about the reason for the bookshop, due to her divorce, about her five children, about her own writing and the book on her brother she was preparing to write. I had a few minutes to marvel at the varied life of this woman before she came back into the room.

She resumed the conversation with the same interest and excitement as if it could go on forever. Our lives, hers and mine, were more mingled now with the dialogue on books. Strands of my obscure provincial New England life were being inserted into the general pattern of Mme Psichari's Paris existence. Thanks to my love of French, she was binding me to problems of French letters, to the personal problems of her own life. Never had a first meeting gone so far for me in establishing a design of sympathy and understanding. Mme Psichari seemed to be motivated by a will to give some color and contour to my approach to France, and I was motivated on that afternoon by a will to justify her confidence.

When I returned to Paris two years later, in the summer of 1934, many changes had transpired. I had rejected the poetry of Sainte-Beuve as a thesis subject, and had replaced it by a project on Ernest Psichari. Professor Morize, my thesis director, had welcomed the change, and Professor Ford, chairman of the department, had given his approbation largely because Psichari was a son of the philologist Jean Psichari. By correspondence I had secured permission from Mme Psichari to write on her brother and an assurance that when I returned to France, she would give me access to documents necessary for my research.

I tried not to examine too closely my motives in undertaking this particular thesis. My reading of Psichari, pursued at Harvard, had focussed my attention on subjects that were of deep personal interest. I wondered if I would be able to write objectively about such a figure as Psichari. And also, my attachment to the sister, Henriette Psichari, had grown during the two years since my meeting with her in the bookstore. Her letters had kept alive and strengthened the bond of understanding which had begun by such miraculous chance. How could I ever compose a book worthy of her belief? Would not her own book, about to be published, lessen the need and the reason for mine?

The tone of her voice over the telephone on the day of my arrival helped to reassure me. We fixed a rendezvous for five o'clock the next day at the Café des Deux Magots. When she appeared in the doorway of the café, I went forward to meet her and at the same time all fear in me subsided. Her first smile swung me back to the summer of two years earlier when I had stumbled into the rue Denfert-Rochereau and tied myself up with her brother's discovery in Africa, with the grandfather's history and the grandson's revindication.

Mme Psichari asked me first about myself, but my recent life had been so dominated by the study of her brother's books and the study of the first fourteen years of the century, that we were soon talking quite naturally about her own life and her family's. I began to realize that the drama I was trying to comprehend in the life of Ernest Renan and Ernest Psichari was reproduced also in this woman who sat opposite me at the small table.

The following day, on the invitation of Mme Psichari, I arrived at her apartment in the early afternoon to begin my study of the family documents on her brother. She had explained that she would not be there but that the housekeeper, Mlle Jaffry, would let me in and show me the room where I was to work. As I entered the courtyard of 22, rue Beautreillis, I remembered that once Baudelaire and Jeanne Duval had lived at that address, and that once Cézanne had lived there. Mlle Jaffry led me through a hallway and dining room into a living room that overlooked the rue Beautreillis. The meticulous order of the room reminded me of the sobriety in taste of the bookshop. On the table a neat pile of letters and notebooks awaited me. I sat down and began the irreverent task of reading personal letters and early manuscripts.

This continued each afternoon for several weeks until I had exhausted the supply of documentation. Each day about five o'clock the three sons of Mme Psichari came in for their *goûter* and I usually joined them. The oldest son, Jean-Gabriel, greatly revered his uncle Ernest Psichari. The second son, Michel, had already made for himself an enviable record at the lycée. The beauty of his mother and the Greek features of the family had been transmitted to him. He spoke about his studies at the lycée with the detached air of a connoisseur. The youngest son, Olivier, was a mere lad and was not paid much attention by his brothers, provided he kept his place. It was obvious he was the indulged favorite of Mlle Jaffry, whom everyone called Maffry.

When the note-taking labors were over, and there was no further need for the afternoon visits, I began returning to 22, rue Beautreillis for the evening meal. The miracle of the supper scene was the continuous animation, always supplied by Mme Psichari herself. It was the moment when she wanted to find out from each son the achievements or the failures of the day. She seemed to know exactly the courses each boy was taking and the characteristics of the teacher of each course. Everything was narrated and commented on in a full lusty spirit of joking and irony, of lightness and wit. But the facts were revealed, and the maternal advice transmitted despite the pattern of hedging and cajolery.

Michel's record was always impeccable, and he could be quickly disposed of and then enrolled either in his mother's service of inquisitor or on his brothers' side of the inquisitioned. Jean-Gabriel was stubborn and difficult to break down, but he so thoroughly enjoyed a play on words and a verbal castigation of his teachers that he would betray himself. If Olivier were worried about a composition to write, the subject would be seized upon by the rest of the family and tossed verbally back and forth over the table until ideas filled the room and Olivier's cheeks glowed with creative fervor. Later in the evening his agony would be renewed when, seated before the white paper, he would try to form the actual sentences that might contain the ideas so easily improvised at dinner. And even then, from the part of the room where his mother and I talked, he was directed and encouraged by her questions. She followed at a distance Olivier's composition while at the same time she urged me toward another kind of composition and discussed her own literary projects.

The evening quiet in the small apartment was of a nature unlike any I had known. Work, for Mme Psichari and her sons, was the prolongation of the studious life and accomplishment of Renan. He figured freely in their conversation, not because of pride but because of familiarity with him. Once, when Olivier was really trapped by some *devoir*, his mother read to him a page from Renan's *Marc Aurèle*, a glowing lyrical page, that stirred the boy and sent him back to his table reinvigorated by Renan's rhythm and language. There was an ancestor in this family circle. He existed in the uniformly bound volumes of his work, and also in the tenacious spirit of inquiry and in the courage with which his granddaughter and his great-grandchildren faced the problems of existence and work.

That same summer I attempted to meet and interview the friends of Psichari who had influenced his work. The friend whose advice I needed the most and whose approbation I hoped to secure was Jacques Maritain. He invited me to come one afternoon to his home in Meudon. The walk from the station to 10, avenue du Parc was auspiciously sun-flooded. The house rested on the flank of the small hill overlooking Paris. The city from which I had come was there spread out, distantly veiled by smoke or haze. No one else was walking in the street. The houses, modestly secluded behind plane trees and lindens, were quiet and seemingly closed off from the afternoon light and air.

I was shown into a long sparsely furnished room. Each object was delicate and gray. The atmosphere was almost cell-like, cool and dulled (by contrast with the sunlight outside), but the few chairs and the table and especially the few pictures converted the natural austerity into a room of subtle refinement. The house seemed totally silent as soon as the maid had closed the door behind me. I walked to the end of the room to look at a very poignant sketch of a face I recognized as Baudelaire's. It was strange to come upon the tormented features of Baudelaire in a room of such great peacefulness.

After a few minutes M. Maritain came in, closed the door behind him, and moved rapidly across the room to greet me and then sit down in the chair nearest to mine. I had seen faces resembling his in paintings of Modigliani. The broad line of the brow and the lower part of the face tapering to a fine point emphasized the importance and almost autonomy of the head. The shock of graying hair falling across the brow and seeming to incline the face to one side, added a youthful expression to a face that belonged to no particular age.

His presence and his words led me into myself. I began saying things I had not consciously thought before. The questions I had prepared in my mind, and on paper too, began to appear irrelevant or to answer themselves, and in their place, problems, more exciting and central and imperative, formed without my knowing precisely in what manner. Maritain's attentiveness helped mine. He spoke of Psichari from such a reserve of memory and with such intensity of feeling that he had to hold himself constantly in check for fear of going far beyond the questions I was asking in my relative ignorance.

What he said was not the mere rehearsal of memory. He reiterated the fact that Psichari's adventure lay beyond his reach and comprehension. He minimized his own role in his friend's life and deliberately turned aside all the human and historical explanations. Since that first meeting at Meudon, I never saw Maritain's face so docile to the inner spirit. It became incandescent: a face that retained no vestige of disquietude. The example of Psichari was an absolute for him, a pure example of God's entrance into a human being.

As soon as I brought up the name of Péguy, I realized I had unwittingly broken the spell. The actual expression on Maritain's face did not alter. Only the texture of his skin deepened, and roughened. We were still within the framework of the same problem of God's intervention in the existences of men, but in this new case the resisting will of man had been stronger, the combat between time and eternity more resolute. Péguy was close to Maritain's heart, but he had been difficult. In Psichari's case the human drama had been resolved and had changed into the divine drama. In Péguy's case the human drama had continued, always appropriating more depth from the life of prayer, but never completely absorbing or converting the stubbornness of the artist.

When the conversation was ended, Maritain accompanied me along the path to the metal gate opening on the sidewalk. Sensitive to the rich pattern and significance of his words, I was puzzled during those last minutes as to how I might terminate our conversation and at the same time indicate my gratitude and my adherence to much of what had been said. Maritain took this problem out of my hands. He ended his sentence which was still a part of the discussion and then added, as he turned to go back, "Priez pour moi."

This was the first time anyone had made that particular request of me. The words were not said as a mechanical formula, and they gave me an overpowering sense of oneness with the world and creation. I was blocked and garrotted. The steps I took down the street toward the Meudon station were no longer those uniquely personal steps I had heretofore taken all my life. My being seemed merged with all others, with the movement of the universe, with the past of France, whose meaning, like that of a palimpsest, I was trying to decipher.

Thanks to Mme Psichari and to M. Maritain I met several friends of Psichari who helped me to see more clearly into his character. I met with no adverse criticism and no hesitancy of approval as concerned my subject. Psichari had been loved by his family and friends. In only one book had I come upon a sentence expressing doubt on the question and example of Renan's grandson. This book was Le Voyage au Congo by André Gide. My curiosity was stirred to hear a more detailed version of Gide's criticism. In my notebooks I had a rich collection of testimonials of praise and appreciation and gratitude for Psichari. And not a syllable of censure. I knew that Gide's attitude would be different, and valuable as antidote. So, in a letter composed of very precise questions, sent to his publisher, I requested his counsel. His answer came back almost immediately: a thin sheet of paper on which the small delicately written words mounted almost up the page from left to right. "Venez me voir mercredi matin à 9 heures. Je ne peux pas mettre par écrit ce que j'ai à vous dire." ("Come Wednesday morning at 9:00. I can't put in writing what I have to tell you.")

That Tuesday night I was sleepless through anxiety and anticipation. Gide was one of the contemporary writers I had read the most carefully and for whose position as artist I had the most unqualified respect. His work had revealed to me much more than a system of moral evaluations and psychological insights. His books remain alive because of the unique quality of his sentences. They are penetrating without being dogmatic. I had learned to read them as examples of an art form consubstantial with the tormented questioning of man's mind, with his tireless search and curiosity, with his attentiveness. Gide had ended this first letter to me with the words *bien attentivement*, and that had seemed to summarize succinctly his attitude.

When I arrived at 1 bis rue Vaneau, it seemed preposterous to ask the concierge for M. Gide's apartment. But without any surprise, she directed me to the right floor. A maid showed me into a small anteroom, and in a very few minutes I heard Gide's voice in the hall as he approached the door. His greeting was simple and almost businesslike. He ushered me into a very large room as he said: "I shall keep you only five minutes." With those words as warning, I plunged immediately into the most crucial questions that disturbed me about Psichari. Gide's first answers were so direct and luminous that they incited me to other questions of a more general nature, although for some time I continued using the name Psichari as motif. Soon he turned questioner. "Do you know the Psichari family?" he asked, and when I replied affirmatively, he said, "What a pity! Now it will be hard for you to write this book for yourself; you will have to write it for the family. They will help you, of course, but they will obligate you also."

Many more than five minutes had passed, when with a nod of my head— I could not interrupt our speech because there was a steady flow of words by then—I indicated that perhaps I should leave. But M. Gide, with a firm gesture of his hand, indicated that it was no longer necessary for me to leave.

This first conversation with Gide remained literary, and passionately so. He condensed his thoughts on Psichari into faultless sentences. I remember his concluding sentence of that first topic: "I should like to have met Ernest Psichari in Africa." Those words relieved Gide's former sentences of their tinge of dogmatism and critical stricture. This happened to every part of the conversation. What resembled the formulation of dogma or canon would be achieved, only to be followed by a sentence of such deleting quality that when all was said, the problem remained nude and trembling, as unsolved as when it was first articulated.

We moved from French literature to contemporary American writers, and here Gide became insistent and eager, almost avid in his questions. He made me feel I knew much more than I actually did about the literature of my country. I do not believe he was affecting any enthusiasm. My own attention was divided between the effort to say something cogent about whatever book was being discussed and the effort to follow the use to which Gide was submitting this conversation. No matter how inept or inane my remarks were, Gide would make something out of them.

As the conversation proceeded, I was able to settle more easily into my chair and observe my surroundings. We were both very far into the room: Gide seated behind a large desk or table, and myself at the side of the table. There was much space and depth. On the walls hung a few decorative objects, ostensibly from Africa: masks and spears, shields and other hunting instruments. The Algerian and Tunisian scenes in Gide's writings, as well as the Congo, flashed through my mind, and I found it difficult to imagine in such settings this man whose gestures were those of the cultivated Frenchman, whose voice was clear and incisive as he spoke of contemporary writers.

The only connection I was able to establish between Gide and the African objects on the walls was the darkened color of his skin. His face and hands had been exposed to the sun. His head was bald, and the skin was drawn tightly over the bone structure. If I half closed my eyes, his head and face seemed that of an Egyptian mummy: a brown baked complexion and clear small features. Age was depicted on his face: years of living and thinking and self-cultivation. But the present also was depicted there: the agitated restless present moving against the past. The present imperiled the stability of the past. Every minute a new light came into Gide's eyes that contradicted their permanent color as if the acquired wisdom of a lifetime were suddenly questioned and about to be supplanted by a newer insight. As his words reduced or expanded whatever was being expressed, so the expression of his eyes reflected the degree of fervor his thoughts incited. In conversation Gide resembled my idea of him as a writer. His oral sentences were not unlike the written sentences of his *Journal*. The same quality of aliveness characterized them.

[62]

When I stood up to leave, my watch marked 11:30. I was overcome with remorse at having stayed so long. I asked Gide if he would ever consider coming to America. He smiled as if he understood the personal thought that lay behind my question, and said, "You will come back here. The winds do not blow me in that direction." The masks of the African medicine men supported this statement, and Gide's own face, a living mask of intense concentration, confirmed it too. I knew he was a man who had constructed for himself a precise pattern of life within which freedom of thought and experience were also forged and then destroyed in a daily delirium and justification of self.

In August I went to Perros-Guirec, in Brittany, where the Psichari family had always spent their summers. During the latter part of Renan's life, he had occupied a large house called Rosmapamon, on the opposite side of the bay from Perros, and there he had surrounded himself with his children and grandchildren. But his daughter, Mme Noémi Renan, had of recent years purchased a small house, called Saint-Jacques, in Perros itself. Directly opposite this stone cottage stood a large ordinary looking building which was the convent of Saint Jacques, most of which was divided into rooms for boarders. There, Mme Psichari, who, with Olivier, was living with her mother, secured a room for me.

She must have told the nuns I was writing a book on her brother because I was welcomed at the door by the Mother Superior herself, flanked by two younger and smaller Sisters, and informed immediately that I was not the only writer in residence at the convent. When I heard the name of the "other" writer (little did they suspect that I was merely a graduate student from Harvard, of a race not in the least unusual!), my first impression was that they were having a little canonical joke with me. I heard "Monsieur le Comte" first, and then the fuller name, "Monsieur le Comte de la Haute-Chambre." Their voices were so low and respectful that I could not quite make out whether they were directing me to my room or really announcing the man whose small figure was by then shoving a way through the group of nuns.

His opening sentence was of exceptional length and ornateness. It provided me time in which to observe his physical aspect—he was dressed in tweed knickerbockers and a white sport shirt opened at the neck—as well as the keenly alert expressiveness of his face. His complexion was ruddy and his head round and large, crowned with a circle of white hair.

He seized my bag and dragged me to the stairway. His speech, composed of seventeenth-century periods, was uninterrupted. When we arrived at the door of my room, he left me abruptly with a final sentence: "Nous aurons le temps de nous feuilleter" ("We shall have time to turn one another's pages"), which I did not know whether to interpret obscenely or imagistically.

I liked the bare white room, as cell-like as any I had heretofore inhabited, but left it almost immediately in order to go across the street to pay my respects to Mme Renan. I found her alone in the tiny garden attached to the house. The chair on which she was seated sagged to one side with the sloping land. The house had fastened itself resolutely into the slope, but the plot of garden with its few bright orange blooms and single fruit tree was precariously slanting.

The fleshiness of her face, brought on by her advanced years, had not concealed the traits of purity and regularity in her expression. The spectacles she wore came so far down on her nose that I could see her eyes. The light of the Breton sky was favorable to them. They were a faint blue, or rather a bluish green, a color transmitted by her ancestors who had watched the sea and had looked into the marine depths during all their lives. The color of the sea did not exclude from her eyes flashes of gaiety and wit. But always the steadiness and calm of the ocean persisted: whatever was ephemeral and momentary in her eyes was drowned in the abiding stillness of their real color.

She spoke especially of the early years of her marriage, when she was Mme Psichari, and came each summer to Rosmapamon with her husband and their four children, Ernest and Michel, and the two girls, Henriette and Corrie. There they lived in the presence of the aging Renan, and close to the simple lives of the Bretons. She gave me directions about reaching the house and told me not to fail to visit the little coppice of hazel trees behind the house. There she and her children spent many of the hot afternoons of midsummer because of the coolness of the spot. The example of the illustrious grandfather was clearly fixed in the minds of the children because their favorite game in the woods was the writing of a composition, the subject of which was announced by their mother when they had propped themselves up against a tree. A prize was offered for the best composition. They applied themselves to the art of writing, which they knew to be the family art. The silence settling down over the woods while the children were writing was so total that they could hear the squirrels descending and mounting the tree trunks. To this day in the family the spot is referred to as *le salon des écureuils* (the squirrels' parlor).

On several occasions I took the autobus from Perros to Tréguier. Even if I left the convent in a moment of sunlight, the sky of Tréguier was always gray, the very color of its granite houses and its roofs of slate. In the center of the town, where the bus made its principal stop, stood the cathedral, whose stone had a color such as I have never seen anywhere else. It was pink and gray, of such delicacy that I wondered how it buttressed itself against the space of the sky. One afternoon Jean-Gabriel led me through all parts of the edifice: up to the top of the tower, along the galleries, behind the choir, until I grew familiar with the color and the shape of the stone. Inside the nave the light was warm and revealed every corner. It was a golden light that turned the stone yellow and provoked a constant air of celebration, of incense and high ceremony. The tinge of pink on the outside walls gave the aspect of the outer world, of the material vegetable world.

From the Cathedral of Saint Yves, I would go for a brief interlude into the small public garden which is adorned principally with a lifesize statue of Renan. The figure is seated, in an almost collapsed position, on a bench, as if weighed down by its large bronze belly. The statue is that of the celebrity, of the native son who grew into the academician and the professor at the Collège de France. But then I willingly turned away from the sculptured form of the aged thinker to the house of his birth, about one hundred meters' distance from the park and the cathedral.

It is a humble peasant house, built in the early years of the seventeenth century. The earliest bill of sale that has been preserved bears the date of 1623. There, Ernest Renan was born in 1823, in the room on the first floor which was both kitchen and bedroom. I learned that the house was first opened to the public in 1923, one hundred years after Renan's birth, and was to be made a public monument in the summer of 1947.

The house was especially for me the container of Renan's childhood. More than the portraits, the autographs and caricatures, and the mould of Renan's hand, I liked the desk on which he wrote as a child and the prizes from the Collège de Tréguier. The meaning of the house seemed to be summarized in the copy of Fénelon's *Télémaque*, a history prize from the fifth class. The small room on the third floor, with the one window opening onto the garden below and the house tops of Tréguier, where Ernest Renan wrote his school exercises, seemed more hallowed than the glass cases filled with academic and scholarly honors. One object, more than all others in the house, attracted and held me. It was the green shawl of Renan's sister Henriette, which he had once described as sheltering his sister's proud poverty.

These first meetings with members of Psichari's family and the visits to places where he had lived had made of my thesis documentation an adventure rather than a labor. When I returned to Paris from Perros-Guirec and Tréguier, I asked permission to call on Mme Geneviève Favre, whom I wanted to meet on several counts. First, she was the mother of Jacques Maritain, whose advice had encouraged me to continue work on Psichari. Then, she had been an admirable older friend and counselor to Psichari. But the important part I knew she had played in the life of Charles Péguy attracted me to her the most. When I did meet her, I realized within the space of very few minutes that Mme Favre was by herself and in herself one of the most striking personalities I had had the privilege of meeting in France.

Her apartment was at 149, rue de Rennes. Five long flights of stairs had to be climbed in order to reach her door. The housekeeper Thérèse always opened the door and looked at me penetratingly as if to measure the worth of my being and judge the adequacy of the reason for my call. Each time her look was less hostile, but imperceptibly so. I did not fit into the category of the great who gained admittance through her. When sufficient time had elapsed for me to be kept waiting, she ushered me into a small room where I found Mme Favre on a chaise longue. Once—I believe it was my second visit—Thérèse forgot, or pretended to forget, that I was waiting. A full hour passed in the waiting room, and I had just risen in order to find my way out, when she opened a door and entered the room as if looking for something. If her surprise was simulated, it was well performed. She mumbled some brief apology about having too many things on her mind and watched me calmly as if to gauge the degree or the lack of my irritation.

Mme Favre was a diminutive woman who always sat propped up on a kind of couch. As I came into the room, she extended her right hand with a great urgency of her body and held it outstretched until I had time to cross the room and accept the hand. All the time she bore on her countenance a cordial expression of welcome. As soon as I placed my hand in hers, she turned her hand over palm upwards and placed her other hand on top of mine. It was done with the precision of a pact-making or the sealing of a great promise. This took place on my first visit and on every subsequent visit, and the same ritual was repeated at the end of each call.

Her voice was deep, and she spoke her words with studied slowness. The more significant phrases were punctuated with long silences during which she prevented me from intervening by concentrating her expression on what she was to say. She was somewhat deaf and accustomed to speaking uninterruptedly. Her large prominent eyes accentuated a look of childishness and innocence. Her hair was the most striking element of her appearance. As if to heighten her small stature, she wound her brown hair in a series of coils of decreasing size on the top of her head. It was a pyramid of hair so insecure that it might have been a hat rather than a coiffure.

Each sentence was physically so much of an effort for Mme Favre to articulate that it was more pointed and telling than a usual sentence in conversation. She felt no need to spare my feelings or flatter or conceal any of her own sentiments. Her age, her deafness, her intelligence and the important people of France with whom she had been connected afforded her the right to frankness. My letter that had preceded my first visit had announced my interest in Psichari and explained the primary reason in my wishing to meet her. She entered into the subject almost immediately with the question, "Are you a Catholic?" When I answered, "no!" she seemed relieved. I thought it only right to tell her I was deeply interested in Catholicism and felt myself temperamentally close to it. She waved my words aside with a wand-like gesture of her hand and said, "So are we all. But that does not alter the immense difference between those who are intellectually Catholic, like you and me, and those who are Catholics and hence dominated by priests, as Ernest Psichari was, and as my son is."

Mme Favre began talking about the character of Psichari, and soon I realized that what she said was in terms of her hero Charles Péguy. She described especially the luncheon gatherings on Thursdays in her apartment when her son brought home with him both Péguy and Psichari. The ideological causes of the past interested her the most. On one of my visits she greeted me by saying she had just written to President Roosevelt and to the pope in Rome. Each year she saw the reasons for war grow inevitable. The last years of her life were consecrated to the founding of a vast organization of the mothers of the world by which, if it grew strong enough, peace might be maintained. Her letter to the pope was a plea for him to exact from the faithful that they put down arms. I remember the agonized tone of her voice as she said, "Why doesn't he answer me? It would all be so simple if he insisted on peace!"

The picture of this little woman, in her high apartment on the rue de Rennes, writing to the great of the earth and puzzled that they did not answer her and accede to the simple cause of righteousness was a vision of heroic determination. In the midst of the war years, news of her death reached me in New Haven. Many of us had the opportunity of seeing her son during those years in New York where he gave all his time and energy to the cause of peace. I never entered his Fifth Avenue apartment without recalling his mother's in Paris. The speech of the son and the mother had the same intensity. I recognized each in the other and always liked to believe that I was recognizing also the ancestor, Mme Favre's father, Jules Favre, one of the founders of the Third Republic, and whose passion for justice and love of the people had been transmitted to his daughter and to his grandson.

In the unpublished correspondence of Psichari I had come across references to a chapel in the rue Monsieur where the singing of the Benedictine nuns was of exceptional quality. Curiously, the first verbal allusion to the chapel I heard was from Mme Favre. She mentioned it in some connection with Psichari during our first conversation. It was the end of the summer of 1934. The two months I had just spent in France had been the richest and most stimulating of my life thus far. The last event of the summer was appropriately the most significant. Eveline Garnier, granddaughter of Mme Favre, offered to take me to mass at the chapel on the rue Monsieur.

We arrived several minutes before the *Asperges me*. The chapel was small and every seat was taken. I was struck by the reverent attitude of the congregation. In other churches I had noticed a constant coming and going at the back, a perpetual changing of places and seeking of places, but here the people had come ahead of time and were actually preparing themselves for mass. They were praying or reading from their missals. The chancel was spacious and broad. To the left was a high grill with a curtain drawn behind it.

So imperceptible that they seemed merged with the silence itself, the first notes of the plainchant, coming from a great distance, reached me. They gave a breathing swelling form to the chapel's silence. The nuns who were singing must have been far off, in a court or within the convent itself.

[68]

As the voices came nearer, their purity and solemnity grew almost over-powering. The plainchant I had heard as a boy, sung by the Harvard Glee Club at the museum concerts, had not been like this. This was no concert, but worship. At those moments when the music became almost dramatic, when the vibration of a note grew into almost a personal accent of fervor, it would be cut off abruptly. Then the next notes, without any quavering in them would continue and repeat and embellish the phrases they followed.

Clearly visible and detached against the space surrounding the altar, the acolytes, the two deacons and the celebrant moved with the slowness and the faultless precision of the notes that were being sung, now in fuller tone since the nuns had taken their positions behind the grill and had drawn aside the curtain. Nothing existed now but the drama of the mass. The men who enacted it and the women who sang it were not performers but participants. The green vestments moved back and forth slowly in front of the altar. The plainchant, almost continuous, seemed to translate the drama into another realm, and yet it was never separate from the visible gestures.

I remembered Psichari's comment about the chapel, and his embarrass-ment at seeing there so many celebrities. Their proximity prevented him from concentration on the mass, and he worried that people attended the chapel for esthetic rather than religious reasons. I looked about again, and recognized no one save the young girl with whom I had come. In Boston, when I attended the Anglo-Catholic church of St. John the Evangelist, I had experienced the same feelings that Psichari had in the rue Monsieur. There I used to recognize in the congregation Ralph Adams Cram, T. S. Eliot, John Wheelwright, Austin Warren, and others whose presence, mo-mentarily at least, was a distraction for me.

The crowded summer weeks I was ending that Sunday morning in the Benedictine chapel of the rue Monsieur seemed already distant and unreal to me. I had spent my time trying to reconstruct the life of Ernest Psichari and to follow his search for the absolute. The people who had helped me the most—Henriette Psichari, Mme Renan, Mme Favre, Jacques Maritain, André Gide, Eveline Garnier—had so befriended me that too often I had lost sight of the real motive for my seeing them . . . . Here at the Bene-dictine mass I felt closer to Psichari than I had at any previous time during the summer, closer to an understanding of his particular search.

VI

Bennington College, 1935–40   Ecole du Sacré-Coeur
Robert Penn Warren

When I arrived at Bennington College in early September of 1935 to occupy my first full-time teaching position, the college had been functioning for only three years. No other change of place in my life was so completely new and unpredictable as the change from Harvard to Bennington. Not even France, because I had carefully prepared for France and knew something about it before I left New York harbor. But all was new at Bennington: the Vermont landscape I had never seen; the red barn on the crest of the hill, where I was shown my office and where I was to teach; the miniature library that filled one wing of the same barn, where I saw only a meager allotment of French books; the 250 girls everywhere on the campus, all of them attractive and many very beautiful; the forty-odd members of the faculty I had to meet and know and become friends with.

The previous four years I had taught on a half-time schedule one of the elementary French courses at Harvard while at the same time I was studying at the graduate school and writing my thesis. The course, of which I had two sections each year, was a firmly fixed course of readings from the celebrated authors: Corneille, Racine, Molière, Rousseau, Chateaubriand, and the like. My method had been to dispatch as quickly as possible the routine subject matter of the course—the check up on reading and general comprehension of the text—and then to spend most of the time on an analysis of the text as literature. My goal was to have the readings felt and apprehended as an experience. I did a very uneven job. I had not been taught that way, and I had to experiment constantly with method and

[70]

technique. My early teaching method must have been extremely florid in approach. One day after class a student who had been visibly impressed with the lesson came up to the desk and said, "Sir, you are the most lyric teacher I have ever had." I began to modify my method.

At Bennington I found myself the entire department of French literature. Courses which at Harvard had represented the sacrosanct privilege and property of Professors Morize, Babbitt, Grandgent, now depended on me. But the drastic doctrine of the new progressive college became clear when I realized I was not to "offer" a course; no, not even suggest a course. The idea and the desire for the course must come from the students. My role was to wait patiently in my office from nine to twelve in the morning and listen gratefully to whatever request might be made.

The waiting began in the low-ceilinged office on the second floor of the red barn. I was just over the entrance. From my window I could see girls coming and going, and that spectacle gave me the disturbing impression that every other teacher was being visited and tapped, so to speak, for some subject. After an hour's wait, my door opened abruptly, and in rushed a very excited young lady who spoke in French and informed me I was to be her "counselor" and that she wanted to work on the French classic theater. She explained the counselor system and emphasized the fact that she was to come alone for the work on Corneille, that no other student was to be admitted. Then she gently indicated that the counselor conference was to be just as much about her as about the French playwrights. Her name was Peggy. She was very attractive and an ardent convert to the Bennington method. I felt I was within my rights to ask why she wanted to study the seventeenth century, but she turned aside my question as if it were inane. So I did not insist on basic motivations, but felt grateful to have at least one student who had not only chosen a familiar subject to study but was quite ready to indoctrinate me in my new position.

Not many minutes passed after she left, when the door again opened, this time gently, and a beautiful blonde girl appeared on the threshold. I thought instantly of medieval figures I had seen on tapestries in Angers, of young girls and unicorns. She told me she was studying romanticism and that she and a few other students would like to have a class on the French romantic authors. Her whole manner was apologetic as if she were taking my time from countless girls waiting outside to interview me. She must have known that the corridor was empty. So I asked again the question I felt more than suitable in this school of avowed motivations: "Why are you studying romanticism?" She smiled then for the first time. "I don't know. It is proper to have a reason for everything here, but why isn't romanticism as proper as anything else? I hope you don't mind." Then she added, when she realized I was not in the least dismayed, "Romanticism has lost ground so much with the moderns, that I thought it might be just good fun and perverse to reinstate it."

This unicorn-girl's name was Prudence. That seemed appropriate because her appearance was allegorical. During the next two years, wherever I met her: in the buildings or especially along the country roads, her red gold hair flamed higher than any other color on the landscape. The composure of her features formed the only picture of human peacefulness I discovered at Bennington. She was beyond systems and even romanticism. She existed somewhere else—oh! how I hesitate to define what I only imperfectly understand!—mysteriously centered in life, in those deep currents of life that count more than our attachments to human beings and institutions. For the first time in my life I was able to speak with and walk beside my childhood heroine with the red gold hair, for behind Prudence, in her shadow, I recognized Pearl White of the serials and Mary Garden as Mélisande and the Titian Europa.

After a few days of interviews, during which I had reason to hope some students were coming my way, the hour dawned for the first meeting of the first class. It was a freshman group, in modern French literature. Twelve girls had enrolled, many of whom I had not seen. I remember that the day was a Wednesday, that the hour was nine in the morning, that it was early in the month of September, the air mild and warm, and the sunlight showering over the valley from which it had scattered most of the fog.

When I entered the room, the girls were all there, seated quietly around a large table. Only one chair was vacant in their midst and I went to it. This was their first class and mine at Bennington. An embarrassed silence fell over us all. I had to pretend to be busy with a few books and papers in my hands, which I arranged and rearranged in the small space of table before me. I began speaking, without knowing what I was saying, save that it was something I had not planned to say. I wanted to tell them not to listen to those first sentences, that they meant nothing. But the girls politely concentrated on my vacuous words. Their shyness disappeared before mine did, and then they set about to put me at my ease. They accomplished that by feigning a great interest in French authors.

The summer sun had changed their complexions to the same tan. Their lips were all rouged to the same degree. My persistent impression told me

I was not at school but backstage with a chorus. When the second hour began, I had found some kind of pattern of mannerism and speech. The usual kind of glib historical generalities about literature, which, as a student, I had been reared on, sounded inane in the Bennington classes. More philosophical generalities dealing with the meaning of literary form seemed more appropriate.

Their state of mind was always paradoxical to me. On the one hand, they wanted to be with a teacher who knew where he was going in a class discussion, who had formulated in himself some rigid view of the subject, but they also wanted to feel that they were creating and achieving the discussion themselves. They wanted a sense of final independence in the attainment to an idea and that moment of exhilaration when they could look at the teacher from their distant post of discoverer or creator. I could lead them just so far—if the class was to be successful—and then they wanted to accomplish alone the last trek.

During my first year I lived in the town of Bennington, three miles away from the college, in the Mayflower Inn. It was a large angular white house, set back from the main street. Mrs. Kelley owned and ran it with the help of one girl, who lasted only a part of the year. I grew very fond of Mrs. Kelley. She had had a hard life. Her acquisition of the inn was the culmination of her life, and she was more devoted to it, to the multicolored paper she chose for the walls, to the furniture she bought at auctions, to the floors she scraped and waxed, than to the people who occupied her rooms. If some task of decorating or cleaning occupied her, the meal would be put off, and then finally something easy to prepare, scrambled eggs and sardines, for example, would be concocted in a flash. I became fascinated by Mrs. Kelley's fervent attitude toward the house, which was her creation, and her detached attitude toward people, who became obstacles in the adornment of her house. Other boarders were not so intrigued as I was, and during the year I watched them come and go.

My nightly return to the Mayflower was release and repose for me. The days at the college on the hill were long and filled with "talk": classes, conferences, meetings, and meals too when the talk continued. Theories of education combined with theories of art walled me in from the world. When dinner or the last evening meeting was over, I crawled into my car and turned on the motor with the feeling that I had strength only for that. My body relaxed in the seat, and the car seemed to direct itself down the hillside onto the main road. Then gradually, in the night air, with the distances the darkness gave to the fields and the sky, I revived and turned my thoughts to the town I was approaching. Bennington is a dismal non-descript town: a few mills on the outskirts and then the lines of standard stores in the center with the one movie house, The General Stark. But it became for me at night, after the long day of red maple furniture at the college and the endless talk about theory, a wondrous arena of liberation.

Early in my first year at Bennington, I was asked to recite a role in a very original dramatization of *The Eve of Saint Agnes*. The lines of the poem were divided between two narrators, a man and a woman, who stood at either end of the stage, and the action, corresponding to the lines, was danced. This was my first part in a long series of dramatic presentations during the next few years.

The director of dramatics, Francis Fergusson, whose genius and un-paralleled patience became immediately very real to me, fashioned and justified each of my experiences on the stage at Bennington. His own imagination had so deftly constructed whatever role he was directing, that the actor's principal task, during rehearsals, consisted in drawing it from him and perfecting the mere technique so that it might harmonize with the master conception.

In my second year, I made a translation of Molière's *Les Femmes savantes* and played the part of Chrysale. The presentation was lavishly mounted and enriched with a Lulli ballet. On that occasion, more than ever, I felt the synthesizing power and sensitivity of Francis Fergusson. In French, the great scenes of Molière are tossed into the air, where they are danced and sung because they are composed with the mathematical pre-cision and varied tempi of a Mozart symphony. My English of the text was heavy by comparison, and any approximation to Molière we reached was due to the director. He timed our movements and organized the group positions that came together and fell apart in rhythms not unlike the musical rhythms of the ballet surrounding us and encouraging us.

The part of the father, which I played, in a family dominated by "in-tellectual ladies," afforded me a few moments of excessive loneliness on the stage: the loneliness of a man thinking of the well-being of his body ("cette guenille m'est chère") and realizing that the members of his family had moved into realms different from his own. There was a moment in the final scene when I stood in the center of the stage and watched all the members of the cast move toward me as if the center of the family had been once more reaffirmed in my potbellied bewigged personage. But, more important than that action, was the focussing of all the spectators in the theater. As the actors rushed toward me in a semicircle, behind them and the light falling on them, the shadowy forms of the public seemed to be rushing toward me too, until I felt locked within a physical space. I felt in me the enjoyment the spectators and actors felt in the seeing and the forming of a pattern. The experience was over in a flash, but in each subsequent part I played I strove to realize it again, as the highest reward for acting.

The following year I had two parts in a dance recital presentation of Hart Crane's poem *The Bridge*. In the section called "Ave Maria," it was the role of Columbus. The dancers fell apart and opened up the stage for me to walk down facing the audience and reciting the Columbus lines. The red velvet costume, the strong light, and the even stronger richness of the lines created an almost excessive weight in me. I was completely outside the familiar actions of living, and completely within the world of acting where speech, gesture, movement were timed and deliberately projected. Every tie with my ordinary life of teacher and member of a college community was severed during those minutes of "Ave Maria." (One of the girl dancers, chubby at that time, Carol Channing, destined to become in the sixties and seventies one of our most gifted musical comedy stars, had the habit of falling at exactly the wrong place. She blocked my entrance at rehearsals and performances, and I had to step over her recumbent body. Each time I looked down at her on the floor under my feet, and each time she managed to wink back at me as if she were saying, better luck next time!)

There was a wait of thirty or forty minutes between "Ave Maria" and the other section of the poem I recited. I removed the heavy layers of red velvet and put on the very lightweight costume for "Southern Cross." It was simply a pair of black trousers and a deep blue shirt opened down the front. When I walked on the stage to recite the love poem, I was pinned down, not by a costume this time, but by the darkness which filled all the stage except a center white light into which I moved. I was detached, as if I were made of the light in which I stood, and my voice came to me from far off, from the namelessness of the world and of woman with which the lines of the poem were concerned. I had felt previously on the stage other kinds of loneliness, but never before, this light-filled limitless form when all the rest of the theater—stage, pit, walls, ceiling—was sunken into immobility. The girls of the chorus were on the floor at the two extremes of the stage. On my right, down stage, the figures of four men moved their bodies very slowly, without walking, in the shadows. Between them and myself there was no relationship, and yet there was always a striving on my part and on theirs to communicate.

In between the major productions there were always a few evenings given over to a series of scenes from plays, often directed by students. These were like exercises, which had more chance of being perfected. My final Bennington performance was a scene which Kathryn Henry and I did in French: the beginning of the third act of Cocteau's *La Machine infernale*. The scene between Oedipus and Jocasta, on the marriage night, has an exceptional unity in the childishness that passes back and forth between mother and son.

My lines became meaningful only when the set was prepared. Then I was able to move about the stage and feel that I was moving within the pattern of a myth. The low white bed, the mirror and Jocasta's crimson dress resembled elements of a vast painting which needed Oedipus as pre-cipitant. Jocasta was a thin slip of a girl, wondrously beautiful and child-like. I tried to convert her black hair into the red gold hair of Mélisande and Louise, of Pearl White and Prudence, but this time she was more than heroine and spouse—she was maternal too. She preceded me, and I was never able to get back of her or to look at her for the first time.

The actual sets on the stage of the Bennington College Theater, where I spent so many evenings playing so many different parts, are today con-fused in my mind with the permanent site of the college itself, with the buildings and the lawns, the red barn where I taught, the Swiss chalet, built by Barbara and Lewis Jones, where I lived after the first year. Even in my solitary corner of the library, by the French books, I never ceased believing I read and took notes as if I were enacting a role. I would be hard put to define exactly that role. After all, the literal hours of teaching and acting were not as numerous as all the others when I studied or wrote or talked with the students or visited with faculty friends. The word *com-munity* was used a great deal in Bennington conversations. It always op-pressed me as being a concept without reality, one of the catchwords intended to discipline forces that could not be disciplined in any usual way.

Students and faculty were so aware of the newness of the college, so fearful of what might be considered traditional in education, in behavior, in taste, that at times I felt divorced from the past, isolated in a present without a past. This feeling disappeared to a large extent during the course of my five years at Bennington when the students' misunderstanding of the present turned them toward the past and they began requesting courses on

[76]

Dante or Pascal. But the first year I seemed to be immersed in modernism, so devoid of foundation and reason, that my evening return to the Mayflower Inn seemed a reassuring recovery of a part of myself which the day's occupations had obscured. The architecture of the house and even the wallpaper I disliked related me to strands of my New England past. Mrs. Kelley's eager conversation about the goings on in the town, about her newest acquisitions for the house, and even about her general philosophical observations on life in our century, reinstated me in a wider and more natural context.

Directly behind the Mayflower, on the next street, was a red brick school building that bore over its main entrance the French words: *Ecole du Sacré-Coeur*. The familiarity of these words, when I had first seen them from the sidewalk, dissipated all feelings of strangeness about the town and my new life at the college. Often on late Saturday afternoons I would go into the school. The chapel was in the basement. The priest, whom I had met and talked with, Père Campeau, would be in his confessional box. I remember especially one cold dark afternoon of Advent season.

The chapel was far from beautiful. One row at the back was filled with children and a few adults waiting for their turn at the confessional. The altar had purple decorations. On the wall over the altar was a heavily painted inscription: "Aimé soit partout le coeur de Jésus." Under the words a red heart pierced with a flaming cross and dripping blood upset me. The devotion to the Sacred Heart I had never been able to understand because of the atrocious pictorial realism associated with it. I preferred to look at the stand of candles dominated by a small painted statue of the child Jesus bearing a large gold crown and draped in a heavy royal mantle.

It was cold in the church. The tall green windows let in a colder and colder light as it darkened outside. A dozen candles or so were lighted on the stand and their tiny flames lent a bit of warmth to the front of the church. Half of the penitents, on their knees, were praying, and the others were looking into space. A child left the confessional box and another took his place. In a few seconds the boy had reached the front of the church and knelt at the altar rail. I wondered what sins he had just whispered and what new purity filled him . . . . I was in a strange house which permitted me a union with many lives, with many millions of lives. The child at the altar rail was clutching in his left hand a dark blue ski cap, and his heart was speaking to eternity. This penitence in a church I had never known. I had never waited in line for Him, and I had never heard Him speak in a little half-minute accorded by some human sense of justice.

It would be easy for me to say that Bennington took on the form of an exile. It did, but so has every other place where I have lived, including native Brookline. I have felt exiled in the cities I have loved the most: Paris, Rome, Dresden, London, New York, New Haven, Chicago, Durham. I have never really unpacked my trunk and settled down. Exiled from what or from whom? My answer to such a general and persistent state of feeling must necessarily be general too. My work as teacher and writer has forced me into a life that has no geographical site. I have looked at streets and buildings, rooms and apartments, with the deep knowledge that I must not form any attachment to them, that I must never consider them my own.

My first act, upon entering a room where I am to live, in a friend's house, or my own apartment, or a hotel, or my family's Brookline apartment, is to sit down at a desk or table and write some sentences in whatever work I am engaged in at the time. The act of writing, as soon as I enter a new room, releases me from it and makes out of it, not a home, but a place where I work. The architecture of my life has been formed by my daily act of writing. Whatever else happens to me may be more exciting or more disturbing, but it is less permanent.

During the Bennington years, the weekend visit each month my friend Walter paid me, underscored my feelings of exile. His appearance forced me back into the few previous years and reminded me that I was a stranger at Bennington. He came, by various means, over the Mohawk Trail, in answer to a need and sense of friendship. His arrivals told me that I was in exile and that I was spiritually still fixed in the state that had preceded exile.

During my third year in Vermont, in order to facilitate and hasten and make dangerous the trip from Boston to Bennington, Walter acquired a motorcycle. I was waiting for him on a Friday evening when he was making his initial flight. It had been dark for several hours, and I was worried that the new vehicle had broken down. Barbara and Lewis Jones were out that evening, and I was alone in their house. I had left my own room in order to sit in the living room. Then, from afar off on the country road, I heard the motorcycle and followed its pounding until it gasped and snorted and stopped outside the house. I heard Walter's rapid steps on the piazza, but I was there at the door to greet him. I expected to see him in some familiar guise and recognizable, but it was an angel who spoke and laughed as Walter did, Azrael perhaps. The figure of the friend was encased in a pure white rubber suit, a kind of modernized Gilles, standing taller than ever before, looking as if he had come, not from Newton Center and the Mohawk Trail, but from an unknown planet. I was suddenly rescued from exile by an angel-clown. Never was my feeling of exile so real and so dissolved at the same time. I had known gratitude before and I have known it since, but never so deeply as that night in Bennington when Walter-Azrael crashed through the night on a motorcycle. He emerged from the night as magically as a white clown emerges from a burning hoop. What I had defined to myself as danger—the night, the thumping two-wheeled monster —was only the door he opened into my exile, the painted stylized danger of a stage set. He laughed as he took off his angelic costume, and the walls of my cell collapsed.

It must have been in Iowa City, on one of my June visits to Austin Warren, that I first met Robert Penn Warren. He had been teaching that year at the university as a visiting professor. Austin had spoken so highly of him that I was anxious to meet him. At that early date I associated him especially with the founding of the *Southern Review*.

My first memory of him is a sunny late afternoon when I called on him and his wife Cinina in a small rather miserable looking house in Iowa City. He was on the porch enjoying the sunlight and talking with a student. He explained that work stopped for him usually mid-afternoon when he exercised vigorously by swimming or walking, and then a relaxing drink when friends were invited to drop by without invitation. On that first visit one other student came by soon after I arrived. When the fellow had settled into his porch chair, a drink in hand, Red Warren asked him: "How many hours did you spend at the typewriter today?"

The student answered, a bit sheepishly, "Only five."

I was more than impressed, but Red said, "Not enough. I told you to get it up to eight hours a day."

"But I dry up when I stay that long in front of the typewriter. The damn novel grows stale in me."

"That's because you stay too long with one kind of writing. When you get tired of the novel, then go to your short story, and after that to your essay. A writer should be working on three or four kinds of writing at the same time." Then Red summed up his advice by saying to the student, who gave evidence of having heard the advice before, "Long working hours and vigorous exercise—that's the regimen you have to follow if you want to be a writer."

Poet, novelist and especially today in the seventies, one of our best literary critics, Robert Penn Warren has justified in his own accomplishments the way of life he described to the aspiring student-writer in Iowa.

The following spring I received a note at Bennington from Red asking me to rent for him for the summer a small house in Bennington in the vicinity of the college and near a lake if possible. Swimming was his favorite exercise. I did find a suitable house in North Bennington which had a front porch. There, late afternoons, I continued making visits similar to those I had made in Iowa City because a few young disciple-writers followed Red wherever he went and made late afternoon reports on work accomplished during the day.

At the end of the summer—college was about to begin—Red told Francis Fergusson that he had finished writing a play in verse and would like to hear it read by the student actors Francis was training. Enough of us were around (students and faculty) who had played in some of the Fergusson productions, to make up a cast. We met one evening in the barn and sat around a table. Scripts were handed out and we read at sight. The text which contained choruses, seemed impressive to us. Francis and Red listened attentively for two hours to . . . . *All the King's Men.*

When the reading was over, Red thanked us and turning to Fergusson, said, "Francis, if you would like to give this play its first production here at Bennington, I would be honored."

It was a dramatic moment for all of us, but Francis replied with words I instinctively felt he was going to say, "Red, I don't think the text is ready yet for production." Red Warren's reply came quickly.

"Perhaps you're right. I'm going to shelve it, and tomorrow morning I will begin to write it over again in the form of a novel."

I was lecturing one day at St. Catherine's College in St. Paul. Red had invited me to spend the weekend at his home in Minneapolis where he was resident writer at the University of Minnesota. I remember the house as being large and rambling. My room was at the head of the stairway. Saturday night he told me he would take me to mass Sunday morning and would knock on my door fifteen minutes before we would have to leave. The knock came. I opened the door and said I would be down in a few minutes. Red pointed out a chair at the bottom of the stairway and said he would be waiting there. I noticed a notebook on the chair just before I turned to go back into my room. As I finished dressing I wondered whether he intended to write as he waited for me. In ten minutes I opened my door and went down the stairs. He was writing and fully absorbed. I asked him whether, knowing he had only ten minutes to wait, he was working on some serious writing. He answered me that it was serious—the ending of a chapter he had been having a hard time with. At some off moment, such as that morning, he was often able to put together sentences that had been recalcitrant heretofore.

On another occasion, I visited Red Warren in New London, Connecticut, where he was teaching a summer course at the College for Women. My memory of the visit and of the place is vague except for one moment in our conversation when Red and I were alone and when he asked me in all seriousness, "What do you understand by allegory?" On hearing the question, another question flashed through my mind that years earlier Jorge Guillén had asked me: "What is poetry?" This time I was determined not to be glib. I was older and had less confidence in my ability to answer such a question. So I hedged, and rightfully so, because I am still puzzled over what allegory means. I reviewed with Red the medieval meaning of it that Dante explicates, namely the relationship between an event and the life of Christ. Red and I agreed the Dante interpretation makes good sense, but can it be used in an unbelieving age?

Ever since that day in New London, the word *allegory* has been associated for me with Robert Penn Warren, and I examine each new critical piece of his, as it appears, Coleridge, Hemingway, Faulkner, Whittier, to see if he has hit upon a meaning as intelligent as that of Dante's letter to Can Grande.

VII

16, rue Chaptal, 1938, 1939   Noémi Renan
Jacques-Emile Blanche

There is a regular procedure in the resurgence of my memory of France. It begins with a flash of sunlight. Often it is light refracted against the walls of a building, and always it is southern France I see, which is the real kingdom where the sunlight marries the stone of edifices. I often see the blaze of yellow into which the sun converts the walls of Aiguesmortes as if it were eternally celebrating the departure of Saint Louis to deliver the Holy Land. And I often see the more subtle pink sunlight on the walls at Avignon rising up from the city as if to herald the skies themselves. More persistently still do I see the flat white sunlight on the villas at Argelès-Gazost in the Pyrenees, and even the white dust of the path I used to climb in order to get to the top of the small mountain called Balandraou.

My memories are provoked by the same sun of Provence that Valéry in "Le Cimetière marin" immoblized over the graveyard of his ancestors at Sète and the shimmering tiles (or waves) of the Mediterranean where white doves (or sails) move in some ancient celebration of life and light. It is the same sun whose reflection on roofs of red tile was immobilized by Cézanne in his paintings of L'Estaque. Cézanne created a dimensional world in his fruit, his bathers and his Mediterranean harbors, all of which are sun-filled objects of Provence, as perfectly luminous as my own memories of the Midi.

As soon as this first transformation is established in my mind by means of a flashing light, the opposite vision of France can easily come before me. The grayness of Paris and the rain of Brittany may quickly replace the sun of Provence and the dry lightness of the Pyrenees. Here again, since I am describing the involuntary procedure of my memory, the same picture of a little courtyard in Paris comes to my mind each time the grayness of France is remembered. It is just off the rue Chaptal at the beginning of Montmartre midway between the Place Pigalle and the Place Blanche. At one end of the courtyard is Ary Scheffer's studio and opposite it, the small provincial looking house where Mme Noémi Renan lived. During the two winters when I occupied a room on the first floor of her house and worked at the same desk where her son Ernest Psichari used to write, I remember the rain falling on the cobblestones of the courtyard with the same insistence that it used to fall in Brittany during the summer I spent at Perros-Guirec. When in Paris, at lunch with Mme Renan, and in Perros-Guirec, at tea with her, I habitually commented on the rain falling outside, she, with an evasiveness reminiscent of the writings of her father, would always answer, "Mais non! il ne pleut pas aujourd'hui."

Twice I arrived in Paris on the last day of the year, in 1937 and 1938. I spent Christmas at home with my parents, left Boston late Christmas Day for New York and sailed on the *Normandie* on the 26th. Each year we arrived at Le Havre late afternoon of the 31st. The boat train got into the Gare Saint-Lazare about eight-thirty in the evening. I went by taxi to 16, rue Chaptal where I was to spend the winter. Mme Renan had already left the house, to spend the evening, the *réveillon*, with her daughters. Esther, the housekeeper, who had opened the iron gate at the sidewalk, talked volubly as we walked up the cobblestone driveway. The closed gate and the high walls on either side shut me off from the streets of Paris, the station, the boat, Boston. I knew I was entering a new year. As soon as Esther showed me into the small bedroom I was to occupy, she announced she too was off to spend the *réveillon* at her daughter's. In a few minutes I was alone in the house.

That house, resting on the slope of Montmartre and cut off from the noise of the Quartier Pigalle by the driveway, was built in 1830 by Ary Scheffer. On each side of the courtyard two large studios remind one of Scheffer, whose paintings, once bought up by all the museums of Europe, have now fallen into disrepute. Born in Dordrecht, in Holland, at the end of the French Revolution, Ary Scheffer was one of those foreigners who became French in their heart. I felt very close to him while I lived in the house he built, close to his generous nature and his love for France. His studio was kept up by Mme Renan as a kind of museum. There, Lamartine used to come to pose for the painter. At the last sitting Scheffer asked the poet what he thought of the portrait. Lamartine's haughty answer, reported to each succeeding generation in the house, came without hesitation: "Vous avez bien rendu mon front magnifique et mon expression royale."

Mme Renan often referred to the special place occupied by Lamennais in the house. His deep sense of charity and political passion had endeared him to Scheffer. Nightly they played chess together, although the game usually ended in a quarrel when each player hurled the chessmen at the other. Chopin was welcomed by Scheffer as the representative of oppressed Poland. And Liszt, who came from Hungary about 1840, was literally promoted and introduced to Paris by the painter. In the Scheffer home, Liszt forgot his worldliness and was beloved by the family for his sensitivity to art. For thirty years the little house and the studio formed a veritable center of art and politics. Mme Renan never tired of listing the celebrities who came there: Gobineau, de Tocqueville, Ingres, Turgenev.

The revolution of 1848 marked the collapse of Scheffer's political ideas as well as the loss of his fortune. He was left with his house, his talent as painter and his friends. After the initial period of political fervor and artistic glory, the house on the rue Chaptal was to become the site of another kind of drama, for there Ernest Renan met Cornélie Scheffer, niece of the painter, and fell in love with her.

The historian Augustin Thierry was responsible for this meeting. He was proud of his discovery of young Renan, and brought him to the Scheffer salon one evening. It was in 1854. Renan was living with his sister Henriette in a small apartment on the rue du Val-de-Grâce. Their life was peaceful and studious. Behind Renan lay his troubled early period when he left the seminary, and behind Henriette lay her long exile in Poland. The sister was watching over the early fame of Renan, dispensing tenderness and direction to her brother. She had decided that Ernest (then thirty-two years old) would marry much later in life, that his work had to be accomplished first. He was already publishing scholarly works: *Avverrhoès* and *L'Histoire des langues sémitiques*. At thirty-two he was a member of the Institut.

The Scheffers received on Friday evenings. In her advanced age, Cornélie Scheffer, who was to become the wife of Ernest Renan, often told of that first meeting in her uncle's salon and of the impression the young savant made on her. Renan was far from resembling the hero of a novel. He was timid and awkward. His nose was large and his flat long hair gave him the appearance of sadness. His clothes were ill-tailored and poor. But everything changed when Renan began speaking. His blue-green eyes sparkled, and the magic of his words effaced the first impression of awkward constraint.

Renan became one of the regular Friday evening visitors at the rue Chaptal. But it was not easy to court a young lady at that time. It was impossible to see her alone. It was forbidden to write long letters to her. Cornélie was able to interpret the assiduousness of the young writer and the concealed emotion in the brief notes he sent. She must have wondered at the slowness of his proposal and the constant references to his sister Henriette. A drama between brother and sister was being played nightly on the rue du Val-de-Grâce. Henriette was saddened that Ernest was finding happiness elsewhere than with her, and such violent reproaches were spoken that Renan announced to Cornélie he would no longer return to the rue Chaptal. When Henriette realized the grief she had caused, she repented and came to beg forgiveness of Cornélie.

Two years after Renan first came to the home of Ary Scheffer, he married the niece Cornélie, on September 13, 1856. The ceremony was performed both in a Protestant church (le temple de l'Oratoire) and a Catholic church (Saint-Germain l'Auxerrois). The history of the little house was far from complete at that time. It was to revive later at the period of *l'affaire Dreyfus* when the daughter of Ernest and Cornélie Renan, the young woman who bore the name of Noémi, was occupying the house with her young husband, Jean Psichari. Both Clemenceau and Jaurès visited the Psicharis at that time. The generation to be sacrificed in the First World War had just been born. The two sons of the Psicharis, Ernest and Michel, grew up in the atmosphere of the Scheffer house and the passionate controversy waged over the Dreyfus Affair.

The Mme Noémi Renan whom I knew spoke with equal familiarity about the living and the dead. She often talked of people outside her family: of M. Berthelot, of M. Taine, of Hérédia, who in her salon used to recite his sonnets, of Victor Hugo, who once when she was a little girl gave her his seat at the Comédie-Française. But most often she would talk about her family: about her father as professor at the Collège de France or as the kindly sage at his summer home of Rosmapamon in Brittany; about her son Ernest Psichari who fell in Belgium in August 1914; about her second son, Michel, who married the daughter of Anatole France and who was killed in a trench in northern France in 1917; about her grandsons, one of whom, Michel Revault-d'Allonnes, lost his life in a submarine off the coast of Africa in 1942, a few months before her own death occurred in Paris. All of those lives were in her, and they were transposed, whenever she spoke of them, into figures of real dimensions and attitudes. She spoke as understandingly of the simple Breton folk in Tréguier, as she spoke of the literary talents of her son Ernest or of the latest production of Dullin in his Paris theater. Her ancestors were Breton fishermen, and she had inherited from them the magical power of seeing far behind her and far ahead. The silence and fidelity of the sea had never been lost in the transplanted life in Paris, and even there in her quiet salon on the rue Chaptal she could hear the bells of the Cathedral of Ys during the seconds when the waves parted and allowed the sound to mount up from the ocean depths.

My bedroom was the smallest I have ever slept in. Each day began with Esther appearing over the bed holding aloft the breakfast tray. Emerging from sleep, I pushed the pillows behind me and sat upright. Esther placed the tray on my lap as if I were a child. I was awakened each morning by her voice and by the rich smell of coffee. I drank it at first greedily, and then slowly in order to make it last. On those winter mornings I understood so well a passage in Proust where he describes his breakfast coffee in its white porcelain pitcher and the miraculous courage it gives one to begin the day.

As recompense for the smallness of my sleeping quarters, Mme Renan provided me with the use of a small study at the end of the hall. It was referred to as *le petit salon* in contrast to *le grand salon* where she received her guests. My habit of writing in the morning I had always possessed, as far as my program of classes would permit, but during the two winters on the rue Chaptal it was carried out without interruption. The morning silence of that little house, which began with Esther's coffee, and which ended with lunch about twelve-thirty, taught me many things about my capacity for work and the particular ritual I needed in order to write.

Mme Renan and I met in the dining room. For both of us this was a first engagement in conversation in the day, since the few words exchanged with Esther were hardly conversation. The shift from silence to speech was difficult for me. But from her very first words on, Mme Renan was remarkably fluent and engaging. She never began by trivia: the weather, the previous night's sleep, our hunger (which we both felt if I judged by the quantity of food we ate). She began instantly on some topic of politics or literature, usually in connection with an article she had read the night before. She never questioned me about what I thought on whatever topic

[86]

she was discussing, but I soon learned that I was expected to interpose, and vigorously so, my opinions.

At one lunch our conversation had somehow gotten on to opera and from there to singers. The name of Povla Frijsh flashed through my mind (as it always does when I think of singers), but I decided there was little chance that Mme Renan had ever heard of her and that her importance to me would be too complicated to explain. But at one moment, when it seemed my duty to initiate a new part in the conversation, I asked her whether she had ever heard of the Danish soprano, Povla Frijsh. She looked at me for several seconds without speaking, and then began, to my amazement, "Mais je pense bien. What surprises me is that you ever heard of her. When she first came from Denmark to study singing in Paris, she came to this house. We secured a teacher for her and organized her first concert which was held in the studio. We believed in her art and loved her. Then one day, she left abruptly without saying goodbye, and from that day, which was several years ago, until now, I have heard nothing about her and have never known where she was."

After lunch I went into the studio alone in order to see it again with the new knowledge about Frijsh's first concert in Paris. I tried to imagine her as a young woman standing by the piano and singing "Infidélité" by Hahn, and not knowing what her future was to be. I felt omniscient and closer than ever before to one part of the past of Ary Scheffer's studio.

Dinner with Mme Renan was different from lunch. She was more tired, and hence her speech and movements were more slow. The light from the center lamp fell obliquely across her. When she bent her face in order to eat, it came into the light and was beautifully illumined for a moment. And then, as she straightened up her head, it rose back into the shadow from which she spoke. For the occasion of the evening meal she always wore a black dress and added to it some slight scarf neckpiece which she varied. There was a black jet collar, which lay flat on her dress and gave her a regal severe look. On other nights she wore a detached wisp of black gauze-like cloth appearing like a circle of darkened foam around her neck.

The food itself, always expertly prepared by Esther and served by her silently, I felt should be commented on and praised more abundantly than Mme Renan would permit. I am confident she enjoyed as much as I did Esther's cooking, but she was determined the conversation should not be wasted on such topics. She possessed such an admirable sense of hierarchy and order that there was even a marked distinction between lunch and dinner conversation topics. At noon we talked about politics and Paris and personalities. In the evening the talk broadened and deepened into more general speculations: philosophical and literary. Whatever proper names were mentioned, were brought in to justify some idea or theory. So, I had to reserve for the following morning, when Esther appeared with my coffee, my fullest thoughts on her cooking.

On the evenings when I had no early engagement, I accompanied Mme Renan to the *grand salon* and continued there for an hour or so my visit with her. This marked still another shift in the tone and tempo and subject of the conversation. From her armchair my aged friend commanded a view of the entire room. I sat on a low chair in front of her and beside the table where stacks of current periodicals and books waited for the longer more solitary hours of Mme Renan's evening. These moments were more relaxed. Indirectly she spoke about me. She never once asked me a personal question of any nature, but she asked about my writing, or rather about problems of writing. I eagerly encouraged this subject. Mme Renan was not a writer, but she had spent her life close to many writers. Her speech was the most elaborate, varied and engaging of any I have ever heard, with the exception of the speech of one Frenchman whom I was to meet a few years afterwards at Yale, and who turned out to be a fervent admirer of Mme Renan: Henri Focillon.

Curiously enough, when I think of a Paris room, of the inside of a Paris house, and of a salon, no one of the particular rooms I knew well and really lived in, comes first to my mind. It is always a salon where I went only once and where I spent only one hour. Through some reflex of pride, it occupies a preeminent place in my memories of France because I experienced a triumph in a literary debate.

February 1939: Mme Renan had taken me to a tea at the home of an old friend of hers, Mme Dietz, in the rue des Mathurins behind the Opéra. I had been lured to the tea by the promise of meeting the painter Jacques-Emile Blanche, whose painting of Gide as a young man in Algeria I had admired the year before when I had come across it in the museum of Rouen. The room was long, narrow and crowded. When M. Blanche entered —he was the last to arrive—there was considerable flurry. I was introduced as a younger teacher from America. I stood in the center of the room facing M. Blanche, who insisted upon standing during the ensuing conversation. The other guests I felt behind me massed as spectators. Even

Mme Renan, whom I could see out of the corner of my eye, seemed to be watching a performance.

With each succeeding question of M. Blanche, a little more of my life was revealed. By the tone of his questions he made each of my answers seem preposterous. To begin with, it was preposterous I was an American. Preposterous too, that I was a teacher, that I taught French literature, and to young ladies, and in a place, Bennington, Vermont, that he, Jacques-Emile Blanche, had never heard of. "Qu'est-ce que c'est que le Vermont?" I remember as one of the more haughty questions. As they continued, all my latent beliefs in Bennington progressivism and modernism became real, and I began to defend the faith of my beautiful students on the Vermont hill. When M. Blanche insisted I must be teaching Alphonse Daudet and Pierre Loti to American girls, I took pride in insisting I taught Gide, Mauriac, and Proust. "Vous enseignez Proust aux jeunes filles?" I followed this up by speaking of the poetry course in which Mallarmé was the principal poet studied. This, M. Blanche interpreted as insolence.

"Vous dites que vous expliquez Mallarmé?"

"Oui, Monsieur."

I sensed that the ladies seated behind me had given up their conversation and were following the duel in the center of the floor. They were certainly impressed when M. Blanche informed us all that he had been a pupil in one of Mallarmé's classes at the lycée, that he had read Mallarmé all his life and that he had not yet understood him.

This clearly made me out an impostor. M. Blanche decided to rebuke me. He announced that he was going to give me a line of a Mallarmé sonnet and ask me to interpret it, to give the American interpretation I might have given "dans le Vermont." There was a pause during which M. Blanche seemed to enjoy my discomfort and during which I prayed to hear recited a sonnet with which I would be familiar. This was the case, fortunately. He quoted the first line of a sonnet which I had not only taught, but had had the good fortune of discussing with the two American poets Louise Bogan and Léonie Adams.

As I heard the line,

M'introduire dans ton histoire

I felt both jubilant at recognizing it and perplexed about what degree of frankness I could use in my answer. But this answer was to make or unmake me. I would have to use with Jacques-Emile Blanche in Paris the same crass psychological speech I had been trained to use with American girls in a progressive New England college. The distinguished painter continued insisting that the image of this first line of the Mallarmé sonnet meant nothing. More than myself was at stake: there was Mallarmé too, and Bennington College! So I blurted out that although the profound meaning of the poem doubtless concerned the creative process in art, that first line described on a purely literal level, the sexual act.

There was a brief embarrassed silence, and then the reluctant but audible words of M. Blanche gave credence to Mallarmé, Bennington, and the American impostor: "Mais oui, en effet, ah! c'est curieux!"

This is the picture that dominates my memory of conventional Paris, of the austere politeness of elderly Parisians, of the finely traced elegance in their features. The people that day in Mme Dietz's salon resembled portraits by famous painters. The ladies in black coats with tightly drawn veils over their faces might have modeled for Manet or Toulouse-Lautrec.

The two successive winters spent on the rue Chaptal had about them such precise and appealing patterns that they appeared to me at the same time and have continued ever since in my memory, as autonomous periods of living, completely cut off from the rest of my life. During the best hours of the day I was able to devote myself to the work I wanted most to do. I was able to preserve the deep silence of the morning hours because I knew it would be followed by the lunch conversation with Mme Renan, and then, later in the day by further conversation with other friends. Never had I kept such silence, and never had I talked so much.

So Paris became the city of silence and of speech. Each day that I closed the iron gate behind me on the rue Chaptal, I faced a challenge that involved my behavior, my utterances, the very way in which I walked down the street, the very manner in which I asked for postage stamps at a *bureau de tabac*. I answered the challenge of Paris very imperfectly, but I learned to understand its reality and its value. Back in America it has continued to exist. From the various houses where I have lived, which have no iron gates before them, I have gone out into the New England or the Chicago street with a feeling of excitement and awareness so strong that if I closed my eyes for a second I might be transported magically to the rue Chaptal.

VIII

Amboise, 1939   Sacré-Coeur   Café Flore   Hudson River

The summer of 1939, which I spent in France, had about it an apoca-
lyptic strangeness. On my previous visits, there had been much talk about
the state of the world and the threat of war. My friends to whom I returned
had ceased talking about the prospect of war. It was already taking place
in their minds. Their real thoughts were submerged within them, and they
continued to exist in those days of such achieved physical beauty, by
giving no articulation to their thoughts. They continued to talk about
ideas, art, literature, and about their families, but dispassionately.

The steadiness of the sunlight that summer accentuated the constant
sombreness and concealment of the French spirit. Anxiety seemed to be
covering the land of France. The vineyards grew heavy with grapes that
summer in the prolonged dryness and sun. In Touraine and Anjou where
I spent some time, I watched the vineyards more closely than ever before.
The green clusters of tiny grapes brought me some vague notion of relief.
I walked beside them alone in order to sense their permanency and their
quiet growth in the sun. The plants of the earth that summer were the
only signs I found of foreordained peace.

And yet the world of men still functioned with utter charm. The speech
of France was more rich and more harmonious than I had ever heard it.
And because my friends avoided talking about the gravest problems, we
talked exclusively of books and paintings, and of related subjects. The
entire summer was a respite. I was reminded many times of that moment
of waiting in a Greek tragedy, when there is nothing for the characters to
do except to exist until destiny declares itself.

[91]

During July in Paris I began to feel this tension wherever I went: in the cafés and gardens, along the quais and in the museums. When August came, the fatal month of invasions in the history of France, I went to the country, and there I followed each day the growing anxiety. I settled down in Amboise in order to be near Henriette Psichari, who occupied a small house outside of Amboise, and also to be near another friend, Alice Coléno, who was living in Amboise.

On arrival I had difficulty in finding a room. No hotel management wanted to assign a room to one individual. As I was turned down at the hotels near the Loire, I moved into the center of the city. I stopped in the heart of the commercial section, at the point where an arch supporting a bell tower stretches over the street. The bell was ringing, and I paused to listen to it and admire the shops around me. On my left was a large handsome hardware shop (*une quincaillerie*) and opposite it an enticing looking *pâtisserie*. A woman from the *quincaillerie* was standing at her door. We began talking. Behind her I saw a spacious well-ordered store. I asked her if she knew where I could fine a room. By her evasive answer I knew she knew of one, but wanted to talk a bit longer in order to get a better impression of me. Finally she offered to rent me a room over the *quincaillerie*.

A circular stone stairway led up to my room from a side street. It had only one window, which opened on to the narrow side street and an opposite wall of stone. I placed the table at the window and worked there each morning. The light fell directly on my page from the small patch of sky above.

When I finished work about noon, I walked over to Alice's hotel, and then we set out together in order to choose a restaurant for lunch. After a few days' explorations, we fixed on one to which we returned daily and where we became known by the proprietor and the waitresses. The French, who on first meetings are the most suspicious and even defiant of people, become, when reasons for suspicions dissipate, the most cordial and warmly exuberant.

Lunch over, Alice and I walked about for an hour or so. We investigated each section of the small city until, as in the case of the restaurant, we discovered the most suitable walk, to which we returned each day. It was the *mail*, the well-ordered strip of park that went along the Loire. The city lay on our left, as we moved away from it. The château was at some distance behind us. After crossing the *mail*, we continued along the embankment of the river, lined with sturdy plane trees. Alice was the first friend to whom I spoke about plane trees. Literature had demonized both of us, but me more than her. I was unable to mention plane trees without referring to Valéry's remarkable poem "Au platane."

The first day, in the presence of a particularly magnificent tree, I tried to recite the poem, but got no farther than the first line: "Tu penches, grand Platane, et te proposes nu." So, on the following day I brought along the volume, and seated on the stone wall of the embankment, under the shade of a plane tree, we read the poem together. We saw how the nudity and whiteness of the tree were held by the earth ("Ta candeur est prise"), and how the earth might be conceived of as a venerable hydra binding and holding all the other living trees in the vicinity ("pressens d'autres vivants liés par l'hydre vénérable"). There was no wind that day in Amboise, and we were unable to hear the language of the tree Valéry speaks of, but we could understand why he ended by choosing the plane tree as the imposing character of a park. "Je t'ai choisi, puissant personnage d'un parc." We labored painstakingly through the poem, I more exultant than Alice, who, when the last line was reached, asked: "Que fait le poète dans tout cela?" It was a cry from her heart, spoken so impetuously, that I laughed and inscribed the question in the volume at the end of the poem.

Toward the latter part of the afternoon I met Henriette, who came in each day in her Peugeot to do the marketing. I knew the approximate time she would arrive in Amboise and the various stores where she traded. Every other day, when the shopping was over, we visited in a café, and on the alternate days I drove back with her to the little house outside the city where she was spending the month.

A small vineyard surrounded the house, on the slope of a hill. The extensive view across a valley resembled the wooded background of a typical eighteenth-century landscape painting. I looked at the scene without real interest or emotion. In former summers I had developed a predilection for the Angevin landscape, and there is just enough difference between Anjou and Touraine to make me regret the first.

During the endings of the long afternoons, we sat outside of Henriette's house on the edge of the vineyard and watched the haze on the valley as we talked. Olivier was painting water colors that summer. He did many studies of his mother as she sat in the garden chair that unfolded like a deck chair. We talked about the landscape and Olivier's paintings. Henriette read to us from the novel she was writing. The days passed in luxuriant warmth and in an outer semblance of happiness. Never did a summer possess such a pattern for contentment, for work, for companionship. Yet the richness of each day declined as the sun did, and when night finally came, I found in myself a relationship with it. Amboise then became for me the small town of France vulnerable to time and invasion. At the embankment I paused often in my night walk and tried to listen, through the perfect quietness, to the tumult of the future.

During the octave of the Feast of the Assumption, the château was illuminated each night. I would arrive ten minutes before the lights were turned off. The details of the stone were more visible than in the daytime. The entire structure stood out so clearly against the blackness of the night that I would easily forget a town existed behind it. But more than architectural designs I watched the white bodies of owls flying lazily and intermittently about the very top of the château. The illumination was an irritant for them. It penetrated into their nests. They rose up from the whitened cornices into the total blackness, where I lost sight of them until they swooped down again to some part of the stone.

When the switch of the floodlights was turned off, the white beauty of the château vanished. Only the mass and general outline of the building remained. I turned away from it and from the Loire, and traced my steps back into the center of the town.

The silence of Amboise at that time and the darkness of its streets were different from the silence and darkness of American towns. I came to believe that the difference had something to do with the age of the place and the centuries that had spent themselves there. At night in France the houses are closed up and barricaded more than the houses of my country, and hence the streets have a more deserted appearance. The houses with their closed metal shutters resembled tombs. I often imagined myself to be the last inhabitant in the town. At times, after passing by so many closed doors, I wondered where I was and whether I was walking in a nightmare.

I returned to Paris at the end of August. My boat was to leave on the 31st. It was there in Paris that the threat of war became suddenly real and grew hourly. The air was permeated with the anguish of waiting for the worst. The day was marked with the successive editions of the newspapers. I was unable to stay in my room more than an hour at a time.

Only one of my friends was in Paris in that last week of August, Eveline Garnier. I had met her a few years previously at her grandmother's, Mme

Favre. Since that time she and I had often gone to Meudon together to visit her uncle and aunt, Jacques and Raïssa Maritain. Eveline had many devoted friends. I had observed their devotion to her which had been generated in the wake of her own extraordinary devotion.

I used to meet her at the end of the day during my last week in Paris. She felt all the horror of the waiting which those last days represented, and yet she felt also a force beyond the horror. I brought to her each evening the confused sum of my anxieties, and she was able each time to give them some order within a greater order. After dinner we walked along the Seine in the very heart of that Paris I felt was doomed. Never had it appeared more peaceful or more singular in its beauty. The faces of the people who passed were drawn and tense. They looked straight ahead as if they could no longer bear to look at the city itself.

When my last full day in Paris came, the 30th of August, I no longer pretended not to look at the sky. My eyes were on it constantly, and the conviction lodged firmly in my heart that the day would not pass without an appearance of the planes.

Eveline left her work in the afternoon, and we went to Montmartre to-gether. When we arrived in front of the basilica, the crowds had grown to such an extent that lines had formed outside. We took our places there and gradually moved up until we were inside the nave. I had never before been in such a large crowd of people all of whom were engaged in prayer. Even at Lourdes I had not sensed the same degree of concentration. There were not enough candles to suffice for the one prayer, but the church seemed ablaze with the tiny flames. Everything I had been taught about prayer as a child was now revealed to me in one experience of utter simplicity. In terms of my childhood, the scene on Montmartre was foreign and Catholic, and yet I was participating in it because of its urgency. No affectation and no strangeness disturbed that moment. It was not only the culmination of my summer and of my experiences in France; it was also the culmina-tion of my prayers as a boy when I prayed for individuals. No single name was on my lips then, but all of mankind. The word enemy ceased to have meaning. I prayed for all the living.

On coming out from the basilica, we paused at the top of the stairway that led down into the city. It was crowded with people moving up and down. The women were dressed in black. I watched the contrast of their clothes against the gray stone of the steps, and, turning around, watched the even greater contrast of their dresses against the white stone of Sacré-

Coeur, as they entered the church. The oriental aspect of the edifice and the light blue sky of that particular day made it difficult to realize I was still in Paris.

That last full day in Paris was almost the microcosm of my life in France. I had spent the morning at work in my hotel room. In the afternoon Eveline and I went to Montmartre, and in the evening we joined a friend of hers, Roger Livet, who was an artist-photographer. For some time I had looked forward to meeting him, on Eveline's insistent recommendation, but I was not keen on meeting him my last evening because my thoughts at that time were sick with their confusion. There before me in the crowded Café Flore was a new character, highly sensitive and cultivated, whom I was expected to meet in that spiritual midway of *sympathie* and attentiveness. At first, secretly, I resented his presence.

Roger Livet's voice was subdued. Eveline and I both somewhat ill at ease over this meeting, but for different reasons, spoke glibly. Livet urged us into his manner of speech and into the quiet manner of his feelings. He was the only Frenchman I had met at that time who demonstrated an unashamed interest in American matters: films, books, art and what I suppose might be called the American temperament or spirit.

Livet had that special kind of passion for poetry I shared and understood. During our conversation about American letters and films, he had been testing me. In many ways I was inferior to him on those subjects, both in knowledge and enthusiasm. Then, the discussion shifted to French poetry. We met evenly on the obvious grounds: Baudelaire, Rimbaud, Mallarmé, Valéry. The actual texts were more present in my mind than in his, and in a short time the air around our small table was charged with the verses of poets, remembered and recited in some need to reaffirm permanent values. The rehearsal turned into a game. He wanted to make sure of me on every point and brought up the slightly more obscure names of Audiberti, Patrice de la Tour du Pin, *Divagations*, *Chimères*. The examination went well for me, although I kept reminding him that French poetry was my *métier*. It was difficult for him to realize that an American could live in America and live at the same time in a constant study of French letters.

The subdued smile on his lips broke into an authentic one when he announced that he had remembered the name of a poet who might well have escaped me. Before naming him, he described him in terms of hermeticism and modernism (although he was not a recent poet), and I knew that the poet my new friend had in mind was Maurice Scève. With absolute assurance, I said the name to him. Thus the final step was made. I believe I was more moved than he in the discovery of our mutual admiration for Scève.

The very lights of the Café Flore seemed more intense and luminous as I looked out over the heads in front of us, across the wide sidewalk and the darkness of the night beyond. The space where I sat was an island. The sentences I heard and the words with which I replied to them cut me off from the rest of the world just as much as the physical limitations of the café table. The French language was an island from which I saw the world differently, as the poetry of Scève was a new gauge and measurement of human experience for me.

From out of the darkness suddenly appeared, on the very edge of the lighted sidewalk and the first row of tables, a large man leading by his hand a little girl. It was midnight, and I was confused at seeing a golden-haired child enter that particular sphere of light. A commotion started at the tables closest to the strange couple. They were greeted vociferously, and the man, who had a massive leonine head, shook hands with the many who extended their hands to him. The girl followed him and curtsied before each table. The picture was charmingly surrealist, and I was not surprised to hear Livet explain that it was André Breton and his daughter who appeared nightly, at this particular time, at the Café Flore. I watched them wind in and out among the tables, Breton speaking in low but cordial tones to his friends, and the little girl, silent, but her body very expressive as she curtsied and rose upon her toes. The celebrated writer and his daughter did not pass close to our table.

I remembered the pages of *Nadja* that trace a pattern of chance meetings and illogical separations, and I considered the passage of that extraordinary couple in the Flore as if it were directed at me, as the symbol of continuity and faith and endurance. The poise of Breton's middle age and renown and the grace of his golden-haired fairy child were the preoccupations of the hour, as if all the anxieties of the real hour had been recognized as false and terminated. Age and youth passed by me in a marriage of such simplicity that I knew France to be all over again the land of permanence and regeneration.

Eveline and Roger left me at my hotel door, but I did not go upstairs immediately. I crossed over from the boulevard Raspail to Edgar Quinet where the walls of the Cimetière Montparnasse line the sidewalk. The goal of my walk was the spot at the wall on the other side of which I knew Baudelaire's monument to be. This had been one of my earliest goals ten years previously on my first visit to Paris. At that time I had entered the cemetery in the daylight and had seen the actual stone and carving of the monument. But now I was reenacting the Mallarmé sonnet on Baudelaire's tomb. I had followed the street lights and their skeletal shadows on the walls, until I paused like some vain shade close by the greatness of the poet. He was no longer the voyager, but I was, and I knew that part of my actual voyage had been chartered by him: "Dites, qu'avez-vous vu?" The precious lines came to my mind. What he had said about Mariette's tomb, I was saying about his: "Les morts, les pauvres morts." And I listened, as he had told his child Grief to listen, to the night walking toward me: "Entends, ma chère, entends la douce nuit qui marche."

On the following day, the 31st of August, the train ride between Paris and Le Havre was the first part of a pattern of separation and return. It seemed that almost instantly we were passing by Norman farms, red-tiled roofs and the gray city of Rouen. The swiftness of the train became exaggerated as the housetops and patches of fertile land flashed by in a jerky cinematographic procession. I saw men and women working in the fields, and wondered what age-old faith kept them there.

As opposed to the train, the boat seemed to be immobilized. A slight storm arose the second day, and I was ill in my cabin where I completely lost any sensation of progress. The movement of the boat seemed to be circular. I remained on my back, half somnolent, half sick, as if waiting for some decision to be reached. Two days passed thus. On the fourth morning the sea was calm, and I knew that the boat must be moving in one direction. On the way from my cabin to the deck, I learned from bits of conversation I overheard, that war had been declared.

The train ride from Grand Central to North Bennington paralleled the ride between Paris and Le Havre. I was again able to turn my head away from the inside of the train and the passengers and keep my eyes fixed on the moving land. These were to be the last hours of solitude before the new life—that life framed by war—was to begin. It was eight-thirty in the morning, and the ride would take until one in the afternoon.

The sky and the day were the same as those of the train ride through Normandy. But the aspect of the countryside had changed. The Hudson River flowed through a land that was still new, a land that was not yet divided up into small farms. It still resembled an uninhabited country, wooded and unexplored. From time to time we passed a barge on the river, and once on an island a mock medieval castle rose up as in a dream. I remembered then that the river was not the Rhine but the Hudson, and the castle was a beer factory. In the Normandy ride a few days previously I had watched every vestige of cultivation and property as if it were menaced by some hideous dissolving force, but in the New York ride the breadth of the river and the majesty of the West Point cliffs converted me into the sightseer. I was returning home as a tourist, with the lightness of heart of a tourist who senses no danger in the country he is visiting.

Each billboard we passed, each stationary freight train bearing some American name I had not said or seen in months, revived a pattern of recognition. Albany came, then Troy, and soon after that the landscape began to resemble Vermont's. The sun might well have been that of Amboise or Normandy, but its light fell on a countryside wilder and more irregular. The shape of the towns and the houses belonged to another world. The old self that was re-forming in me recognized them and accepted them back. Their drabness had still some meaning. It related me once again to the austerity and puritanism under whose diluted influences I had been reared. The small station of North Bennington was almost deserted.

IX

Old Bennington, 1940   Martha Graham

At the beginning of 1940 I occupied for the first time in my life an apartment of my own. It was in Old Bennington, the residentially aristocratic part overlooking the poor commercial town of stores and mills and drab houses. The structure in which I found an apartment had been built in the Greek revival period. It was a massive white house with both large and small columns decorating the façade. The college had purchased it and cut it up into apartments. Mine was on the ground floor. It was composed of two large strangely formed rooms. The living room, which followed part of the piazza and then plunged solidly into the center of the house, was dark. The main door from the piazza opened directly into it. On either side of the door were long windows or French doors, the sole source of light in the daytime. This room was always dark, and hence I never used it in the daytime. At night when I turned on the lamps, it became a new or forgotten room and my quarters doubled in size. The other room was equally long, and it followed the adjoining side of the house so that my two rooms formed one corner. This room, both sleeping room and study, had many windows and the flood of light from them was always excessive. There I slept at night and worked during the day when I was at home.

For this first home I purchased from a factory in Gardner, Massachusetts, some pieces of white modernistically designed furniture. A desk I placed at a window in the second room. It was reserved for my personal writing. Opposite it, against the wall I placed a large table I had bought at an auction and painted black. On it I corrected papers and prepared my classes. The white desk and the black table divided my studious life

[100]

into the creative and the academic, in much the same way that the two rooms of my apartment divided my life into day and night.

In the farthest corner of the night room, at the extreme point of my apartment which seemed to end in the center of the entire house, where there was no recourse to light from the outside, I placed the one precious object of my possessions: my clavichord. I had bought the instrument a few years previously from my friend Austin Warren, who had acquired it from an aged lady in Cambridge, the first music major at Radcliffe. The clavichord was one of a series made by Arnold Dolmetsch in 1906 for the Chickering Company of Boston. It bore the number 9. I had kept it in my room at the Joneses' house at the college, and when the harpsichordist Ralph Kirkpatrick came to teach for a semester at Bennington, I asked him for some lessons. I remember his looking amusedly at me and asking if I had a clavichord. I described the instrument and mentioned Dolmetsch No. 9. The world of clavichords is so restricted that the real initiates know the address of each instrument. Kirkpatrick's face glowed at that moment. "I had wondered where No. 9 was. You have one of the best clavichords. It is quite possibly the longest in the country." He insisted upon coming to my room to see it.

After walking around it, touching it reverently, tuning it with great patience, he decided to communicate with it and began to play the first prelude of *The Well-Tempered Clavichord*. He continued with the fugue, and then the second prelude, and so on, until he had played most of the entire first volume.

I was a mediocre student of the clavichord that semester, but I derived pleasure from my imperfect playing. I would come to the clavichord in the evening, as I would come to the room itself in order to change the tempo and the way of my living. When I turned on the lamp beside it and the full light fell on the dark cover, the room assumed its complexion, and the change was completed from one act to another. The keyboard, diminutive in size, each key of which seemed fragile, and the fan-like arrangement of strings, all represented a deep silence that was to be broken. When I began to play, the silence had become so complete in the room that the softest tinkle was audible to me. The room encased the sounds, and as I played they grew in clarity and forcefulness until they filled all the space. Because of the brevity of the sound, I was tensed to hear it more accurately. The instrument had to be "touched" in a particular way by me, and I had to be receptive in order to hear what I had imperceptibly instigated.

I created and planned the solitude of my strange apartment. I arranged

[101]

it according to degrees and hours, according to the course of the sun and the capacity for work I felt in me. The first silence of the day was the writing period. When, from there, I moved in the middle of the morning to the black table, I often spoke out loud the lessons I prepared and particularly the verses of the French poets I was continually memorizing. That was the first voice I heard in the day, my own, reciting not my own words, but those of Racine or Baudelaire. This second period was no longer silence, but it was another kind of solitude when I moved within the world of the poet. When I left the house and moved into "life"—the streets in Bennington, the classes at the college, the activities of my colleagues and town politics—I felt I had left the real part of life for its caricature.

With the breaking of spring, I began regularly on my free days to take a noon walk in the center of Old Bennington. The town is still today a perfectly preserved specimen of early New England. Industry and commerce have kept themselves down below in the town of Bennington itself. The adjective "old" added to the name, marks a difference of caste and appearance. Old Bennington is a museum town stretching out under its obelisk monument. A long green fills the center of the street. The First Church, white and stark, in the most prominent site, has been restored inside and out and kept freshly painted. It is on the topmost crest of land. Beside and behind it the sloping cemetery reaches half-way down the hill. The dead are preserved from any dangerous closeness with the more humble folk below.

The tombstones forming the first line after the white fence are the oldest. They stand closest to the street and to the church. From the sidewalk I often read to myself, or out loud if there was no one nearby, the epitaph carved in the stone marking the grave of the first pastor:

> In memory of the Revd. M. Jedidiah Dewey,
> First Pastor of the Church in Bennington,
> Who, after a laborious life in the Gospel Ministry,
> Resigned his office in God's Temple
> For the sublime employment of immortality
> Decmbr 21st 1778
> In the 65th year of his age.
> Of comfort no man speak!
> Let's talk of graves, of worms,
> And epitaphs, make dust our

Paper, and with rainy eyes,
Write sorrow on the bosom
Of the earth.

I had admired the beauty of the lines. One day at lunch in the college "commons" I mentioned them to William Troy and asked if he did not agree that they sounded like the best of eighteenth-century English verse. (He and his wife Léonie Adams had once occupied my apartment in Old Bennington.) He told me that he too had been impressed with the poetry on Jedidiah's tomb, and when once he praised the lines to Léonie, she quietly replied, "They should be good. They are from *Richard II*."

Summer came as the third season I was to know in my Old Bennington apartment. Classes stopped in June. My two rooms became more than ever a retreat. Their emptiness and lack of color, the thin tones of the clavichord and the paper bound French books I kept near me forced me to believe, more than ever, that the substance of my life would have to become those words I consigned each day to paper. There in the apartment I tried to realize the news that France had fallen once again into the power of the German army.

As I walked on West Road in the direction of Mount Anthony I remembered walks along the parapets of the Seine over which solitary fishermen dropped their lines or where the *bouquinistes* exhibited their varied wares. All that was closed off now. The world had been diminished. The entries I made in my journal concerned the eclipse of France and my consequent estrangement from that source. Abruptly what had been central to me for so long, was deviated. I began living according to a new regimen of conviction that was assaulted each day and each week by the facts of the world and the news from Europe.

At the college, four miles away, a summer session on the dramatic arts had begun. The work was to culminate at the end of the summer in two productions: a play version of *Huckleberry Finn*, written and directed by Francis Fergusson, and a new dance of Martha Graham, which we learned was to deal with the life of Emily Dickinson. I had a small part in the third act of *Huckleberry Finn*, the role of the brother who came from England and whose sixteen lines helped to precipitate the dénouement. This meant I had to attend very few of the rehearsals. It was a stock character I played, and quite early, under the direction of Francis, I had fixed the tone and movement of my one scene. It remained steadfast at each rehearsal, and I could enjoy on my infrequent visits to the campus and the college theater the other scenes and the dances that were composed and rehearsed by Martha Hill. I was glad to have some tie with the summer performances.

There was more excitement during the final week when the full dress rehearsals began. Even my small role was being affected by the beat and tempo and precipitation of the entire work. The separate scenes suddenly fell together and fused. The dancers began enjoying the dances when they no longer had to count their steps. My entrance was a kind of dance movement itself. I was made up to be a fat potbellied fellow dressed in a white and pinstriped vest. When I appeared in the extreme right upstage corner, several characters rushed at me, almost lifted me in the air and escorted me in a flash, as if they were pushing a balloon, to a platform downstage from which I was to speak my lines. For two minutes my rotund personality became the center of the action. I was the English brother who towered above his more moderately sized American brothers and dispensed to them a few clipped British syllables.

That summer I turned to the poet who had become essential for me, to Mallarmé, in whose verse I had discovered the enchantment and symbolism of objects and closed rooms, the drama of language in its search for understanding, in its cult of mystery and night. The memorizing of his poems became a spirtual exercise. Mallarmé's metaphors are so constructed and so absolute that they channel the mind into themselves and allow no divergence from them. That was the discipline I needed in the summer of 1940 when the fate of France was being shaped and questioned. The pure rigor of Mallarmé's art restored me daily to a faith by which I had lived since my first visit to Paris.

I found myself returning every day to the sonnets on the golden hair. They formed a cycle in which I came upon an almost forgotten aspect of my childhood. The poem beginning "La chevelure vol d'une flamme" became obsessive. Certain of its phrases became fixed in my mind as key elements, not only of Mallarmé's vocabulary but also of my early life in films and opera: the flight of flame encircling the beloved's head like a diadem; the cloud of hair seemingly alive with its fire; the sowing of rubies in the air which a toss of the head accomplished; the torch both radiant and protecting. These phrases, as they settled into their fixed pattern, went far beyond Méry's hair, and I saw the blond hair of Pearl White. Her hair had once held me spellbound as it accompanied her frenzied actions, and years later, the same spell came over me in the elliptical sonnet of Mallarmé.

The sonnet "Victorieusement fui le suicide beau" was another daily exercise of my 1940 summer. In it the image of golden hair became ruddy, and the flame metaphor of the first sonnet became the love metaphor in which the abundant hair of the beloved drops over a cushion as if its redness were roses falling from a warrior's helmet. The heroine of my youth became in this second sonnet the heroine of my adolescence. Mary Garden replaced Pearl White. I moved from the screen to the opera stage, from my childhood dream of action and blonde heroines to my adolescent infatuation for opera and Mary Garden's depiction of red-haired Mélisande.

My continuous recital of Mallarmé and the rehearsals of *Huckleberry Finn* were two extremes of the same histrionic exercise. As the summer wore on, I became increasingly aware of another extreme in dramatic self-projection, in which I had no part, but which was being prepared at the college. It was the new dance of Martha Graham, which we knew was being composed and rehearsed in secret and which would be performed publicly in the final week of productions.

Even before coming to Bennington, I had seen Martha Graham dance in Boston. Each year she produced a new work. I had marvelled at the steady progress of her art and at the enthusiastic faithfulness of her public, which grew in size each year.

During the course of the summer months the rumor grew that the new dance was to touch on some aspects of the life of Emily Dickinson. We heard next that certain lines of Dickinson were to be recited during the actual dancing. The dancers rehearsing the work were pledged to silence about it, and we were never sure whether what we heard was fact or invention. I was envious of those who professed to know her well, who had the chance of working with her. The summer idyl I formed around Martha Graham had its source in my admiration for her performances and the courage she proved each year in the development of an art difficult to accept. She had become a dancer in spite of a hostile public. She had forced attention and adherence from an audience prepared to make fun of her.

By now I have seen so many times the dance on Emily Dickinson, *Letter to the World*, that I no longer distinctly remember its first version in August of 1940. More accurately than the dance itself, I remember the place in the audience where I sat and the excitement of my feelings during the minutes that preceded the first curtain. My memory of the dance on that occasion of its first performance, is the dual apparition of Emily Dickinson: the girl in white (Jean Erdman) who moved infrequently across the stage, and who recited fragments of the poems, and the girl in red, who was the dancer Martha Graham giving form and movement to the inner turmoil of the poet. The white dress and the unaffectedly read lines of the poems served as background for the red flame of the spirit and the bodily movements. The dance seemed to be the way of rejection: the immediate world images in the poet's life were being rejected one after the other, and after each episode of rejection, the lines from the poem were spoken as the way of affirmation.

Emily Dickinson, interpreted by Martha Graham, became the reincarnation of my heroine. But she now had black hair, which fell away from her swaying body as if it formed a dance by itself. I recognized the hair, but not its blackness. *Letter to the World* provided me with so different an image that I felt a new age or new cycle had begun. Martha Graham's hair was like the night itself, made real by the whiteness of her brow and the redness of her dress. I followed it no longer as light but as darkness, and it guided me through a well-known labyrinth toward the still center of the heart. At ten I watched the blond hair of the girl in *The Ruby Ring*; at fifteen, the red hair of the singer when it fell into the hands of Pelléas standing under the tower window; at twenty-five I first read the sonnet on the presumptuous treasure of the child empress's hair; and now at thirty I watched the dancer's black hair obscure all the earlier gold and flame as if night had enshrouded my dreams and drained off from all the artificial skies of the stage the last glimmer and streak of light. The diadem was now of ebony, and the flame across the sky was now a cloud, not ignited but darkened.

X

In the early fall of 1941, I moved to New Haven, in order to teach at Yale. This was another world and the beginning of a new period. The shift from Harvard to Bennington was now repeated in reverse. The move from Bennington to Yale completed a cycle. I had returned to where I had begun, but everything was changed. At Harvard I had risen painfully from the status of undergraduate to graduate student and instructor. Instructors on a half-time basis, who are preparing a doctoral thesis, live on the fringe of a university, in a special limbus where desire and ambition have to be submerged, where the permanent faculty treats them as students and criticizes their first steps in the sacred ritual of teaching. The students sense the insecurity of such instructors, whose lives are divided between the tasks of elementary teaching and the meticulous and often sterilizing labors of a thesis. And they watch these ghosts or slaves of the profession dismiss their classes and then withdraw from the world of sunlight into some obscure corner of the library stacks to pore over, not the great writings of the world, but the dustiest and driest of the volumes in whose territory they are entombed.

I had forgotten, during the Bennington years, much of the Harvard initiation to scholarship and teaching. There, in Vermont, I had taught only the major works of literature and had paid the minimum attention to scholarship and literary history. Back once again in the city, I considered the streets, the stores and the people with relief and an old familiarity. This was my setting and my atmosphere, even if it did recall the closed-in cubicles of the Widener Library stacks. Before I visited the Sterling Library of Yale, I wandered about New Haven in order to see the city first.

I suppose there is no city of New England that can rival New Haven in ugliness of architecture. The large houses seem to have been built as defiances of any laws of proportion. They are massive lumps constructed without taste. The public buildings create no harmony with one another and when taken separately are nondescript. Only the churches, at least those in the center of the city, have a character and placid dignity of their own. Christ Church, built on a kind of island formed by the crossing of two main streets, is a distinctive baroque-looking edifice. It is an Anglo-Catholic church, whose appearance reminded me of Trinity Church, Boston. By walking down either one of the two parallel streets, Elm or Chapel, one comes to the city green, cut into two large squares. At one end the early buildings of Yale and the site of the old "fence" stand as an intellectual embattlement against the city proper. At the other end, the city hall, of similar architecture and color, and the more modern stores line the entrance to the lower city.

In the center of the green, three churches, evenly spaced, provide a pause and a reminiscence of the past. Two of the churches are early Colonial style. Center Church, if I remember correctly, harbors the remains of the first Yale presidents, a reminder of the original union of university and church, of learning and piety. Just one block from the solemn line of three churches, the intersection of Church and Chapel streets provides the contemporary aspect of crowds and traffic jams, of stores and banks. That is where the Italians of the city mingled with the Irish, where the Irish directed the movements of the few descendants of the early New Haven families, where the Yale students brushed by the high school girls. Liggett's drug store, dominating the corner, was the common meeting place and the first spot in the city I learned about after moving into my rooms at 32 High Street.

The New Haven apartment was far different from the one I had occupied in Old Bennington. Its living room was just large enough to contain the clavichord and the white desk. Into the bedroom I was able to place my beds and black table. I thus maintained two places at which to work and separated school work from writing. The rooms were so restricted in space that I did not recognize my furniture, and on the slightest occasion I left the apartment during the first days to enjoy the free space of the streets, to make necessary purchases and drop into a movie.

Both the art museum and the library of the university were on High

[108]

Street. During the first few weeks I enjoyed the confusion of the buildings. I played the part of the newcomer who was bewildered. It was almost a game to search out the classrooms in Harkness and to pass so many faces in the corridors, not one of which I recognized. The types of faces I remembered from my Harvard years: the same manner of dress, dark trousers and a bright tweed coat, the same large notebook used for classroom note taking and held in the same fashion of studied nonchalance.

Memories of Harvard were present on the surface of my mind, but they lacked the pain and the anxiety of the ill-defined role of instructor-graduate student. My role was clearer at Yale. I was an assistant professor, and one of the three courses I taught was entirely my own: sixteenth-century literature. I had been working all summer on the course and vaguely imagining a large room of a hundred students. At the first meeting I discovered that only six students had elected the course. My pride was humbled.

My other two courses were sections of large freshman courses. One of them was directed by the head of the department, M. Henri Peyre, who each week gave one lecture to all the assembled sections. This weekly lecture I attended with increasing admiration for the skill and brilliance with which Professor Peyre expounded each topic. I had never heard, even from Frenchmen, such fertility of speech. And yet, despite the abundance of ideas and facts, the elaborate lesson fell into its parts and discovered its form. The rapid speech was not haste. It was an ardor with which Henri Peyre renovated and adorned his subject. Allusions and examples were drawn from every century and many literatures to expose the theory of classicism. At such lectures the listeners found literature to be a vast complex experience, involving many worlds. M. Peyre was able to convince others of what he believed, that literature is an expression of what is deepest in man. I followed avidly the dual experience of watching languid listeners transformed into excited students and of feeling in myself a reaffirmation of my own faith.

The most modest of my three courses, known as "French 30," gave me my greatest pleasure during the first year's teaching at Yale. The class was composed of twenty-five freshmen, all quite unknowing of the ways of literature. The excitement of the course for me was to watch first reactions to a story of Voltaire, or a play of Musset, or a poem of Baudelaire. The students soon developed an eagerness to see what could be seen in a text, and it became my duty then to restrain them from leaping beyond the text into some imagined theory. In a way, the climax of the course came with Flaubert's "Un Coeur simple." We fixed on the symbolism of the

[109]

parrot as if it had become the text of the entire year's work. Every part of that miraculously composed story was illumined with the richness of meaning we found for Loulou. I remember how meager my notes were for that lesson when I entered the classroom, and how they grew in the class discussion. My neophytes had turned exegetes, or their encouragement had become so subtle that I no longer knew who was finding the meanings, they or myself.

I began taking my evening meal two or three times a week at the Faculty Club, housed in a small white building on Elm Street, opposite the green. It was one of the oldest houses in the city and still preserved some of its original aspects: low-ceilinged rooms and a vast fireplace in what was once the kitchen. Both mind and body were tired when I arrived at the Faculty Club for dinner. The uniformly good food served there helped somewhat to restore me. I looked back on the day, at the inadequacies of my teaching and writing, and tried to measure the signs of friendliness in the students and colleagues. My distant memories of food are very few, but the Faculty Club ice cream and coffee are among them. From childhood the hot rolls baked by my grandmother and which we ate with the Saturday night beans, baked also in her oven, are my first memory of food. Then at Quiberon one summer in Brittany, after a long walk with Henriette Psichari and two of her sons, we ate oysters with fresh bread, still hot, and drank cool white wine, whose taste I can still recall.

On my first Sunday in New Haven, I was invited, through the mediation of the Peyres, to luncheon at the home of Mrs. Mabel Lafarge in Mount Carmel, just outside the city. It was a courtesy of welcome. She had read my book on Psichari and had heard from the Maritains that I had come to Yale. Mr. and Mrs. Charles Hendel, of the philosophy department, were also among the guests at that luncheon.

That first visit to Mount Carmel is now confused with countless other visits. During my years in New Haven, I called on Mrs. Lafarge almost every week. She became a good friend. Many things joined us. Her early life about which she willingly spoke had been spent in New England. She was born in Cambridge, Massachusetts, the daughter of Edward and Fanny Hopper, and niece of Henry Adams. In fact, she was one of the nieces to whom *The Education of Henry Adams* was dedicated. In 1898 she married Bancel Lefarge, the painter and one of the three sons of the distinguished painter John Lafarge. From then on until the beginning of the First World

War they lived much of the time in France where she brought up her five sons. There, for many years she observed the Catholic faith, of which she had read an expression in her uncle's book *Mont-Saint-Michel and Chartres*, and finally accepted the religion of her husband's family and was received into the Church. On her New England Unitarian background was grafted a tender loyalty to Catholicism such as she had found it especially in France and in French writers. Every time we walked through her garden, she combined a story from her childhood with a story of some French artist. Claudel had once stayed at Mount Carmel and had talked with her at length about the mysterious origin of his play, *Partage de midi*.

I often think of Mrs. Lafarge's paintings which were always of flowers from her garden. She transported them to boxes of earth in her studio and watched over them until their blooms had sufficiently opened. She painted them at their highest moment of beauty. And she colored around them a dark background so that they would glow dramatically in their own blaze.

She encouraged me to bring small groups of students to Mount Carmel for picnic suppers: Roger Shattuck, Boone Porter, Harvey Buchanan, Ted Morris, Philip Walker. I enjoyed all parts of the ceremony, repeated so many times during two or three years. It began with the long bus trip on Whitney Avenue. Then came the walk along the country roads until we began to climb the hill. Gradually through the trees we could see the house, and always on the lawn, when we reached the top, stood Mrs. Lafarge, thin and fragile, anticipating our advent and eager to welcome us. She led us on a tour up the path behind the house to the barns and stables that she and her husband had converted into studios when they first came to live and work at Mount Carmel. She showed us paintings of her husband and of her son Tom. And then some of her own paintings, usually the most recent ones, flowers whose living models were still there in the studio. Then we would come down to the lawn where we had supper. The conversation always turned to Europe. The students were about to leave for war or were already in uniform. I knew how full her mind was of the possible sacrifice of their lives. She inquired about their courses and readings, about their thoughts on the war and their plans for the future.

She understood many things, and other things she always failed to understand. Once when we were alone, she made the extraordinary statement, "I wish *Hamlet* had never been written." She was saying much more than simply, "I don't know why you refer so much to *Hamlet* in your writings and conversation, but I wish you wouldn't." She was denouncing us all,

all the pseudo-Hamlets and the sons of Hamlet, all the Henry Millers, the D. H. Lawrences, the Rimbauds and the Prousts, all the writers and readers who remained children and who never completed the rite of initiation. One day she asked me about a Mallarmé sonnet that has the phrase *mauvais Hamlet*, and I tried to tell her what I believed about the clown and the *pitre châtié*. But she did not understand.

Gustave Cohen of the Sorbonne was visiting professor of French the year I arrived at Yale. I was acquainted with some of his writings, especially his explication of Valéry's "Cimetière marin," and I had heard about his teaching from students in Paris. I knew of his great interest in the medieval theater and of his particular predilection for *Le Miracle de Théophile* by Rutebeuf, productions of which he had sponsored at the Sorbonne.

We met first in the restaurant Mory's, situated close to the Graduate School where he lived. He was seated at one of the tables when I came in, and as he extended his hand to me across the table, he spoke a few words I have always remembered, "Nous avons beaucoup de choses en commun, et surtout un amour de la poésie." His speech was always ceremonious and dramatic. From our first conversation, I was fascinated by the ease and eloquence of his diction, by the skill with which he converted simple episodes into significant actions. To talk about something, for Gustave Cohen, was to elevate it, to endow it with some important meaning. His enthusiasm and energy were limitless. He would extol an obscure medieval text as vehemently as *La Jeune Parque*.

I was summoned one day to Professor Cohen's rooms and made to feel that the revelation was to be momentous. Before the preliminary remarks had ended, I realized the proposal was to concern *Le Miracle de Théophile*. With that realization came the direct words of request, "Will you play the part of Théophile at Yale?" If M. Cohen had been offering me his chair at the Sorbonne, his voice would not have betrayed more pride. The text of *Théophile* had curiously become his own. Rutebeuf was an obscure thirteenth-century *trouvère* whose play existed in the twentieth century thanks to this aging scholar. Cohen had never actually played the part of Théophile (he had suffered a serious leg injury in the First World War) but I am certain he had infused his spirit in the various Théophiles of Paris and elsewhere. His love for the Middle Ages, his scholarship, his histrionic talent and his unspoken but very real devotion to the Virgin,

[112]

were all present in his transposition of *Le Miracle de Théophile* and the many performances of the play he had instigated.

I told him how honored I would be to play *Théophile*. The old desire to act started up again in me. A copy of the text in my hand, I returned to my apartment and began reading it out loud. It was a stubborn, difficult and awkward text. The archaic words and inversions made it almost impossible to give the short lines any flow and lyric cohesion. In a week I returned to Cohen and confessed my discouragement with the lines. He asked me to begin reading the opening monologue in which Théophile speaks to God and vituperates against Him. I had scarcely uttered the first syllables when he took over and became Théophile. He read the part with an almost terrifying participation in it. After every long speech he would see me still there beside him and ask me to begin reading the next speech. But as soon as he heard my weak articulations, he would repeat the words for me and then would forget he was giving me a lesson and continue with the speech. Not only was the text his, to such a degree that he often said, "I don't know where Rutebeuf ends and where I begin," but also he was Théophile, in a savage possessive way. I wondered at that first lesson, which was to be the only one, how Professor Cohen had ever allowed anyone to play his *Théophile*.

His reading helped me prodigiously. I realized, as I listened to it, that his interpretation could not be mine, but it revealed to me that the text was capable of interpretation. My own way was not clear when I left Gustave Cohen that day, but I felt confident I could discover a way. My major worry was over. Soon began, however, a host of minor worries. According to the original plan, Cohen was to direct the rehearsals, but he was frequently out of town for lecture engagements. Time was passing, and no rehearsals had taken place save an initial meeting for distribution of roles. Finally, he asked me to take charge of the production and direct the play as I saw fit.

This changed everything for me. Heretofore I had always been directed. Now I was responsible not only for Théophile but for seeing the play as a whole and organizing all the parts around Théophile. The strange stiff quality of the text induced me to conceive of the work as a ritual, as a ceremony to be stylized. There were brief dramatic scenes uniting the long lyric passages. There was a dance to be composed for Théophile and the devil. Paul Hindemith was generous and helpful in choosing suitable music for this dance, in making a record of it for me to rehearse by, and in training a chorus to sing backstage, for the opening and close of the play, the Introit, *Sederunt principes*, composed by Perotinus for the feast of Saint Stephen, on the 26th of December, 1198.

I plotted out the action of the scenes and even the details of the speech. At rehearsals themselves, with the living actors before me moving and speaking, I brought changes to the first plans.

A week before the performance, M. Cohen returned from Canada where he had been lecturing, and asked to see one of the rehearsals. I had been dreading this moment, aware that whatever my production had become, it was vastly different from the Paris version. We went through the play without interruption, and then I dismissed the cast. When Cohen and I were alone, he said in a totally direct way, "It must not go on that way. It will have to be changed. You have turned my *Théophile* into a *ballet russe*."

I had expected remonstrances but not of such a total order. It was not merely a case of director against author. It was almost pupil versus professor. Any infringement against the sacred tradition of *Théophile* was blasphemous. Much was at stake, and above all, the performance scheduled a week off. I reminded Professor Cohen that I had never seen a Paris performance and that he had given me no indication as to its style. Moreover he had told me to direct the play according to my own ideas. I even reminded him of the theory he had once exposed to me, that since *Théophile* ranks among the great plays of the world, it can be variously interpreted. Then I begged him to have confidence in the cast, saying that when we were in costume and makeup and acting on the stage, this particular stylization would appear different to him.

My role of director disappeared—I forced it to disappear—when the chorus began singing the music of Perotinus at the performance. We were waiting for the curtain. Not until then did I feel I had the right to think only of the part of Théophile. I no longer saw the other members of the cast and forgot about the directions and the drills. As we moved into the opening procession, I moved into that terrible separateness from myself and from the others. When the music stopped, the actors withdrew and left me alone on the stage. A moment of silence was sufficient for me to become Théophile and I began reciting from out of that silence

"Aï! Aï! Dieu, roi de gloire."

Then began the strange experience of reciting a text and hearing it issue forth stronger than ever before because there was an audience present. I was reciting Théophile's role and hearing it for the first time. I was no longer alone with the text. The audience was silently participating in it.

When it was over and the backstage confusion somewhat subsided, I looked around for Professor Cohen. I was no longer fearful of encountering him now, because the performance had been well followed and appreciated. He broke through the barricade of friends and colleagues, and as we moved toward one another, I felt I was resuming the part of Théophile in order to receive a final benediction. He bestowed a Gallic accolade on me, and, kissing both of my cheeks, said I had understood better than he how the play should be presented to an American public. This epilogue scene was a reconciliation when the American Théophile was absolved from a waywardness not included in the old text of Rutebeuf.

Early in 1942, soon after Pearl Harbor, I visited Professor Henri Focillon in his suite at the Taft Hotel. He had been for some time confined to his room with illness. During the fall I had gradually realized what a prominent and beloved figure he had become in New Haven ever since he had been dividing his time between the Collège de France and Yale University. Of his work I knew especially *La Vie des formes*, but I remembered him from an incident in Paris of New Year's Day 1939. I was at Mme Renan's house on the rue Chaptal. She had told me at lunch that she was receiving that afternoon one of her cherished friends, Henri Focillon, the art historian and critic. I was in my room late in the afternoon when the bell rang. He had to pass by my door to reach the salon, and I heard him speak to Esther as they went down the hallway. Thirty or forty minutes later, the salon door opened, and again I heard his voice, this time addressing Mme Renan. Up until that moment Mme Renan's speech had been the richest I had heard in France, but on that occasion her voice was almost silent, and I heard a still richer expression of thought and sentiment.

The name of Mme Renan occupied a large part of my first conversation with Focillon. He called me one of the privileged of the earth when he learned I had spent two winters at the rue Chaptal. One of the many reasons for his devotion to Mme Renan was the moral support she had given him at the time when he was thinking of presenting his candidacy at the Collège de France. He was professor at the Sorbonne and hesitant about requesting entrance to the Collège de France unless there were assurance of a large vote in his favor. He sought counsel from Mme Renan, who urged him to have faith in his destiny. "I am a Breton woman," she said to him, "and all Breton women are magicians. I know you will be elected with an overwhelming majority." ("Je suis Bretonne et toutes les Bretonnes sont magiciennes. Je sais que vous serez élu à grosse majorité.") Her divination, of course, was exact.

As I heard Henri Focillon quote the words of his friend, I felt transported to her salon and the quiet evening conversations which, already, since the occupation of Paris, seemed to belong to another world and another period in time. The room at the Taft Hotel and the bed from which he spoke, were transposed instantly by his words into whatever setting he happened to talk about: a romanesque church, a Flaubert short story, the genius of his beloved Général de Gaulle.

At the end of my first year at Yale, I was invited to inhabit a spacious and ornate suite of rooms at Trumbull College (one of the ten colleges of the university) where I was to serve as resident fellow. On my first visit with M. Focillon after my installation, he asked me how I liked the change from the modest small apartment on High Street to the Trumbull suite. I answered hesitatingly that the new elegance was not quite appropriate to my nature and that it might take some time to adjust to it. He explained this by saying I was really a monk, and when I protested that after all I was not that, he quieted me with a raised hand and pronounced: "Mon cher ami, cessez d'être moine et devenez cardinal."

The fall of 1942, my first in Trumbull College, was the last period during wartime when Yale functioned in its usual way. One felt everywhere a gradual dying off of normal college life. I inhabited in fairly austere solitude my apartment, 1248 Trumbull, until the period of farewells began, just before Christmas vacation. It extended over several months, well into the spring and early summer when one by one the students dropped out from classes to leave for training camps. The ritual of departure was always the same. As I left the classroom after a lesson, the student would stop me and ask permission to call at my apartment that evening to say good-bye. Each week I went through a similar scene two or three times. The student would call at the time set, and we would talk in my vast living room, an ironic picture of space and comfort, about the books he might take away with him, about the courses he might take on his return to Yale.

Each visit was different from all the others, each one had some particular variation on a familiar pattern, but all were the same to me in the unspoken anguish one felt over the uncertainty of war. War as a spirit of illness and depletion grew around me. The heavy entrance door of the apartment, with its figure of 1248, became the background of so many scenes of good-bye that each time it closed, I felt being cut off from one further part of the world. Only the noise of the streetcars continued on Elm Street below, as if they were rumbling through a hollow world.

After a few months in early 1944, spent in New York where I was employed by the Office of War Information, I returned to Yale to find it functioning on a wartime basis. An army detachment of the ASTP occupied Trumbull, but I was allowed to inhabit the 1248 suite. The Navy V-12 program had taken over several of the Yale colleges and there was an urgent need for men to teach sections of one of the required courses in American history. I was the delegate from the French department and began teaching a subject about which my knowledge was limited. The majority of the forty sailors assigned to my section had just completed a high school course in American history and were far more conversant with the facts of the subject than I was. My waking hours were spent trying to learn the details of each lesson and then to prepare some discussion beyond the facts, which might give the students a semblance of a fresh approach. I confess that I fell back on all possible French relations with America: Jesuit explorers, Lafayette, Jefferson and the Encyclopedists, Franklin in Paris, etc. One evening, waiting in line in the Trumbull dining room, I overheard two students talking about the history course and referring to my section: "They shouldn't call Fowlie's course 'American History' but rename it 'What We Owe France.'"

The first commission to write an article had come to me from the surrealist magazine in New York called *View*. The topic suggested seemed at the moment beyond my powers, but I had just finished an essay on the theme of Narcissus, and knowing it to be a favorite with surrealists, sent it to *View*. It was accepted and appeared with illustrations as the leading article of an issue. Soon after its appearance I received a letter from Henry Miller expressing satisfaction over "Narcissus" and asking if he might see other writings of mine. A modest postscriptum informed me he had published two books in Paris. I had already read some of his books, especially *The Cosmological Eye*, which had left a deep impression on me. In my answer I told him how important his work had appeared to me. We struck up a correspondence. His letters contained a warm friendliness and enthusiasm, an eagerness to converse, a total freshness of approach to books I had forgotten might exist in the world outside of university walls.

His letters were frequent and long. They made him into a very real person for me, a friend equally solicitous about problems of writing and about the diverse minute facts of existence. Through his letters his personality became so strong and pervasive that I felt it would never be necessary to meet him. Just at that time, in the fall of 1944, he announced his arrival in New Haven and his desire to stay a few days with me.

I was to see Henry Miller and talk with him directly, but what had already transpired between us was so vibrant and salutary that I dreaded any diminution, any risk of failure. After a few minutes with him, I realized that the experience of knowing him was to provide me with a further illumination on mankind and a strengthening of friendship.

I had been expecting his arrival all one morning. He telephoned from Bridgeport and said he would get in about two o'clock. At exactly two, the bell rang. He was standing in the hall, quietly withdrawn into himself. He expressed surprise at not recognizing me. He had not had lunch, and I invited him into the kitchen while I set about making coffee and scrambling eggs. Gradually Henry Miller put me at ease. His voice was low and exceptionally resonant. Each phrase he uttered was poised and precisely filled some function.

When we finally settled down in the living room, he spoke with that deepest kind of grace that comes from concern with what is central in the person addressed. Henry fixed himself comfortably in a large chair and then said with a smile of expectancy, "Now tell me all about acedia." He explained how he had come across the word for the first time in one of my essays and had been fascinated by it. In reply, I actually said very little, but he seized upon it and began developing it himself. Henry needed no teacher. I watched both the transformation of the word and the exhilaration of the man who played as he created and learned.

One of my students, Jesse Clark, had pleaded more insistently than the others to meet Miller, and I arranged for him to come in on the second afternoon. Jess had distinguished himself to me by a temperament and imagination I recognized as being authentically those of an artist. He had shown me passages in his journal that were explosions against the world and against himself, passages possessing a moving power close to that of literary creation.

At first Jess spoke reservedly to Henry. I had tried to explain Jess before he came in, and saw soon that all explanation had been unnecessary. Henry turned his attention on the boy as if a bond of understanding existed between them. At one point Henry turned abruptly to me and said, referring to Jess, "His head is just like Van Gogh's. Have you ever noticed the resemblance? And his hands are those of a painter."

In recalling the week Henry Miller spent at New Haven, I have no impression of a sequence of days. It was a long conversation in multiple parts with multiple interruptions. His kindness and attentiveness were overwhelming. I had never before observed a man able to remain so alert and fervent in every aspect of living and thinking. I was aware that week of recasting and reassessing themes and problems of my entire life. Many strands seemed to be joining together. Whether we talked of Rimbaud, of Chaplin, or the circus, or D. H. Lawrence, the subjects all fused. My initial debt to Miller came from the encouragement he had given to my writing before he knew me personally. Then, after our meeting, a new debt became apparent to me, and has not ceased growing ever since: that unity he feels in himself and which he is able in part to transmit to his friends.

With Henry's departure, apartment 1248 recovered its solitude. My steps, as I walked down the hall, actually echoed. I continued seeing him move lithely from room to room, and I continued hearing him marvel at the austerity of the building. "How can you stand it? How can you stand it?" he used to say, speaking almost to himself.

My answer today would be clearer than it was in 1944. Every apartment and every room, big or small, I have occupied, has been hollow, and has resembled an empty stage, boards on which to walk and from which to recite. The words I say out loud (of my favorite authors) and those I assign to paper (of my own mind) have always converted whatever space I dwell in into the scene of an enactment. Words create their own spot lights, and the public . . . . It is there too, the living and the dead, just beyond the gaping pit, that magnificent dark pit where I had sensed such indefatigable waiting. I walk alone on the set, but with many ghosts whose actions are still real for me, and whose accents resound in my own speech.

XI

June 1955: memories of high school
a teacher's vocation   Austin Warren

A visit to the home of a Brookline friend, on a June evening in 1955,
brought back to me with the force of a sudden revelation an entire period
of my youth. My friend's young brother Stephen, to whom I was introduced for the first time, was reading a book on American history when we
entered the living room. Stephen shook hands with me politely enough,
but we were interrupting his reading, and the music he was listening to on
the radio—Beethoven, if I remember correctly—had to be turned down,
and ultimately switched off.

To lessen the effect of pure intrusion, my friend explained to his brother
that I too was a graduate from Brookline High School, and to me explained that Stephen was graduating the following Friday night. Proudly
and rapidly he listed the year's achievements of his brother, among which
he gave full importance to the editorship of the *Sagamore*. That word,
more than "Brookline High School," released the flood of memories. I
could see the long format of the paper and the black letters of the word
Sagamore. In my day I had felt rather aloof from the *Sagamore*. I had
not "gone out" for it, feeling it was too journalistic, too commercial, too
little focussed on literary matters.

The word *Sagamore* and the actual *Sagamore* Stephen showed me, the
final issue of the class of 1955, brought up before me a picture of waste.
On the day of its distribution, it would be read in every corner of the
buildings, like any newspaper. Then, the following day, the copies, crum-
pled and dirty, would be everywhere, on chairs, in books, on the floor. The

[120]

first secret doubts I felt for my teachers came from their seeming acceptance of the *Sagamore*, of the waste of time and money that publication represented to me.

I questioned Stephen about his teachers. We were both startled to discover that, despite the difference in our ages, we had some of the same teachers. We compared notes on them, and I was moved to find in Stephen the same reverence for teachers I had felt. Semidivinities they were. Even today I am unable to think of high school teachers as purely human. Their knowledge, by comparison with my own at sixteen, the mysteriousness of their personal life, the absoluteness of their judgments, all made them into a race apart.

Stephen and I spoke especially of Miss Alice Spaulding, head of English, who taught at Brookline for more than fifty years. The prestige of her high position impressed me, but I was more impressed with the dignity of her walk, the detachment and aloofness from students and daily affairs. She taught without effort, because she insisted on teaching either the most advanced group, college preparatory fourth-year students who would work hard anyway because they were taking college board examinations at the end of the year, or first-year general students who were not well-equipped, and who would learn from anything she said. I was in the senior college preparatory class, and the major unit of the course was the study of plays. The readings were well chosen and chronologically organized. We read the plays carefully at home. The class discussions did touch on them somewhat, but our principal delight was Miss Spaulding's indulgence in generalities, in remarks on life and daily living.

On one occasion Miss Spaulding said that if a man knew his Bible and his Shakespeare, he would be learned and understanding of life. Whenever I grow avid to read more and more books, whenever a trend toward pedantry shows itself, I recall the simplicity of Miss Spaulding's bibliographical recommendation and tell myself it is more important to know profoundly one great book than to read one hundred less important books.

By the time I reached Miss Spaulding's class, I had made a determined splurge with French. From the viewpoint of the English department, I must have been looked upon as something of an alien. I felt guilty about this, and vacillated between believing Miss Spaulding wanted to win me back, and believing that she was indifferent to the situation, which she looked upon as eccentric or affected or ludicrous. I worked hard in her class and usually succeeded well in the written work—and even, at graduation, was awarded the English prize. But once, she taught me a lesson, in a slightly sadistic way. It was one of the rare moments of distress and failure for me at high school.

That day I was enjoying a privilege of the Honorary Society and studying in an empty classroom rather than in the study hall. At one moment Miss Spaulding passed by the opened door. She must have seen me working inside, because in a few minutes she came into the room and handed me a composition she had corrected and to which she had given an "E", which was a failure. She had no intention of discussing the matter. She did not even stop, but said simply, "They were all mistakes in spelling. The composition itself was up to your standard." The one mistake, circled in red pencil several times, was *profond*. This she referred to, as she said, "Look out for French, it can play tricks on you." When she had left the room, I puzzled over the severe penalty she had given such a mistake, and reasoned that it must be jealousy or vindictiveness. I learned for the first time the harsh lesson that every choice we make brings in its wake a loss.

Speechless before Miss Spaulding, I was loquacious in the presence of Miss Louise Gambrill, head of the French department, and, by my senior year, loquacious on many subjects: on the teaching of French, on grammar, on France, on French traits, and on the first literary texts I was reading that year—*Le Cid, Le Crime de Sylvestre Bonnard, Cyrano de Bergerac, Maria Chapdelaine*. In her own way, Miss Gambrill was as impressive as Miss Spaulding. She was a very beautiful woman, and her overportliness enhanced her power, her authority, her worldliness. She was an American woman, of French ancestry, and she had learned to speak French well, and had developed, as the best French teachers do, all her tastes in terms of France and of the frequent trips she made there. She taught *Cyrano* each year to her senior class because she had seen as a young girl in America a performance which Parisians had never seen: Coquelin in the role of Cyrano, and Bernhardt in the role of Roxane.

Miss Spaulding was not the performing kind of teacher. She sat back and waited for the brightest students, and sometimes the least bright, to propose an idea or ask a question that might interest her sufficiently to heed it and discuss it. I always had the impression she was withholding her richest thoughts concerned with the lesson at hand. She was eternally reserving the best for the next day, or for some day when we would be worthy of her best. Miss Gambrill, however, more histrionically-minded and trained, "performed" each French lesson. Of course the nature of teaching a foreign language required this. We had been brought up on the oral method. The senior class was the sixth year of French for many of us. We handled the language well by then, and we were being initiated into French culture, to literature and history. This part did not move fast enough for me. I supplemented the meager assignments with additional reading of my own. I was discovering the public library, which had numerous histories of French literature, histories of France, complete sets of Balzac and Hugo. The footnotes in the school edition of *Le Cid* we used in class furnished me with some information concerning the reign of Louis XIII, and the life of Corneille, and the three unities of classical tragedy. But when I came upon these subjects treated in longer works of scholarship in the Brookline Public Library, I was amazed at how complicated such subjects were, and planned to present my knowledge to the class in as dazzling a form as I could when I made my oral report on *Le Cid*.

I never believed in Miss Gambrill's knowledge and critical ability as much as I believed in Miss Spaulding's. But I admired her pedagogy much more, and the fact that she used a foreign language in class and succeeded in getting most of the pupils to do the same. She entered her classroom from her office, and never until after the bell had rung. She walked rapidly to a stand bearing a phonograph. On the top of the closed phonograph she placed her book, opened it and began the lesson. It was prepared and organized meticulously. She knew in advance each question she was to ask, and she knew the kind of answer she would require. Nothing was forgotten, and every point was recapitulated several times—and throughout the year. Each new word explained would recall a former word. Each point of literary history would involve some linguistic definition and some practice in reciting dates. If the lesson was on grammar or composition, some literary allusions would be made and provide reviews. She stood throughout the hour, and resembled an orchestra leader with the open score before her, bent upon drawing from us the sounds she wanted. And she worked hard to hear the sounds articulated in as perfect a way as possible. Teaching was not perfunctory for Miss Gambrill. It was a vocation. France was a cause. She knew that it could be a source of enlightenment for us, as it had been for her. To enjoy her lessons, one had to accept the premise of the importance of France, to realize there was a French way of looking at things, a French answer to each problem. Her class was the initiation into a strange exotic way of life and manner of expression. We began to realize that our American reactions and customs were, after all, those of only one country . . . .

I did not mention Miss Gambrill to Stephen because she had died several years earlier, and because I learned in our conversation that he had not studied French at high school. Stephen seemed unshakable in his judgments. He had ended high school with considerable triumph, as I had, and I must have had at his age a similar self-confidence. My high school years fell in the decade following the First World War, and Stephen's in the decade following the Second World War. Mine was a decade of greater euphoria and security in the world. Without having to ask him, I knew that Stephen would be more reserved, more cautious in his attitude toward life in 1955 than I had been in 1928. The depression had not begun, and we had no foreknowledge of the various anxieties the thirties would bring.

High school had offered to Stephen, as it had to me, a full life, a full world in itself. The *Sagamore*, the Honorary Society, Prize Speaking, the courses themselves, the striking personalities of such teachers as Miss Spaulding, Miss Gambrill, Miss O'Brien, Miss Lewis, Miss Allen. An absorbing world for the complacent, industrious, somewhat passive student. A microcosm of the bigger world outside, but effectual only to a limited degree in preparing an adolescent for the complexity, ruthlessness and insecurity of the larger world . . . . Stephen would learn, as I had, something of all that. I watched his sensitive face as it bent down over the book of American history and imagined that he said to himself words that were similar to my unspoken words about him. "This man is too removed from high school, too old to know how it is run today. There is not much point in arguing or discussing. Only those teachers, like Miss Spaulding, whom I see every day would understand what I am and what I think and what I want."

No vocation, such as that of a teacher, is without its spiritual peril. At the end of a course, with the punctuation of the final class, I usually experience some degree of satisfaction that the "material" held out to the end and that the next semester there will be a new group of students not familiar with my views and methods and manias. The work will then start up again, more fresh and more vigorous, it is to be hoped. One learns to diminish and enlarge the subject matter of a course as one gives it. One learns what works and does not work. But with the September opening when the same students, those still at the school, do not elect the new course, but turn to some newer or older teacher, I experience pangs of not having succeeded as solidly as I thought. This is the beginning of the teacher's personal anguish: the realization he is not necessary to anyone, the belief he should not be necessary. One studies with a teacher to learn how to do without him, to offset his values and views with those of some other teacher.

The notes of the teacher are the background for the unpredictable, for the creative, for the moment of illumination. As his knowledge of the subject increases, the teacher finds it more difficult to arrive at the central points in a single class meeting. He spends longer and longer getting into his subject. An introduction to a subject, such as the background of a writer to be studied, or the early writings of an author, are much easier to teach, to organize and to explain, than the central books. It is easier, for example, to analyze what Stendhal made out of the eighteenth-century philosophers than to analyze the technique of *Le Rouge et le noir*. An accumulation of notes over the years for a teacher's exegesis of a novel is bound to exaggerate such topics as the historical moment, the ancestors, the philosophical formation, the childhood readings, until the student may well wonder whether there is any point in reading the major book, which is the reason, after all, for the choice of such an author. Teachers of literature, more than others, I dare say, spend more time in promising and preparing their bouts with the central issues than in staging the actual combat. Suddenly the time is up, and the course stops just at the point where by rights and by promises it should have begun. The teacher of literature plays the role of historian, philosopher, psychologist, sociologist. And the sociologist spends his time discussing novels that have an indirect application to his problems. The term paper, written by the student, may well be the one piece of work in the course that deals unashamedly with a given text.

As a teacher continues year after year with his favorite course, the one he may have written a book about and which finally becomes synonymous with his own name, he retreats farther and farther away from the central issues demanding his most critical powers. Each year his ease grows with his increasing knowledge. He grows finally into the strategist, and by the verbal display of knowledge and information, no longer fears meeting a possible defeat in the arcanic heart of his subject. The scholar triumphs over the critic, as the virtuoso triumphs over the teacher.

Teaching, at its best, is harmonization between the instructor and the instructed. Each is dependent on the other. The instructed, obviously, needs illumination and guidance. He is there to learn and profit from knowledge as it is dispensed at first hand. The instructor needs to be reminded of what is important to learn about his subject, of what is difficult and easy, of what is obscure and evident, of what touches on problems common to all of his students.

How easy it is to forget that students are really more interested in the method of acquiring knowledge and in the significance of knowledge than in the imparting of knowledge! What will serve them the best is the way to read a book and the reason for reading a book. In the last analysis, the assimilation of the book itself is a purely private matter, in which even the best teacher will have only a minimal part.

The teacher presides over what, in all its forms, is a strange marriage between work and pleasure. By nature they are dissimilar, and yet they come together in a joining that is both miraculous and perfectly natural. Socrates says, or at least Montaigne reminds me that Socrates says, that a god tried to fuse together pain and pleasure (*douleur et volupté*) and, being unable to succeed completely, settled on the solution of coupling them at least by their tails!

Soon after beginning graduate school in 1931, I met Austin Warren who was teaching at that time at Boston University. I met him first in his apartment at 36 Garden Street, on the back of Beacon Hill. He later moved to 28 Garden Street, but the furnishings, of a satisfactory kind of elegance, with harmonium and an overwhelming number of books, were the same, and now in my memory I cannot distinguish the two apartments. I am one among many who owe a great deal to his friendship. He was ten years my senior, and became friend and teacher immediately. The roles were so joined as to be indistinguishable.

The basis of our friendship was a sharing of approximate background, temperament, literary aspiration. It was, moreover, a companionship in the spiritual life requiring from both of us constant moral scrutiny and constant communication. It was initially, and has remained through more than forty years, a friendship of many stratifications, of a range of sharings: esthetic, regional, social, temperamental, intellectual, religious.

In all important matters, Austin was my superior: in literary knowledge and critical powers, in musicianship and speech, in generosity of spirit, in loyalty, in moral goodness. I was his superior only in French (which I proceeded to teach to him) and in a few manual dexterities, such as driving an auto and cooking a meal. I was his equal in doggedness and Yankee stamina, in a blind willfulness to be taught on every occasion, in a daily vow so to organize and order my days and nights that there would be every twenty-four hours some tangible accomplishment, some measurable progress in the life of thought, of writing, of spirituality.

He practiced an unusual candor about himself, and forced me, by his example, to try to practice a similar candor about myself. In those matters he stressed specificity, and opposed me whenever I replied in general terms. Austin was so close a kinsman that I listened to his advice, which, had it come from someone else, would have upset me. He knew what my danger as a young writer was: a tendency to admire so generously that by assimilation I would lose my own voice in that of some master. He urged me not to read contemporary poets and critics harmonious with my spirit. He urged me, in fact, to read less, and to read writers repugnant to me. In the early years of our friendship, he helped me to define, and encouraged me to sustain, a literary faith I still look upon as my own. If I paraphrased this faith in his words, it would sound something like this: "I would rather be a doorkeeper in the house of art than to dwell, all confidently and smilingly and blandly, in the courts of erudition and commerce."

I had grown up as a kind of twentieth-century Yankee in Brookline and Boston without having given much thought to the meaning of the term *Yankee.* Austin used the word frequently in his conversation and endowed it with such meaning that I began, under his example and tutelage, to pay attention to it. It is still not a word in my daily vocabulary. Tacitly, through the years, I have come to associate the word, in its moral, historic and histrionic sense, with Austin. He is the living example for me of the Yankee.

Every disappointment in his life he used as a check to turn in on himself. If the disappointment were more serious, a disturbance, for example, he would force himself to make a conscious rehearsal of his hierarchy of means and ends, of instrumental and final values. Austin knew the indulgence of self-pity. The principal vice is the indulgence of moping and whining and whimpering. (These are all Yankee terms.) During the Boston years of our friendship, he was always fearful of being nervous and moody and irritable. This fear was equal to another allied fear, of appearing extravagant and eccentric. His goal, as he would often say, was to be "classical," but this was a strain on him since it was external.

He always labored persistently to make progress in his inner life. His ambitions were of the highest kind. I would list them in the following order: spiritual, intellectual, professional, social. In terms of the world, his pleasures were the simplest. If the weather were good, he would often propose a boat ride around the Charles River Basin, or a walk in the Public Gardens. If the weather were bad, the proposal might be a vaudeville at Scolloy Square or an hour at the Art Museum. I list these in a purposely incongruous manner because Austin liked incongruity, liked it, not centrally, but as a relaxation.

The impulses of his nature and his talents were always being checked by considerations he would define as truth and philosophy. His oral speech is as brilliant as I have ever heard in English. But he has said to me on occasion, "My oral glibness often fools me. Pen and paper show up my incoherences." No one is more touched than Austin by the approval of his fellows, but he has always known that if he genuinely cherishes the pursuit of truth, he will not require the approval of his fellows to justify or crown his pursuit.

When Austin left Boston for the University of Iowa at the time of the war, about 1940, he had to leave many things dear to him: the city of Boston itself, his circle of close friends and disciples, a pattern of life from which he derived stimulation and contentment. He responded to this "call" in true Yankee fashion. He knew Iowa City would be a necessary proving ground and a validation of his intellectual and moral parts. At first he missed the incentive of friends near at hand. At Iowa where there was a large group of brilliant young graduate students, attracted by Norman Foerster's program at the School of Letters, Austin had constantly to give to others the assurance they were writers, without there being one, in turn, to offer it to him in moments of self-devaluation.

Any such change as that from one university to another is a starting up all over again, a proving of one's merits to a new company, and a collecting of new friends and allies. Austin was literally practicing what he had often preached to me, that man is a pilgrim and a stranger. In his letters from Iowa he continued to direct me, and his wit continued to delight me. He would ask me in my Bennington retreat, "How many desks do you have now?" "Do you keep poems and a novel going at other hours than criticism?" "Where is your book on the 'grandeur and the glory of the French soul?'" When he invited me to Iowa, he was careful to state that I would have a front room in his apartment suitable for "bedroom, writing room and oratory."

On his second year at Iowa, I sent him two friends from Bennington to carry on their graduate studies under his direction. Emily Sweetser was one of our most gifted graduates and Sherman Conrad had taught at Bennington. Both had worked in the drama department under Francis

[128]

Fergusson. They became good friends of Austin, favorites of his inner set and leaders of the local literary intellectuals. Emily and Sherman both objected to much that they found at Iowa, and Emily perpetually harked back to Bennington. Austin in his letters to me began referring to "Saint Francis of Bennington." But Austin knew that they were getting far more out of their year in Iowa than they saw, or having seen, would admit.

Before the arrival in Iowa of the Benningtonians and of the other group of favorite graduate students Austin called the Ransomians (Unger, Forgotson, Brantley), he complained that no one thought of him there as a "writer," himself included. He missed that expectation his Boston friends held for him. His labors were heavy: pedagogical, editorial, amical, scriptorial. His students were intelligent, sincere, eager. The people who wanted to be comforted, amused, instructed, inspired, increased in numbers. The students at Iowa were far more demanding than had been his suburban Bostonians. Emily's presence in Iowa helped Austin to reestablish a tie with his past. She represented a Boston dear and prized. Austin used to call it "the Boston of Jack Wheelwright and Rose Nichols."

Both Emily and Sherman attended Austin's parish church, Trinity Church, and both shared his admiration for the rector, Father McEvoy, a man of deep spirituality and humility. In one of his letters he speaks of his joy at having seen that morning Emily in the pew opposite his and Sherman in the pew behind his.

His powers of teacher and counselor were so lavish and unusual that I can understand why his students often forgot that he too was a writer. He tried to console himself by claiming that to be friend and fosterer of poets is next best to being one. First, Austin had to possess wisdom and love, and then he had to dispense them in large stores to his talented young friends.

On one of my visits to Iowa, I attended, with Emily and Sherman, Austin's poetry seminar. This was one of the very few occasions when I saw him function as a teacher in a classroom. Eliot's "East Coker" had just been published a few weeks previously in *Partisan Review*. For that day's lesson, Austin had assigned "East Coker." Each student came with his copy of *Partisan Review*, and we listened for two hours to what I imagine was the first classroom reading and interpretation of the poem. It was for me as stimulating and as satisfying a performance as I have witnessed in a classroom.

At the close of the seminar I walked away alone to think over some of the points in the lesson. But my thoughts kept returning to various comments Austin had made to me about the comparative facility of giving a lecture, and the difficulty of writing the essay. When he was able to write regularly, it was always a counsel of perfection for him, a symptom, an effect of spiritual health. He has always deplored the fact that professors of literature are not encouraged to be men of letters. Foundations give scholars grants only for doing more of the same thing. Austin steadfastly extolled the examples of such friends as Morton Zabel, Robert Penn Warren, Kenneth Burke, men who have combined the scholarly with the creative. He places them in the line of Flaubert, Pater, James, Eliot, because they are concentrated, constantly working, moral in their loyalty to art, to friendship, to the values of civilization.

XII

literary encounters: Jorge Guillén   Marianne Moore
T. S. Eliot   Henri Mondor   Princess Caetani
Saint-John Perse

The same question has come back to me continuously throughout my
life, in many forms. What is poetry? In school, when I first studied poetry,
I was also attempting to write it, and at that time I believe I consciously
avoided posing the question to myself. With youthful dullness and opaque-
ness I felt I had triumphed over pedantry. I had loosed myself from the
bonds of the academy and the philosophers who sought to define poetry
without possessing genius enough to write it.

Then a meeting took place in my life that radically changed my viewpoint. My first bona fide invitation to lecture came to me from Wellesley
College. I was a graduate student, and Miss Manwaring, in charge of the poetry society at Wellesley, pointed that fact out to me when she extended her
invitation. She explained it was her habit to invite each year an unknown
speaker to perform for fifteen dollars, and a well-known speaker for one
hundred dollars. She assigned the topic of my lecture: "American imagism
and French symbolism," on which I worked assiduously for four months.
When the talk was over, and Miss Manwaring was handing me the promised check for fifteen dollars, she told me that her season's celebrity had
been Christopher Morley. On arrival at Wellesley, he had asked what he
was to do, and was told he was to read some of his poems. "But I don't
remember," he said, "ever having written any poetry." Whereupon, Miss
Manwaring presented him library copies of his poems written and pub-

lished when he was a very young man. To earn his promised fee of one hundred dollars, Mr. Morley had only to open and read the volumes of poetry he had no memory of having written.

That story would have unsettled me if I had not been led away at that moment to be introduced to the distinguished Spanish poet who had just come to Wellesley, Jorge Guillén. I had known of his work, although at that time I had not read it, of its high reputation, of its affiliation with the Mallarmé-Valéry tradition of French poetry. Previously I had met only one other poet of such eminence, T. S. Eliot, whose classes and lectures and teas I had attended at Harvard. Mr. Eliot was much more than a poet for me, whereas Guillén was the epitome of the poet, the one whose life was consecrated to the writing of a single book. He spoke in French, and with such friendliness that I felt gratified and happy in this encounter.

His eyes, behind thick glasses, seemed always to be smiling. As we talked, I realized that what had seemed a smile, was actually the radiance of intelligence, the subtlety of mind and wit, and especially the searching directness of the poet's gaze. The shape of his nose was sharp and the texture of his skin pale and clear. He spoke in questions, and this habit gave his entire figure, slight and supple, the manner of humility, of almost excessive modesty.

It was I who by rights should have felt humbled, but Guillén forced me, by his questions and the tone of eagerness in his voice, into the pompous role of oracle. He took me by the arm and led me a few steps away from the others. Then he stopped and facing me squarely, asked the question, "What is poetry?" ("Cher monsieur, qu'est-ce que c'est que la poésie?")

This question, and the tone of simplicity in which it was asked, were enough to interrupt my chatter and glibness. My first reaction was shame for what must have appeared to Guillén arrogance and self-assurance both in my lecture and conversation. I had been used to definitions offered easily and convincingly by teachers and writers. Classrooms and libraries did not pose such falterings as I observed at that moment in the features and tensed attitude of Jorge Guillén. And so finally I too faltered, and the all too ready words stopped in my throat.

But Guillén refused to let me off that easily. He took my arm and said, "I want you to tell me, in the greatest confidence, as to an old friend, what poetry is, what you understand poetry to be. I have thought about this problem all my life, but I have not found the solution or the key."

Whatever I did stammer at that moment about poetry was deranged by the seriousness and humility of Guillén. In subsequent meetings with him,

I learned of his conversations on the subject of poetry with men like Valéry and Du Bos, and of his intimate knowledge of the poems of Mallarmé, not to mention the rich tradition of poetry in his own country. Thereafter, in my own life, as I continued to study the meaning of poetry, I have always kept in my mind the picture of Jorge Guillén as he appeared to me at Wellesley. I remembered not so much the specific question he asked, but the way in which he asked it and the lesson behind the question and the gentle insistence of the man.

Only one other poet, in this case a woman poet, gave me frankly, unembarrassedly the impression of humility before her craft: Marianne Moore. The similarity of Guillén's and Miss Moore's literary attitudes struck me because they are different in every other way. But the differences are of nationality and background and training. They would be bards in any age or in any country. Perhaps because they are so centrally poets, they can be so centrally localized in speech, in manner, in the integrity of their reactions.

On my meetings with Jorge Guillén, I was impressed with the poet's concentration on the deepest, most philosophical problems concerning poetry. On my meetings with Marianne Moore, in her apartment in Brooklyn, I was struck by the way the smallest detail counted for her, by the functioning of her memory that recalled a fragment of a detail whenever needed, a name, a title, a line of a poem whenever they could serve in the conversation at hand. Whereas Guillén was the type of poet concentrated on understanding what he had done in the writing of his verse, Miss Moore seemed to be collecting and arranging precious bits for the composing of a future poem. Guillén meditated on the metaphysical concept to be explored one day in the future. Marianne Moore cogitated on immediate problems, whether they were prosaic details of housekeeping or a successful line in a new poem of a friend. The range of her interests and preoccupations was tremendous. At the end of an hour, a visiting friend might be bewildered by the variety of experiences referred to, by the almost cruel precision with which she fixed a poetic theory or a household need or the memory of a face, a gesture, a word.

I must not allow this report to sound solemn because there was nothing solemn about Miss Moore. No one laughed at herself with more unaffected pleasure than she. No one understood better than she the picture she gave and wanted to give of herself. The lightness, the deftness of the comic were in the punctuation she gave to statements she wanted you to enjoy, and which she said with an expression on her face of innocent seriousness. I remember hearing her speak on the telephone to a friend. She had been ill for several days and was requesting a few errands to be done. She ended the list by asking for one fresh orange, to taste its juice. She had grown tired of frozen orange juice. And since I was in the room, she involved me too, as a real performer involves every member of the public. The statement itself, carefully worded in its exaggeration, the tone of voice used for the insistent plea, and the gaze of fixed attentiveness were so well synchronized that I still enjoy remembering that moment in 1953.

Miss Moore's scrupulosity in slight matters was by no means unrelated to the carefully woven texture of her writings. She is the artist of the seemingly minute detail and the seemingly innocuous syllable. The intricate pattern of a poem and its coherence were not unrelated to her attentiveness in the presence of a friend and to the way in which she faced the world. Her blue eyes looked intently, with consuming interest. And yet behind them, there was a great depth of peace, of spiritual tranquillity. Her awareness of things was extraordinary, but her awareness of people even more so. Her major fear seemed to be that a friend's attention bestowed on her would detract from the life and activity of the friend. She would not recognize the pleasure her friends derived from doing for her. This was a bent of her nature. It was not a reasoned principle.

I speak of Marianne Moore's attentiveness to friends, but that is too limited a category. It extended to all those she met, to all those who paid her a first visit. I know of a Brooklyn College student who called on her in quest of an inscription in one of her books and went away with a thoughtful inscription as well as the price he had paid for the book. I know a young editor at Viking who requested from her an inscription in his copy of *Poems* and who the next day received from her an urgent request in a letter to mail the book to her. She wanted to change a word and a comma in the inscription she had written when in his office. Long before my first visit to Miss Moore's apartment in Brooklyn, I had heard of the bowl of nickels kept in the living room, from which each visitor was to extract his subway fare back to Manhattan. It was already a bowl of dimes when I came, and although I was tempted to keep my particular dime as a souvenir, I did insert it in the subway slot in obedience to the one who had created such a tradition of financial thoughtfulness. On a later visit the dimes had become tokens, each costing fifteen cents, but their beneficent bestower still continued to ease her conscience over the effort in time and money signified in each visit she received. She would never believe that those visits were events of importance and intense pleasure for all those who came flying underground from Manhattan to Brooklyn.

In the early thirties when T. S. Eliot was Charles Eliot Norton lecturer at Harvard, I attended his classes and the series of public lectures he gave, "The Use of Poetry and the Use of Criticism." They were held in New Lecture Hall. Capacity crowds attended each one. It would be impossible to exaggerate Eliot's importance at that time for those of my generation interested in literature and writing. He was the accomplished poet, prophet and guide. Every word he said—and he seemed to speak more and more parsimoniously—had to be construed into a message of significance. We would discuss every statement, and now that he was present in our midst, we would interpret the intonation of every statement.

We had examined so many pictures of Mr. Eliot that when we saw him for the first time, at his first evening lecture, we could almost believe this was the resurrection of a god. When he came through the door at the back of the platform and walked slowly to the podium, we could see the extreme pallor of his face. His voice was not strong, and it was difficult to hear him beyond the first few rows. We learned to arrive early at those lectures in order to sit close to the platform. Mr. Eliot began his first lecture after Christmas by thanking his audience for their greetings of the season. But especially he wanted to thank the two Cambridge ladies who had sent him a box of breakfast cereal with the message that if he ate it, his voice would develop more carrying power, and they would be grateful for that.

The poet's dry humor became apparent as time went on. On Wednesdays, at Eliot House, Mr. Eliot received students at tea. A timorous strained circle gathered. To speak of trivial matters seemed a waste of time. Here was the supreme occasion at which to ask the burning questions about poetry. But somehow it was impossible to formulate them appropriately. And Mr. Eliot's serene, urbane and somewhat aloof manner did not encourage such questions. The implacable presence of the other students was a deterrent also. The question each of us wanted to ask was about the meaning of specific lines. *Ash-Wednesday* had just been published and there were many puzzling details about that poem and allusions we were not sure of. From time to time, after one of the embarrassing silences, a student would clear his throat and dare to ask, "Sir, what do you mean by . . . " and then he would quote such a line as, "Teach us to care and

[135]

not to care." A momentary silence usually followed such a direct question, and then the poet, turning to a shelf of books behind him, selected one, opened it and found a passage he announced with the words, "Well, this critic thinks it means . . . " and he would read an interpretation. This was hardly what we wanted because we were beginning to read the critics on Eliot, and we were too inexperienced to assimilate an important lesson Eliot himself was teaching in his own critical writings, one that stressed the fact that once the poem was published, the poet became simply another reader of his own work.

The god was enigmatical in his personal relationships and in his appearances. This much we conceded, and with the egoism of youth we turned this discovery to our own profit. We looked upon ourselves as initiates because we were at Harvard where Mr. Eliot was living and where he had once studied. We were taking the course on Dante similar to the one he must have taken, which culminated in his essay *Dante* in 1929 and in *Ash-Wednesday* in 1930. We liked to believe that students at other colleges were farther removed from him not only geographically but spiritually. And we welcomed the story of the Wellesley dinner in his honor. A young student, seated beside Mr. Eliot, plied him with questions about the meaning of a specific line from *The Waste Land*. At first he evaded the question, but finally when harassed by it, said, "Miss, it doesn't mean a thing." This story pleased us in Cambridge, and we easily forgot we had been guilty of the same misdemeanor.

Those of my generation who were students in the thirties, and those belonging to the next older generation, who were already teaching literature, found ourselves portrayed in "The Love Song of J. Alfred Prufrock." The lines in this poem, already famous, had become the mirror of our own character. We never ceased marvelling that *Prufrock* had been written after our birth. We had been born around 1910 and the poem was printed in *Poetry* in 1915. As we grew up and moved more knowingly into the social and spiritual problems of our age, passage after passage of *Prufrock* took on clearer meaning. We knew the street of "insidious intent," and the women who talk of Michelangelo, and the coffee spoons and the indecisions. We had felt in our own way the painful private drama of the modern hero, so succinctly set forth in the very title of the poem. We had looked up the passage in the *Inferno* where Guido da Montefeltro speaks to Dante and had discovered the origin of the name *Prufrock* and had began to see the entire soliloquy as evil counsel the modern protagonist gives himself. Prufrock's social fright was ours, and it had become difficult to take a cup of tea or raise a coffee spoon without seeing in those gestures symbolic meanings of our inconsequential life, of our indecisions, of our spiritual inertness. We had not memorized "The Love Song," and yet phrases from it had become parts of our daily speech. We were enacting *Prufrock* as we walked along Brattle Street or in front of Seaver.

Two episodes occurred during the momentous year of Eliot at Harvard that moved me in a personal way, one of an almost comical nature, and the other of a spiritual nature.

I had become interested in the Anglo-Catholic community of the Cowley Fathers whose monastery was in Cambridge, on the Charles River, and who served the parish church of St. John the Evangelist on the back of Beacon Hill in Boston. The liturgy was admirably performed in the Boston church and the music, both plainchant and polyphonic masses, were skillfully directed by the organist-composer Titcomb.

A few friends—graduate students in French and English—and myself attended the Christmas Eve mass at St. John's. We expected or half-expected to see Eliot there because he was a daily communicant at the monastery chapel in Cambridge. When we entered, we did see him in the center of the church, fairly close to the altar. We found a pew three or four rows behind his, on the aisle. The service was solemn high mass. Long before it began, the church was crowded.

When the service was over, the people moved slowly on leaving the church. There was only one doorway, at the end of the central aisle. We waited until Mr. Eliot had passed us before getting into the aisle, and during the slow progress of the crowd we could see him ahead of us. I noticed another student, whom I did not know but recognized, having seen him in the Harvard yard. He was obviously trying to move closer to Eliot. Finally, when he was almost directly behind the man, and, in the silence in the back of the church, he recited in a clear voice Italian words which later I knew to be:

Perch'io non spero di tornor giammai.

Eliot gave no sign of recognition and continued moving toward the door. When we got outside, and people were disappearing in every direction in the cold night, we consulted among ourselves on the mysterious words but could only guess they were Italian.

About a week later, in the yard, I saw the same fellow walking ahead of me. Contrary to custom at Harvard, I approached him, told him I had heard him recite a line of poetry after midnight mass at Saint John's, and asked what the line was. He looked at me scornfully: "Haven't you ever read Guido Cavalcanti?" The tone of his voice would not have been different if he had asked: "Haven't you ever read *Hamlet*?"

I confessed my ignorance of Cavalcanti, and he enlightened me. "It's the opening line of a *canzone* Eliot took over without modification as the opening line of *Ash-Wednesday*. I wanted to let that old possum know that someone else knew where he had found his line."

No critic had as yet pointed out the source of the line. When during that year we began realizing that many elements of the poem came from Dante, we began studying Italian, and believed we were in some way emulating Mallarmé who, in order to read Poe, studied English.

The Harvard students who had associated themselves with the Cowley Fathers were asked to choose one morning a week when they would help "serve" the seven o'clock mass. My day was Tuesday. During his year at Cambridge, Eliot was a daily communicant at that mass and on Tuesdays he and I were often the only ones with the priest in the chapel. (This was the very small chapel used before the large Ralph Adams Cram chapel was built.)

One of those Tuesdays has remained memorable for me. Only the three of us were present. At the time of communion Eliot had risen and come up to the altar to receive. The priest and I had turned back to the altar, and I could hear Eliot rise and return to his place. At that moment there was such a heavy thud, as if Eliot had fallen, that the priest and I turned around. Eliot was flat on his face in the aisle, with his arms stretched out. It was obvious at a glance he had not fallen.

Under his breath, and as if speaking to himself, the priest said, "What should we do?"

I suggested, "Let's finish here first." So, we turned back to the altar.

The one aisle in the chapel where Eliot lay was so narrow that the priest and I could not have walked there in order to reach the sacristy. The priest finally said to me, "I think you should help him up. Something may be wrong." I went on ahead and put my arm under his shoulder. He came with me easily. Almost no physical effort was required on my part to help him back into his seat. As I preceded the priest into the small room at the end of the aisle, I realized that Eliot had just undergone a mystical experience.

A few years later, in New York City, I was doing some translation work for Jacques Maritain in his apartment. One evening after dinner, when our work was finished, he asked me some questions about Eliot's poetry.

Maritain was just beginning to read and study poetry written in English. At one point in the questions, he interrupted them by asking: "Do you think Eliot is truly a religious man?"

I replied affirmatively and told him the story of the Tuesday mass at Cambridge. He was so moved that he began weeping. "I am thinking of myself," he said as he wiped his eyes, "and I am going to tell you a similar story on myself which is not without its comic side."

"It was my first year at Chicago, the first year President Hutchins invited me to lecture at the university. That winter I attended the early mass each morning at five o'clock, in the Cathedral of the Holy Name. Very few people came to that mass. One morning after receiving communion, I had what must have been an experience similar to Eliot's. It was a desire to worship God, and I stretched out face down at the altar rail when I had received. The priest and the acolyte had gone back to the altar which was at a considerable distance. I was praying when I heard a man speak gruffly to me. He nudged me on my side with his foot, and said, 'Hey, we don't allow drunks in this church.' I didn't respond immediately, and he kicked me again and began pulling me up from the floor."

The janitor in the Catholic Cathedral of Chicago did not treat Jacques Maritain as gently or as respectfully as we treated T. S. Eliot in the Anglican chapel in Cambridge. I have always thought of both of them as exemplary religious men in our day. Eliot was the first to die, and Maritain, before his death in 1973, had entered, at an advanced age, thanks to a special dispensation, the Order of the Petits Frères de Jésus, in Toulouse, where he had lived since the death of Raïssa. During the sixties, it was rumored that Paul VI was going to name him cardinal.

In the fall of 1948, I had a year's leave of absence from teaching, thanks to a Guggenheim Fellowship, to spend several months in Paris for the writing of a study on the poetry of Mallarmé. It was my first return to Paris since the war years, and I looked forward to the renewal of old friendships. I was determined to carry out the writing project alone and even avoid discussing it with French friends. Before leaving Chicago, where I was then living, I had purchased the biography of Mallarmé by Henri Mondor. This huge volume was helpful to me in many ways, in the complete story of Mallarmé's life, in the many anecdotes of the poet's relationships with family, friends, artists. There was very little about poetic theory and almost nothing about the poems themselves. The subject I was planning to write was close to an exegesis of the poems. I was moved by Mondor's appreciation of Mallarmé, puzzled by the vast number of documents to which he had had access and had used intelligently. I knew he was a surgeon in Paris and had written his book during the war years.

During my first days in my hotel on the rue Cassette, I decided, through a sense of duty and gratitude, to write to Mondor and tell him of my project. In my letter I spoke of my appreciation of his book and expressed the hope that one day I might meet him. He answered with an invitation to call on him in his apartment the next Tuesday evening at seven.

Mondor himself opened the door that Tuesday. He was a short chubby man, with a round reddish face, bald on the top of his head and gray hair on the sides. He was dressed in a formal black suit, stiff white shirt, and a richly colored silk tie. The apartment seemed vast as we walked through it to his study where the books were and where we sat—he behind his desk and I opposite him. Papers and books were neatly stacked on the desk. I had the feeling he would start writing as soon as I left. A man of order and precision, I could tell that. My persistent thought was: I must not overstay this visit.

The doctor plunged immediately into my project, with questions about what I planned to write and how I was going about it. I stressed the exegetical aspect and the poetic theory, and told him I had already done some writing on Rimbaud. He knew so little about the American university and literary words that I represented a puzzling phenomenon to him: an American attempting to write on Mallarmé.

As the hour went on, Mondor added to our general discussion small but very precise questions about this and that point on Mallarmé. It was his way of testing me, because in many cases I knew he knew the answer. He returned several times to his major point that he was the biographer and not the exegete.

The hour was over, and both of us had been absorbed by Mallarmé. I had thoroughly enjoyed listening to the strong Auvergnat accent of Mondor's French, once I had recovered from the shock of hearing such an accent in Paris in the speech of such a distinguished physician. He had answered forthrightly every question I had asked that could be answered, and I had learned by eight o'clock that le professeur Mondor had in his possession in that room where we sat most of the manuscripts of Mallarmé's poems and many of the letters from which he had quoted so abundantly in the biography.

As I rose to leave, I asked him if at the end of my Paris months—in

April perhaps—I might return to discuss with him problems that would doubtless arise as I wrote the book. He looked startled, even angry, and replied as if I were a wayward pupil and he a school teacher. "No, you will come back here every Tuesday at seven, and make a report to me on the work you have accomplished during the week, and ask whatever question you think I can answer."

I obeyed to the letter throughout the next six months. At first I checked each Tuesday to make sure Mondor wanted me to return the following week, and then stopped checking when he began referring to what I might do in preparation for the next meeting: "Quand vous reviendrez mardi prochain, vous me direz cela." The principal part of our discussion was on meanings of lines, interpretations of poems, and on the close relatedness of themes and symbols in Mallarmé. Mondor was always curious and attentive, although not always receptive to my theories. But often he would return in later meetings to ideas he had at first considered too "far-fetched" and grant me at least a partial approval.

These weekly visits became an enjoyable habit. Mondor remained at all times the biographer and never turned critic. As we became better acquainted, we began talking not only of Mallarmé but of our other lives, he of the medical world and I of university teaching. Early in our conversations I told him how surprised I was by the hour he set for our meetings and how I wondered when he had dinner. There was obviously no servant in the apartment. He always opened the door himelf and was always dressed in the same manner—formal black suit and stiff collar.

He told me he lectured at the Ecole de Médecine early in the morning, and then performed operations the rest of the morning, usually in the presence of his students. In the afternoon he gave consultations to patients who came to his apartment. The woman who cleaned his apartment prepared for him every evening at six o'clock a light supper. At seven his life changed, from a long day devoted to medicine, to a long evening devoted to literature. The habit had formed during the war years when it had been difficult and dangerous to go out in the evenings. To occupy himself and to forget the opprobrium of the Occupation, Mondor decided to write the life of Mallarmé, whom he had always admired, primarily as a man, and then as an artist. His admiration grew as he continued his investigations and he was surprised to find himself writing a long sustained praise of a man whose writings he did not usually understand. The long wartime evenings became a precious part of his new life in literature. He purchased document after document, letter after letter, until his collection was so well known in Paris that during those months I saw him each week, he often received, unsolicited, letters of Mallarmé which the owners wished to add to the principal collection. Paul Valéry had been a friend of Mondor, and already the doctor was writing studies on Valéry, not as extensive as those on Mallarmé, but equally important in a documentary-historical sense.

One morning I read in the newspaper that Henri Mondor had been elected to the Académie Française. The following Tuesday I congratulated him. He was visibly pleased with the honor, and explained his success with the voting by saying that since he had operated on almost all of the thirty-nine members of the Academy, they had felt some gratitude toward him. "Moreover," he added, "when their turn would come around for the next operation, if I weren't one of them, their apprehension would be excessive."

As time went on, he planned little surprises for my Tuesday visits, manuscripts often of poems we had mentioned. On one Tuesday I remember the pride he took in showing me the large format sheets on which Mallarmé had written *L'Après-midi d'un faune*. This time he stood up and came around to my side of the desk in order to hold the pages so that I might see the calligraphy. "For this manuscript," he said, "I paid what you Americans pay for your most expensive automobile."

Then he spread the sheets out on the desk, and we both peered at them closely. "You know, that opening line, 'Ces nymphes, je les veux perpétuer,' I have often wondered what Mallarmé meant by it." This was an indirect question, and so I suggested in my ludicrous role of pedagogue, "Since it's the faun speaking, he wants to copulate with the nymphs, but the poet is also speaking in the line and telling us he wants to perpetuate the nymphs by writing a poem about them."

Two weeks later Mondor told me he had been reciting over and over again that line of perpetuating nymphs, even during an emergency operation when he was opening up the stomach of a man who had swallowed a whole carrot. As he lifted the carrot, still quite intact, out of the stomach, its form reminded him of a penis, and he mumbled, to the puzzlement of the nurses and doctors standing by, "Ces nymphes, je les veux perpétuer."

Dr. Mondor never demonstrated any warmth of friendship. Without being cold, he was always impersonal. Our meetings in the elegant setting of his apartment were solidly based on research and work. There were moments of levity, examples of *l'esprit grivois*, like the carrot story, that reminded me this man was also a famous surgeon.

I cite and praise the example of Henri Mondor as that type of Frenchman, not primarily literary, but devoted to the literature and culture of his country, who extended help and hospitality to a foreigner because that foreigner was a student of French poetry. Mondor knew that I was a pilgrim as well as a worker, and that only he had the relics the pilgrim yearned to see for his edification. He exhibited the relics and gave to me generously of his time and knowledge in what was perhaps for him a distant and faint analogy with those famous Tuesday evenings when the master himself dispensed revelations to younger disciples and pilgrims.

My first visit to Rome in the fifties was part of a lecture tour for USIS. A good friend from my Chicago days, Gertrude Hooker, then working in Rome, had made the arrangements. During the few previous years I had made the acquaintance, through correspondence, of Marguerite Caetani, the princess founder and director of the large international literary magazine *Botteghe oscure*. She had accepted graciously and published four pieces of mine: two parts of a novel, a poem on *Phèdre*, written for a dance at Bennington, and a set of maxims I had written in French. Her letters had delighted and intrigued me. Written by hand on thin sheets of blue paper, they spoke briefly of my pieces and more eloquently of René Char whom she wanted me to meet and write about. Her charming cordiality toward me had something to do with her promoting of Char whom she looked upon as *the* significant poet of the day.

Before I left for Rome I had written to Princess Caetani, telling her the name of my hotel for this my first visit to Rome and saying it would give me special pleasure if I could meet her. There was barely time for her to answer before I left Bennington. No letter did come. As I entered my room in the hotel, with the valet carrying my bags, the telephone was ringing. I answered "allo" since I had come directly from Paris and had forgotten that *pronto* is more usual in Italy. A clear melodious voice said, "This is Marguerite Caetani. I want you to come to lunch tomorrow at one o'clock." The words were so phrased that I interpreted them as forming not an invitation as much as an order. I accepted gratefully. Then the princess said, "Whom do you want me to invite?" A bit startled, I hesitated, and she concluded the conversation forcibly with the words, "I will think of someone."

The next day at noon I walked to the via delle Botteghe Oscure, to the address I had written many times on envelopes. It was a huge square *palazzo*, with the name Caetani cut into the stone on the façade and painted red. Opposite the *palazzo* I watched the Roman cats, magnificent wild-looking animals, moving in and out of the ruined arcades of the Circus Flaminii.

At one o'clock I entered the courtyard and was directed to the elevator that would take me to the Princess Caetani. When the elevator stopped, she herself opened the door to usher me into the apartment. A short frail-looking woman, white hair and features of gentleness and intelligence. Almost before greeting me, she said, "I decided the best person to invite was the ambassador."

I reminded myself that the ambassador was Claire Booth Luce, and I must have revealed an expression of puzzlement. She may have read my mind because she added as if to put me at my ease, "the French ambassador. He is coming with his wife. Just the five of us at lunch." The prince stood close behind her. A pink face, white hair and sharp features. He was more ceremonious than his American wife. Almost immediately Monsieur and Madame Duparc arrived, by the same elevator. As I was introduced, I mentioned my admiration for the songs of Henri Duparc. "C'est mon frère," the ambassador said. We all spoke French throughout the lunch and the visit.

A servant in livery, wearing white gloves, stood behind each of the five chairs. The food was not as exciting as the ceremony of the luncheon, the way it was served, the gold plates. Two of the servants carried large silver platters they seemed to be constantly passing in front of us. I was placed at the end of the table beside the princess. Opposite me was the ambassador and on my left the prince. Mme Duparc was opposite the prince. As we were being seated, I heard M. Duparc ask Prince Caetani, as if it were a casual question with which to begin a luncheon in Rome, "Combien de papes y a-t-il dans votre famille?" Perhaps a casual question for the ambassador and the prince, but it was overwhelming for the visitor from Massachusetts. And still more overwhelming when the prince replied in total simplicity: "Deux seulement."

I asked then, with more than a tinge of school pedantry, "Which ones?" The prince named only one, but there was a question in the tone of his voice, and he looked at me to see if there would be any recognition. "Boniface VIII." I smiled slightly although I wondered if I was discourteous. "What picture comes to your mind?" he asked me. "I see flames licking the soles of a man's feet while he is plunged head first in a hole in the ground." The scene from the *Inferno* was still vivid for me, and I answered as if Prince Caetani were my Dante teacher. I could tell that the prince was pleased that one of his ancestors had been named by Dante, even in a state of damnation.

The ambassador then went more deeply into historical matters when he continued with a second question: "Isn't there another branch of the Caetani family in Naples?" The answer came immediately, and it bewildered me still more in its jumbling of distant history with the present. "Yes," replied the prince, "but we quarrelled in the fourteenth century and haven't spoken since."

To the princess I addressed questions about *Botteghe oscure* and René Char. The promotion of the magazine had become a large part of her life. It was impossible to speak of such matters without making references to earlier parts of her life, and gradually through the visit and the next Sunday visit to Ninfa, the country home of the Caetanis south of Rome, I was able to put together a sketchy biography of this fascinating lady.

She was Marguerite Chapin from New London, Connecticut, when she first arrived in Paris to study singing with Jean de Reské. From that time on, her life was given over to the study of languages, to literature, painting and music. Bonnard and Vuillard both did portraits of her. After her marriage with Prince Caetani, the youngest member of a Roman family whose written history covers 800 years, and who was a composer, the godson and student of Lizst and a friend of Brahms, their Versailles home, the Villa Romaine, became a center of literary meetings and the founding of the literary magazine *Commerce*. Princess Caetani (then known as Princess di Bassiano, one of the titles of her husband) was helped in editing *Commerce* by Paul Valéry, Léon-Paul Fargue and Valery Larbaud. It lasted ten years and published texts of such writers as Saint-John Perse, Gide, Hofmannstahl, Prévert, as well as the first translations into French of works of Eliot, MacLeish, Virginia Woolf, Edith Sitwell.

The Caetanis moved to Rome at the beginning of World War II to occupy the *palazzo* on the via delle Botteghe Oscure where the family had lived since the 1550's. The Princess was already drawing up plans for the new magazine in which she intended to present new Italian, French, English and American works. Friends tried to dissuade her, for practical reasons, from publishing a multilanguage magazine. Especially her cousin T. S. Eliot. But she persevered and won out. Beginning with the fourth issue, four languages were represented. She commissioned directly works she wanted to publish: Jackson Mathews' translations of René Char, Dylan

Thomas's *Under Milk Wood* which appeared under its Welsh title, *Llareggub*, the short novel *Hunter of Doves* by Josephine Herbst, based on her recollections of Nathanael West.

During the luncheon most of my conversation had been with the Princess, but when we stood up, the Prince took my arm and said, "You have been in Rome for twenty-four hours. What has struck you the most?" Something had indeed struck me forcibly during the course of the meal, but I hesitated to mention it. He was aware of my confusion and said, "I am an old man, you couldn't shock me. Tell me the truth."

So I blurted out my first strong impression. "It is the way you treat servants. I noticed it last night in Mrs. Hooker's apartment where she had invited Italian friends, and today at lunch in the Palazzo Caetani. You treat them as if they were automatons or subhuman. Never a word of thanks when they serve you—and you dismiss them with a gesture of the hand or a shrug."

The Prince wasn't in the least disturbed or surprised. "It is you who are right, and we who are wrong. Each January the Pope has all the Roman nobles come before him and lectures to us exactly on that problem. He tells us that if we continue using such medieval behavior with the working class, the communists will take over Italy. But then we say to ourselves that we are all old and everything will change at our death. Après nous le déluge ..."

On the following Sunday, Princess Caetani invited me to Ninfa. Allen Tate was teaching that year at the University of Rome. He and his wife Caroline Gordon drove me to Ninfa where some friends had gathered for Sunday lunch. Again, after the meal, I had a few minutes alone with the Prince who showed me the gardens particularly cherished by his wife, and which he claimed were the only romantic gardens then in Europe. The Ninfa is a stream running through a twelfth-century town that had been wiped out by a plague. It is on the site of one of Hannibal's camps. In fact, the Ninfa still has a species of trout that had been imported from Africa by Hannibal.

Beyond the rose-covered ruins of the garden, I could see the walls of the original town. I asked the Prince about the inhabitants, and he said, as if to conclude the Wednesday talk at the *palazzo* in Rome, "They are my peasants. I own the entire town. Everyone in the town depends on me for a livelihood. The system, as you see, is still totally medieval. But it will all change at my death. Probably for the worse at the beginning. I am kind to my peasants. They are devoted to me."

[146]

At the end of the day, the Tates and I had a few minutes alone with Marguerite Caetani. We were trying to tell her how appreciative we were of her efforts on behalf of the writer in so many countries, of the encouragement she had given to so many young writers, of the help she had extended to so many established writers. She was totally unpretentious, totally dedicated to her work, totally indifferent to polemical literary discussion. She smiled faintly as she listened to us, and then said quite simply, "I live with the belief that the artist is the most important person alive."

In 1948, in the prestigious *Cahiers de la Pléiade*, appeared the beginning of a new poem of Saint-John Perse, *Et vous, mers*. Those three words, used as title, were simply the first three words of the text. In 1950, in the same periodical, a second fragment of the same poem appeared. I read the two selections with interest because I was already familiar with the volume *Eloges*, and especially with the poem *Anabase*. Because of T. S. Eliot's translation and brief commentary, *Anabase* was better known in England and America than in France.

Then in early 1951, from an address in Washington, I received a letter from the poet asking me if I would translate the new poem. He referred to the two parts already in print and said he would send me new parts of the poem as they were completed. He did not know how long the poem would turn out to be, and he had not yet chosen a title. The letter, written in a magnificent calligraphy, was signed Alexis Léger. I remembered that my copy of *Eloges* bore the full name of Saint-Léger-Léger.

I felt honored by this letter. (Years later I learned indirectly that Allen Tate recommended me to Léger as a possible translator of *Et vous, mers*.) Léger had carefully explained that it was his policy to change translators after every poem. He had the reputation of being hard on his translators, of never being satisfied. Eliot's translation of *Anabase*, in particular, had been severely criticized by the French poet. The simple final sentence of the letter had moved me: "Serez-vous mon traducteur?" I answered affirmatively that I would like to try my luck with the poem, and that *en principe* I accepted, but on two conditions. First, that Léger would correct the translation, and second, that if he were dissatisfied at any point, I would give over my place to someone else.

I was plagued by a dilemma coming from my profession of a French teacher and making me hostile to any translation. In the classroom I had ample opportunity to point out how impossible translations are and especially how important it is to read poetry in the language in which it was written. Léger's answer, with its assurance that the poem would appear in a bilingual edition, and that he would correct each passage I sent him and make suggestions if there were need, convinced me to undertake the work. He wanted my translation to correspond as exactly as possible with the French, so that translators into languages he did not know, might consult mine for exact meaning of the text.

He sent me the six parts (*chants*) of the poem's opening he was to call "L'Invocation." I began the work. Thanks to an invitation of Karl Shapiro, I was on the editorial staff of *Poetry* in Chicago, and we published in October 1951 the French text and my translation of "L'Invocation" from *Et vous, mers*. The poet seemed to be satisfied.

New passages continued to come to me during 1952 and 1953. I had completed the translation of approximately half of the poem—sixty pages —when a new fairly long section arrived bearing the title "Amers." On that manuscript Léger indicated that *Amers* was to be the general title of the entire poem. I was anxious to begin work and paid little attention to the title although it mystified me. I wondered about the form of the word. Was it the masculine plural of the adjective *amer*? The obvious relationship between *mer* and *amer* occurred to me, and at one moment I jotted down *brine* as a possible translation.

In each of Léger's letters he had always repeated the plan to arrange a meeting so that we might talk more easily about the translation and discuss at greater length than correspondence allowed, various problems related to the meaning of the poem. In each of my replies I had always repeated my desire to know him personally and my willingness to meet him at whatever place he would designate. I was in Brookline during the summer of 1953. One morning a telephone call came from a lady—Mina Curtiss—who said her house guest, Alexis Léger, wanted to see me. Her house was a few hours' drive from Boston. Would I come on Saturday about two o'clock and stay overnight. That would give ample time for the kind of visit M. Léger wanted. I told Mrs. Curtiss that I had been expecting such a call and that I accepted her invitation.

At precisely two o'clock that Saturday I drove into the courtyard of the address Mrs. Curtiss had given me. She was standing there as if she knew I would arrive at that moment. At least I felt certain the lady waiting there was Mrs. Curtiss. It was. She greeted me warmly in a most charming way. Then, pointing to a hedge, she said, "M. Léger is waiting for you in the garden. You can see the top of his head just beyond the hedge. I will call you about five to have a cup of tea on the terrace."

His head was covered with a béret and he was reading a newspaper. His greeting was as affable as that of Mrs. Curtiss. At the very start of the conversation, which turned out to be a monologue, he mentioned the book I had written on Mallarmé, not in order to comment on the book, but to speak about Mallarmé. Then he spoke about English poetry, and finally about the difference between French and English poetry. I suffered during this discussion because I wanted to jot down the concepts and developments Léger was analyzing. I had never heard previously and have never heard since, a more brilliant explanation of the essence of poetry, and more precisely the essence of French poetry as opposed to English.

Almost three hours went by without any mention of *Amers* and the real reason for my visit. It seemed to me that Léger had been silent for a long time, for years perhaps, over the subject of poetry, and that my presence, avid listener that I was, had given him the necessary reason to articulate his thoughts.

When Mrs. Curtiss called us for tea, Léger took my arm and directed me through the garden, but he continued speaking the final words of his exposition. It was not until then that suddenly I remembered the name of Mina Curtiss. Since her telephone conversation the memory part of my mind had been trying to recall the circumstances in which I had known her name. It was a volume of Proust's letters she had translated and published. I remembered the dedication of the book to Céleste Albaret. When we reached the terrace, I apologized to her for not remembering at first, and told her how much I liked the book and her translation. In a few minutes we were speaking enthusiastically of Proust. She was as fervent an admirer as I was.

Léger had become unusually quiet. When I looked at him, he seemed unhappy. The reason became clear when he exclaimed in an almost petulant tone: "Both of you are giving too much importance to Marcel Proust. He is not that great at all. You are overrating him."

In our turn Mrs. Curtiss and I began expostulating, but Léger paid no heed and continued with a revelation: "Proust wrote me nine letters, and I never answered one of them. I still have those letters." Whereas I was simply surprised at Léger's opinion, Mrs. Curtiss expressed strong dis-approval. When it became obvious that mere arguments were having no effect, she declared as her final reprimand: "Mon ami, the world will remember you because Proust speaks of you in *Sodome et Gomorrhe.*" (A few days later I checked the passage in Marcel's return to Balbec where one day in his room in the hotel two maids, Céleste Albaret and her sister, find a copy of *Eloges* on the bed. Céleste picks up the book bearing the name Saint-Léger-Léger, turns the pages, samples some of the poems and states that they are not poems as much as guessing games—*devinettes.*)

During the dinner Léger resumed his position of principal speaker. Politics in Washington and Paris were the principal themes. Mrs. Curtiss spoke of the preparation for her biography of Bizet. After dinner, Léger and I took a long walk together during which he asked me what I was working on at the moment. When I referred to a study of the twentieth-century theater, he made a discouraging comment: "Why waste your time on that? The modern theater is so dreary and insignificant!"

"What about Claudel?" I asked because I was aware of Léger's attachment to Claudel.

"He doesn't count because he is so far outside of every French tradition. Claudel does not belong to the French garden."

When I left him an hour or so later, to go to the small guesthouse where I was to sleep, still nothing had been said about *Amers* and the translation.

The following morning he joined me at breakfast on the terrace, and there I asked him if he had any advice to give about the translation. "No," he replied, "I simply wanted to see you and talk with you. I can always communicate by letter, corrections and changes I might suggest. Oh! there is one matter I should mention now—the title. 'Brine' won't do. It is not the meaning of *Amers.*"

And therewith he described the meaning of *un amer* as being a natural or man-made sign on land that navigators use as a guide on approaching the coastline. It could be a cliff or wall, a church spire or lighthouse beacon. There seem to be two words in English that translate *amers*: "landmarks" and "seamarks." It was not hard for me to choose "seamarks."

I was properly humiliated for not having consulted a few of the large French dictionaries. In the standard *Petit Larousse* of that year *un amer* did not appear. After the French publication of *Amers* in 1957, it was added, thanks to the poem of Saint-John Perse.

We walked again, after breakfast that morning, and Léger spoke in a more relaxed, more personal way of himself. He had been away from France since 1940. (He was not to return until *Amers* was published—after seventeen years of absence.) American hospitality had been generous to him during and after the war years. A post at the Library of Congress

[150]

had been given him by Archibald MacLeish. He worried that the financial help he had received should have gone to an American poet. Just that past year Harvard had offered him the Charles Eliot Norton lectureship which he had turned down because of his conviction that he could not or should not lecture.

As I drove off that morning, after the one meeting I was to have with Saint-John Perse, I recalled phrases of a letter he had written to MacLeish and which he had permitted to be published. They were phrases I had memorized as representing a supreme homage to France and to the French language. "France is myself, my complete self." ("La France est moi-même, et tout moi-même.") "The French *language*, the only imaginable refuge, the only place I can be to understand anything." ("La langue française, le seul refuge imaginable, le seul lieu où je puisse me tenir pour y rien comprendre.")

XIII

New School and Barney Rosset　　Bennington in the fifties:
Kenneth Burke　　Stanley Hyman

My second period of teaching at Bennington College lasted twelve years, 1950–62. For five of those years I taught also at New School for Social Research in New York (1950–55). My Bennington program ended Thursday at noon. I took the 3:30 train at North Bennington and reached New York in time to teach a class Thursday night. My second course was scheduled for Friday night. Saturday morning I took the train back to North Bennington. A taxing regimen but exciting for me to have five days a week in Vermont, in a community to which I was attached sentimentally, and two days in New York, the city which, after Paris, I prefer to all others.

My first class at New School was small—about twelve students. We sat around a table. The subject was modern French poetry, and I tried to encourage the students to participate in the discussion in French. All my other classes in that institution I did in English in order to attract more students. The salary was calculated on the number of students in each class. One of the fellows in that first class was a bit recalcitrant about talking. He was slender, small of stature, boyish-looking. I could tell by his alertness and facial expressions that he was getting the points of the lessons faster than the others. After one of the classes, he stood in the back of the room until the others had left.

His first words were: "I know you come down from Bennington every week and wonder if you would have dinner with me one of your evenings here in New York. I want to solicit your help and advice because I have just bought a publishing house and want to choose some French books for my first list."

The young man's name was Barney Rosset.

I told him we could meet the next week, and then asked the name of the publishing house. When he said, "Grove Press," I remembered reading about two young men who had founded Grove Press recently and published as their first two books the poems of Richard Crashaw and Melville's *Confidence Man*. That was indeed the press, Barney Rosset assured me, and he intended to maintain the stock of those two books, but emphasize in his new titles books from contemporary literature.

I liked Barney immediately, and we became friends. We met principally at New School. He and his wife, the painter Joan Mitchell, attended my course on Proust the following year. My function at Grove Press was that of suggesting new titles from modern French literature. In March 1953, on my return from two months in Paris where I had seen one of the first productions of *En attendant Godot*, I wrote a long letter to Barney urging him to buy the rights to publish all the works of three new French dramatists (although I was aware of the reluctance of publishers to bring out plays): Samuel Beckett, Eugène Ionesco and Jean Genet. Barney's answer was not too enthusiastic, but he agreed to try one of the three, the Irishman Beckett. In a month he added the other two. It was the only time in my life I was a good prophet.

Now twenty-seven years later Barney Rosset has made Grove Press and *Evergreen Review* famous. Exerything about him is unusual: his limitless energy, his personal involvement in the books he publishes, his extensive knowledge of literature and the arts, his kindness and his sense of justice. He fights for good causes, and he fights hard. He would have made a first rate crusader under Saint Louis. In fact, he would have made a good Saint Louis in the thirteenth century.

Somehow I knew all this that first time he spoke to me in the back of the classroom of New School. After my first question, I asked a second question—far more personal and one I regretted asking as soon as it was voiced. But Barney looked so frail, boyish and innocent that I instinctively said, "I hope you have some solid financial backing—such an enterprise is very costly."

He didn't even smile when he answered my insolent commentary with a story. "I have been spending my time recently on making a film. The other evening I showed it to myself in my apartment, and it was so bad that I took it to the East River and dumped it in. With it went $100,000." That was Barney's gracious way of telling me he had no immediate financial problems. As we walked together out of the building that same evening, we spoke of Chicago and the school he had attended there. It was a model progressive school in those days, and there Barney learned some of the ways in which he could express himself freely, test out pedagogic methods and also support causes of justice. "We even picketed *Gone With the Wind* when the film was first shown because of the treatment of blacks."

I enjoyed Bennington the most when I had this weekly break from the small college community and the placid Vermont landscape. Three literature colleagues from my earlier Bennington period were no longer there: Francis Fergusson, William Troy and Léonie Adams. But there were new recruits, and brilliant ones, who were making the study of literature as stimulating and serious as any program in the country at that time. Three writers had just left Bennington to teach elsewhere: Theodore Roethke had gone to the University of Washington, Stanley Kunitz had gone to New York, and Richard Lewis to Yale.

The oldest member of the literature faculty was the youngest in spirit and stamina: Kenneth Burke. His appointment was unusual, to say the least. He came to the college from his farm in New Jersey every other week for three days, every other year! During the year Kenneth did not come, we would try to prepare a group of students to take his course. We gave them readings for Kenneth's books, and we instructed them as best we could in the Burkian method. We worried whether there would be a good solid class, and then we worried whether the class would hold out. It did always. If the students failed to understand the points of Kenneth's teaching, they were bewitched by his ardor, his wit, his evangelical zeal. He came bringing good news of how to look at literature, of how to read a book, of how to relate "Ode on a Grecian Urn" or *Coriolanus* or *Nightwood* to life itself. Kenneth had a way of turning his students into co-workers for the discovery and the revealing of mysteries. In advance of each semester, Kenneth would send us a new course name, involving the particular author he intended to teach. But among ourselves we referred to his various courses as Burke I, Burke II, Burke III.

When I was a graduate student, Austin Warren had spoken to me about Kenneth Burke and given me *Counter-statement* to read. Before I knew him, I looked upon him as a priest figure, as one consecrated to the service

[154]

of art, as a man set apart from all the rest of us and who, quite literally, celebrated the mysteries in the formulas he devised. When I met him in the flesh at Bennington, I was astounded to find him so friendly, so witty, so likeable. His mind was always fixed on literature, and in the briefest conversation with him there would be innumerable allusions to great and to small books.

The rest of us—Ben Belitt, Howard Nemerov, Harold Kaplan, Kit Foster—figured as satelites revolving around the fixed star. Two other teacher-writers joined us, Stanley Hyman in 1953 and Bernard Malamud in 1960.

Of all the Bennington teachers whom I had the privilege of knowing and working with, Stanley Hyman was the most striking, the most learned and the most willfully enigmatic. He was closest, I believe, to Howard Nemerov and Kenneth Burke, who enjoyed drinking and playing poker. Stanley had taught at the college one year, in 1945, and then resigned. He gave as reasons a feeling that his teaching was not going well and a need for himself and his wife Shirley Jackson to devote more time to complete their first books.

Initially Stanley had been attracted to the Bennington community by the presence there of three critics he admired: Kenneth Burke in particular, a lifelong influence and a friend; William Troy, whose critical writings appeared in the *Nation* during the thirties and forties; and Francis Fergusson, who was among the first American critics to study in Shakespeare and subsequent playwrights ancient ritualistic patterns.

Of all the critics Stanley examined in his first book, *The Armed Vision* (1948), the three men from Bennington were those whose writings had opened up to him methods and critical theories he incorporated and developed during the rest of his life. They were theories involving anthropology, religion and psychiatry which formed the basis of his most famous course, Myth and Ritual. This subject, pursued by Stanley for approximately twenty years, between 1950 and 1970, was everywhere in his writing and teaching. He was planning to write the book at the time of his death. It would have crowned a remarkable career as critic, and it would have represented an achievement of what we called, both seriously and jokingly, "the Bennington school of criticism."

For ten years, between 1953 and 1962, we were members of the same literature division at Bennington, where I watched him grow into an almost legendary figure, into one of his own mythic heroes surrounded by mystery, revealing only what he wished to reveal, separating himself from the rest of us in order to maintain some private integrity. We met often on the campus, at faculty gatherings, at informal parties, and infrequently at his house where he and Shirley were perfect hosts and where he showed me his extensive collection of coins (of which I remember one from Siracusa), and where the three of us discussed problems of publishing.

In the early 1950's, before moving to a larger house on Prospect Street in North Bennington, the Hymans lived in a house on the small hill separating the college from the town itself. Shirley was sitting on the porch one afternoon as I passed by on foot. She invited me to stop and rest for a few minutes on my way to the center of town. The literature division had just asked her to help us out and teach a writing class. "I stopped you," she said, "to ask how one teaches a class. I haven't the slightest idea, and I'm scared."

Already Shirley Jackson was a well-known and much-admired short story writer. *The Lottery* had begun being anthologized. Her skillful dialogue and the eerie tense atmosphere she was able to create, were characteristics of her first books the critics were already analyzing. During that afternoon conversation, I reminded her that some of the critics were beginning to explain *The Lottery* in terms of primitive ritual. Shirley's beautiful piercing eyes sparkled with an expression that was half surprise and half amusement. "The source of that story is simply North Bennington. Just listen to the people here in town and the way they slaughter one another with words and stories and slander."

She kept returning to the problems of teaching, and I kept wondering if she were serious. "How do you begin a class? What do you say first? And then *what* do you teach?" At moments when I felt she was serious, I began making suggestions. But was this a put-on? Was this a strange test of some kind?

Both Shirley and Stanley were shy and at the same time sophisticated. This combination of naivety and massive knowledge helped to explain bewildering moments in bits of conversation with them I still remember. One day, for example, Shirley asked me for some postcards of old houses in France. She explained that she was writing a novel about a haunted house and needed to have a picture in front of her as she wrote. One semester Stanley and I were both asked to speak on some aspect of tragedy in a series of lectures for the drama department. I spoke first on the *Hippolytus* of Euripides and *Phèdre* of Racine. Stanley was in the audience. He spoke to me after the talk and sadly shook his head: "You're a pro, Wallace. I don't dare speak after you next week. I'm going to be sick." He did fall sick, and his talk was cancelled.

Shirley Jackson died in her sleep one August night in 1965. She and Stanley had two sons and two daughters. The year after Shirley's death, Stanley underwent a cataract operation and asked a brilliant young woman and former student to help him with his work. Phoebe Pettingell and Stanley were married at the end of 1966. Between this marriage and his death in 1970, I saw Stanley only once, on a return visit to Bennington. Among other things he declared himself a happy man and a fortunate man because he had had two wives, both of whom were brilliant women and both totally devoted to him.

Stanley worked hard at everything: teaching, numismatics, poker playing, baseball watching; the long twelve-year preparation for his biggest book, *The Tangled Bank*, a consideration of Darwin, Marx and Freud as writers; the weekly writing for the *New Yorker* between 1940 and 1970; the two pamphlets for the Minnesota University Press—one on Nathanael West and the other on Flannery O'Connor; the book reviews he did regularly for the *New Leader* between 1961 and 1965. These articles, now collected in book form under the title *Standards* represent Stanley Hyman at his best. Each piece is a form of revelation conceived and composed under pressure. The unanswered question is how did Stanley find the time to write such weekly or biweekly articles, each one of which testifies to carefully checked erudition, to carefully considered judgment, to a mastery of critical style, to a prophetic tone, as in the essay on *A Clockwork Orange* by Anthony Burgess.

Ever since the appearance of *The Armed Vision*, Stanley has been called a destructive critic. The word applies best to *Standards* where he demolishes a new work if it does not come up to a "standard" of literary excellence, but the examination of a new work was always carried out with such fervent expectation that it is unfair to stress the negative aspect of Stanley's criticism. As a teacher he was both stern and soft-hearted, and more soft-hearted than stern. At faculty meetings he often surprised us by finding in a weak student ennobling and promising traits no one else found.

Stanley collected bits of information about people and subjects, and filed them away both in a literary filing cabinet and in his mind. He read the Sunday *New York Times* from beginning to end and kept clippings of unusual matters that might be used. He once told Howard Nemerov that he had a fuller file of clippings on him than Howard had on himself.

Stanley should have been a theologian. He often called himself a militant atheist—a habit both provocative and untrue because of the deeply religious meaning he gave to his favorite words "myth" and "ritual." In a posthumous article called "History and Sacred History," a harsh review of Jack Finegan's *Archeology of the New Testament*, Stanley demonstrated, a year before he died, his belief that the history connected with the Bible is what the Jews and Christians believed, and not the dubious doings of their divinities. If he insisted that his children often recite at breakfast the phrase "Jesus is a myth," and if later those youngsters came to understand what their father really meant by myth, they would realize that the holy name had not been taken in vain.

His wry humor, his learning, and, quite simply, his likeableness contributed during eighteen years to the creation of an atmosphere in a small college community in Vermont—to such a degree that students and faculty alike looked upon Bennington as Stanley Hyman's community. When physically present at gatherings and meetings, he dominated the scene with the forcefulness and whimsicality of his speech. When absent, we found ourselves wondering what he would say or think, what he would approve or denounce.

XIV

early and late visits to France: Albert Mockel
Céleste Albaret   Closerie des Lilas, 1928
Pius X, 1954   Notre Dame

The wit of the French, their rapid manipulation of ideas, their deft analysis of sentiments often give to foreigners a false impression of facility and even peril. Their facility cannot be denied, and facility, by definition, is perilous. French newspapers announce daily the end of the old order, an uprising of such proportions that every Frenchman will participate and all countries will be involved. But if you look out from the café window where you are reading the newspaper, the street will seem the same as always, teeming and yet orderly with that uncanny sense of precision and elegance and swiftness the French demonstrate on all public occasions and in all private meditations. The new French books each year seem at first dangerous in the very ease with which they upset theories and characters and genres. We forget that the French mind, even the most learned and profound, is always youthful, and therefore always appears destructive and imposing. Other nations are more solemn and perhaps more efficient than the French. They take less time to reflect and converse and form the brilliant abstractions about human activity that constitute some of the glory of French culture.

On my first visit to France, at the age of nineteen, I had been in Paris for several weeks before having any real experience with the conversation and the wit of that country. Then it came to my attention, in full force, on one occasion. Before leaving for France, I had done some work for a friend, Marjory Henry, who was writing her doctoral dissertation on the symbolist poet Stuart Merrill. Through this friend's kindness, I received in Paris an invitation to meet Mme Stuart Merrill, a Belgian lady, at the home of the Belgian poet Albert Mockel, who lived in Rueil, just outside of Paris. I knew slightly the work of Mockel, who belonged to the symbolist group, and was eager to meet him, largely, I must confess, because I hoped he would speak of Mallarmé, whom he had known personally.

The invitation was for lunch. It was a warm Sunday in August. I walked down the avenue from the station and rang the bell at an ivy-covered gate through which I could see nothing. I was ushered through the house to the garden where M. and Mme Mockel, Mme Merrill and two other guests were waiting. These five people, of the same age—in their early sixties—despite their formal manners, tried immediately to put me at my ease. As I spoke with one, the others did not listen. They seemed from another world. The two men were impeccably dressed in black morning suits and the women in light-colored summer dresses matching the perfect French garden. They spoke at first, but casually, of symbolist writers because I had been introduced as one knowing the poetry of Stuart Merrill. They made me feel pride in the fact that Merrill was originally an American. But soon they dropped the subject of poetry and literature, and it was impossible to get them back to that subject during the rest of my visit.

I began, on that occasion, to realize many things about the French turn of mind. Never was indoctrination more graciously bestowed. Throughout our conversation, a tone of reasonableness dominated. No matter what topic was discussed: the quality of the fruit that season or the prose style of Colette, the effort made was always to appear reasonable, equitable, lucid, rather than "right." Sincerity of tone counted above infallibility of judgment. As I think back to that now distant Sunday afternoon, I do not remember any question being settled satisfactorily; I cannot remember the desire on anyone's part to decide an issue. But I remember a large repertory of stories and subjects, and the evident pleasure taken in stirring up problems and exposing them. There was never the shadow of displeasure because no one was interested in forcing an opinion.

The table was in a kind of annex to the house, almost in the garden itself. The shades had been drawn because of the intense sunlight, and the room was in a soft golden glow. The table was long and narrow. M. Mockel at one end and Mme Mockel at the other end, seemed at a great distance from the rest of us seated along the sides. The luncheon itself was my first elaborate French meal. Course succeeded course, and wine succeeded wine. I was bewildered by the organization and the variety, and delighted by the gastronomy. Mme Mockel had announced that at the end of the meal we were to have an American speciality, something unusual in France, and ordered for the day's menu in my particular honor. I soon gave up trying to imagine what American dish could possibly harmonize with that food. I have no exact memory of the culinary successes of that Sunday, but I do remember a fish in a sauce with capers, the like of which I had never tasted, and a roasted guinea fowl with the feathers replaced to give it the semblance of a winged bird.

Finally the moment came for the American dish. Inwardly I was apprehensive, but outwardly I pretended eagerness to behold the prize and patriotic gratitude for this inclusion of an American memento in an otherwise classical French meal. The table was cleared, and plain white plates were put down before each one of us. As soon as the maid came in from the kitchen, we all strained and turned in order to catch the first glimpse. I saw what the novelty was, and my first thought was: this is a bad joke. On a silver platter the maid carried a bottle of tomato catsup! I quickly saw that the Mockels were serious. Mme Mockel, first, daintily tipped the bottle and shook it until some of the contents spurted out on the white plate. Then each of us in turn performed the same ceremony. Nothing to go with it! Tomato catsup alone! I decided not to expose its common use, but to partake of it as the others were doing. Their comments, abundant and laudatory, covered up whatever words I tried to articulate.

It was not the absolute end, fortunately. A gigantic *tarte aux pommes*, composed of what seemed to be hundreds of thin slices of apple glazed over with some amber substance, was served as the dessert. The incredibly rich cream sauce that accompanied it caused all aftertaste of tomato catsup to disappear, and my attention returned to the manners and the speech of my hosts and their friends.

Nature was constantly called upon to illustrate whatever abstractions were under discussion. Or it was used simply to provide interludes in the conversation. The Mockel's and Mme Merrill's knowledge of the symbolist movement and French literary figures did not surprise me, but their familiarity with nature did. The ease with which they introduced comments on the cherry trees in the garden, and the ripening pears along the espalier wall where each pear was carefully encased in a paper bag, and the habits of a pair of swallows who had made a nest under one of the eaves, impressed me. The history of poetry and the art of gardening were so naturally fused that I began to believe this one of the signs of the very old culture I was observing for the first time. The entire scene involving the swallows, a beautiful black cat, a bowl of brilliant anemones, and forays with sentences from which those participating always emerged triumphant, was organically French. I realized this much later when I had the opportunity of seeing it recapitulated on other occasions.

On a return to Paris in 1954, I called on Mme Céleste Albaret, whose name figures in Marcel Proust's novel, and who served Proust as housekeeper between 1913 and his death in 1922. She owned at that time a rather dilapidated hotel on the rue des Canettes, a small street that goes into the Place Saint-Sulpice. I climbed the stairs to the second floor where the hotel office was located, and there against a background of mail boxes and keys I waited until Mme Albaret ended a conversation with one of her hotel guests. At least I imagined it was Mme Albaret from her age and from the authority with which she spoke. When the right moment came, I introduced myself as an American who was a student of Proust's work. She smiled and said she had already known why I was there, that she had seen many of my compatriots and admirers of Proust from other countries. She received me then with a regal air and such serenity, that I had from the beginning of my visit, which was to last two hours, the impression of a great privilege being granted me.

This was certainly true. As I listened to Céleste speak of Proust, I realized she had rehearsed the account and the anecdotes countless times before, but I listened eagerly to the slightest detail and hoped that by some of my questions, I was encouraging her to discuss more than the commonplaces of her knowledge. Through the years her cult for Proust had deepened into a worship that was almost fanatical. "He was my master," she said, "and I think of him now as—almost a saint." The pause she made just before saying "saint" was not to search for the right word, but to mark the emphasis she wished to give.

Montaigne divided French speech into two categories. The first, *le boute hors si aisé*, is the rapid facility of self-expression I heard at the Mockels many years earlier, and which Montaigne claims to be the speech of lawyers and the more prevalent in France. The second is the slow, elaborate, premeditated speech, which Céleste Albaret uses, and which she perhaps inherited from her master. This is the tempo used, according to Montaigne, in the sermons of preachers, *les tardifs*. I do not mean to imply that Céleste spoke with unctuousness. No, it was a deliberateness tinged with dogmatism. She gave the impression of wanting to impress her listener with the fact that her testimony is unique and precious. As well it is! One senses that her excessive kindness is modeled, perhaps slightly, perhaps extensively, on Proust's kindness and on his manner of speech. Through the years when she has received so many visitors, eager to hear about the writer, she has grown into an important personage, almost an oracle, who remembers with uncanny clarity, and who predicts the future of this man and this novel to which she is so attached.

Céleste has met many of the scholars and critics who have written on Proust. She has talked with literary men and members of Proust's family. She spoke especially of Mme Gérard Mante-Proust, the niece and sole heir of Proust, who has three children, two daughters and one son. The daughter Claude married Mauriac's son Claude. More than of the literary work, as may be imagined, Céleste spoke of the character of Proust and of his personal habits. Still today she is upset by the fact that Proust ate so little during those years when she knew him and when he was devoting himself almost exclusively to the labor of his writing. *Il se consumait.* I remember that phrase returning often in her speech. She is proud of the advice Proust gave her repeatedly, to keep a journal and to note down everything she observed about him. He used to say to her that he would be well known before fifty years had gone by. "He used to promise me," she said, "that if he lived long enough, he would put me in one of his books." That statement led me to think that Céleste had not read *A la recherche du temps perdu* and did not realize her full name does occur in the text of the novel in a passage of *Sodome et Gomorrhe.*

At two different moments in the conversation, Céleste reminded me that she bought the large notebooks (*les cahiers*) in which Proust wrote his novel. Whenever one was used up, he would send her out to purchase another. "He lived only for this work," she repeated. "And he arranged the entire room for the writing of the work. Every paper and every notebook was kept in its place." During those last years he went out in the evening very seldom. When he did, Céleste waited up for him. He returned at two or three in the morning. She listened for the sound of the elevator and opened the door for him. He used to say to her then, in a state of great fatigue, "Leave me alone for five minutes, Céleste." After a brief period of seclusion, he would call her back and talk to her at length about the evening. He had a need to relate in detail the appearance of all those present at the dinner party and the anecdotes about them.

Céleste wept a bit when she spoke of Proust's death. She and his brother

Robert were present at that moment. Anecdotes of tenderness alternated with some of cruelty and stricture. Céleste disliked Gide whom she had to admit often to Proust's study. In announcing his visit to Proust, she would always say, "C'est le faux moine." Those who have written about Céleste Albaret have usually called her a domestic tyrant ruling over the daily life of Proust and who might refuse to admit this friend or that visitor. I was curious that she used the word "tyrant" in speaking of Proust, but with such an affectionate accent that I sensed Céleste to be of the race of those who find pleasure in being tyrannized.

More than an hour had gone by when I made my first attempt to leave. Then, Céleste offered me a glass of cognac, "un petit digestif, monsieur," so that we might drink to the memory of her tyrant-master, and so that I might meet her daughter and her husband. Albaret, before his marriage with Céleste, had been Proust's coachman, so actually he had known Proust longer than Céleste had known him. But his memory, because of his age, was very dim, and of course he had never enjoyed the confidence Céleste had enjoyed.

The ceremonial of the cognac and the imminent leave-taking turned Céleste's attention to me. The fact that I was an American pleased her because she owed much to the kindness and generosity of Mrs. Mina Curtiss, who had translated letters of Proust. With deep pride, Céleste reminded me that the volume prepared by Mrs. Curtiss is dedicated to her. That was tangible proof of her participation in scholarship on Proust, on the preservation of his memory, on the growing cult of his name.

The slow steadiness of her speech was now punctuated by the measured and deliberate sippings of the cognac. Like the ending of a Beethoven sonata, which at many points seems to have reached the conclusion, only to begin again with more fullness and vitality, the final part of Céleste's conversation went on and on, and every physical move on my part to leave would be impeded by a fresh intoning and a new theme. I imagined going down the stairs many times before I actually did.

When at last, I was outside on the rue des Canettes on that gray wet February day of 1954, I experienced a feeling comparable to that felt on the sunlit Sunday afternoon of August 1930, when I left the garden and the house of Albert Mockel and began walking down the avenue to the station of Rueil. It was happiness at being finally alone in order to reconstruct the things that had just been said and the pictures of the people and the setting. I feared that all that richness would disappear and be forgotten. I hastened mentally to relive and record it. I rehearsed phrases and intonations I had heard. On both occasions, so widely separated in time, I had had the impression of living a scene in literary history of which some record must be kept.

Now, with some perspective in time, and after a rereading of Montaigne, I realize I experienced on the two occasions of Rueil and the rue des Canettes, the two main types of French speech, the rapid *boute hors si aisé* of the last survivors of symbolism, and the slow *tardifs* in the woman who perhaps best remembers Marcel Proust today. Two extremes of tempi in conversation, and two extremes of French society, and yet one basic level of attentiveness, graciousness and intelligence.

To make sense and form out of chaos has become through the years a daily need, a daily rule. When any semblance of success is reached in this respect, the years in their chronological aspect cease being that. Time present draws into itself all of time past. The anecdotes of the past, the incidents, the coincidences, the painful experiences and the happy ones grow finally into themselves when they transcend time and enter upon some perspective of meaning. The reasons for keeping a journal or writing one's memoirs are doubtless very complex. Among the less reprehensible reasons is that which dictates to each of us the need to understand the past in terms of the partial but fuller light of the present.

My first evening in Paris collected about itself so many unpredictable occurrences that it was only much later, after other voyages to France, that I began seeing those occurrences as an initiation to the city. I was nineteen. It was a June day. The boat train reached St. Lazare late in the afternoon. The pension where I had reserved a room was in the rue Léopold-Robert. Mme Yvet had met me at the door and shown me to my room. Dinner was served promptly at seven o'clock. We finished about eight. I immediately went downstairs into the street where it was still daylight. A few steps and I was on the boulevard Montparnasse. I turned to the right and walked down the boulevard. I tried hard not to recognize and remember, but to feel free from the bits of information stored away in my mind. This effort collapsed when I saw, on the other side of the street, at a crossroads, the name *Closerie des Lilas* on a café.

Even manuals of French literature had referred to that café. In two years I would be taking the general examination for the bachelor's degree, and I had seen on examination papers of past years the name of Jean Moréas and his Ecole Romane who used to congregate at the Closerie des

Lilas. This would be, appropriately, my first café experience. I crossed the street and took a table on the terrace, at the edge of the sidewalk. The arrival of the waiter caused me a momentary embarrassment. Offspring of puritanism and the prohibition era, I had not tasted alcohol in any form. As I asked for a *citron pressé*, I scrutinized the features of the waiter, but he seemed unperturbed. By the time he returned with his tray, I had become increasingly aware of a large crowd of people on the other side of the square reaching to the entrance of what bore the name in glittering letters: *Bal Bullier*. The preparation of my fresh lemonade was performed expertly on my table. The waiter cut the lemon, squeezed the two halves, added the sugar and water in accord with my directions. This gave me the chance to ask him the nature of the crowd, which was by then reaching close to the Closerie.

The explanation was given with a shrug of the shoulders and an intonation revealing some degree of respect. "Gorki is speaking tonight at the Bal Bullier." The words made me feel I was sitting in the front row of the universe, of the world of letters, at least. Would every day in Paris be like this? Each moment the crowd grew larger and more restless. Policemen on horseback began making their way through the crowd. On a return trip to my table the waiter reported that Gorki would not appear that night and the police were trying to disperse the crowd.

Then the fighting began, spasmodically at first. I held fast to my seat in the outer ring of the Closerie until one man was knocked down on the sidewalk at my very feet. The blood flowed from his head. His companion grabbed my lemon from the table and hurled it at a mounted policeman. I decided to disappear. If war had begun—I was ready to believe almost anything at that moment—it was too early in my life and too early in my first trip to Paris, to participate. I made for the inside of the café. The waiters were clustered around the doorway. Only when some of them saw me going down the stairway into what I supposed was the kitchen or the storeroom, did they call after me. I was disobeying rules. Never since have I demonstrated comparable courage in opposing French laws, but ignorance guided me that first evening and the fear I would not see Paris, after all.

I compromised with the waiters, and paused halfway down the stairs. There I was out of the firing range. In a very few minutes the storm abated, and I emerged when the tables and chairs were being straightened out, the new orders being given, and the crowd dispersing. It had been a quick war, but very real to the novice American. The next morning I read the accounts in a few of the newspapers, of the Bal Bullier disturbance. The words used to describe the uprising were *bagarre* and *rixe*, which were new to me. They have always been associated thereafter with the Closerie des Lilas and with the Bal Bullier which no longer exists.

On my first visit to Rome, late January 1954, I spent my first free morning at Saint Peter's. I began the tour of the nave on the left and came almost immediately to a side altar under which a glass casket exposed the full-length figure of a pope. The mummified shape, in full papal vestments, was brightly illuminated. A few people were praying in front of it. On a prie-dieu I saw the name Pius X and wondered if this was the pope who had been announced for canonization in June. I asked one of the devout if it was the body of Pius X. The woman replied evasively and said she thought it was Pius V! During the course of the morning I met no one with sufficient authority to question about this fact. The problem was relegated to the back of my mind as something to solve when the opportunity came.

The last city of my Italian trip was Genoa. I boarded the Paris train in the early evening. The second-class compartment, where I found a seat, was crowded. Near the frontier, a group of *carabinieri*, on passport duty, expelled us all from the compartment. When their checkup was done, about midnight, one of them passed me in the corridor and told me they were getting off the train and I could have the compartment back. Returning to it, I found it empty, save for my bags. I stretched out on one of the benches in unusual luxury for second-class accommodations. At that instant, the door was pushed open and the tall figure of a priest stood there. He asked me in French if I were alone. I said yes, and he immediately took possession of the bench opposite mine. I sat up, to be polite for a while at least, and we engaged in conversation. He was a young Frenchman, a missionary priest assigned to Madagascar, who had been studying in Rome.

It occured to me early in our conversation that this priest could answer my question about the pope in the glass coffin. I described the position of the coffin in Saint Peter's and asked him if it was Pius X.

"It most certainly is," he replied, "the pope who is to be canonized this year. In fact I have a part of him in my briefcase."

He pointed to the rack over his head. He went on to explain that he had a special devotion to Pius X and that he had asked for a relic of the pope for a new altar that was to be consecrated on his return to Madagascar. With great pride, he showed me the relic. He unfolded a white paper bearing in Latin the certification of the authenticity of the relic. Inside was a glass covered pyx in the center of which was a brown speck. I asked if it was a chip from a bone, but he said it was a speck of flesh.

"C'est très bien organisé," I remember his saying. "You can have a relic of almost every saint after the sixteenth century."

Later when we turned off the light and stretched out on our respective benches, I reflected on the incongruousness of travelling in a train with a relic of Pius X carelessly placed in a briefcase on a rack over my head. Some of the thoughts I had had when I looked at the pope in his glass case returned to me then in the train between Genoa and Paris. They were thoughts about the fate of man, thoughts mingling doubt and awe, thoughts which, had they been cast in a firmer language, would have resembled Hamlet's and Montaigne's. I recalled especially a sentence of Montaigne, which has always struck me as one of his most terrifying: "Nous sommes chrétiens à même titre que nous sommes Périgourdins ou Allemands." When I first read that sentence as an undergraduate at Harvard, I underscored it and wrote a marginal note of approval. It came to my mind as I stood in Saint Peter's before the body of Pius X, and it came to my mind again as I travelled with the relic of Pius X in the night train.

In another sentence, Montaigne contrasts the fragility of man's mortal nature with the power of his imagination by which he places the heavens themselves under his feet. Is presumption the basis of all our systems, our sentiments, our science and religion, our values and customs? So many things crumbled for me when I first read the "Apologie pour Raymond Sebond!" No idea was left intact after that ruthless analysis of the weakness of everything. Hamlet was indeed the first victim of Montaigne's *que sais-je?*

Literature, I must remember, is not concerned with the revelation of absolute truths. Fictional characters, even those before Proust's, know the intermittences of the heart, the stagnating quality of habits, the absorption with dreams of the past. *Hamlet* is a work in which everything is destroyed or denied or damned. Little wonder that in my own insignificant personal experiences, such as the manifestation before the Bal Bullier, and the way in which I learned of Mme Yvet's death, and my train trip in company with a relic of a deceased pope and saint, I can never see a full portrait of man such as that offered by *Hamlet.*

All of Paris moves out in concentric rings from its center: Notre Dame. The island of the Cité is the heart of Paris and the cathedral rests on it like a vast ship held solidly on a reef in the midst of the water. Notre Dame may not be the most beautiful cathedral of Christendom, but it is the most loved since it rests in the very heart of the most loved city. It is the church by which all other churches of Christendom are measured and judged. The first church—although there are older, like Saint Julien le Pauvre, so close by it; the best known, although it is far from being the most intimate. I have always been fearful of knowing Notre Dame, shy in its presence, resentful of its bigness and its shower of buttresses. It faces the west, and only when its façade reflects the setting sun does it glow warmly. That is the moment to look at the portal of the Virgin, on the left. There, in the coronation scene, the cathedral demonstrates its deepest meaning for me, a meaning I never feel inside where the awesome shadows and the miracle of the windows bewilder me. But the carved group outside, in the portal of the Virgin, that lives so closely with the elements and bears the color of the wind and rain, shows the human and the divine in such subtle alliance that I often feel no need to enter. The Mother and the Son are seated. The ecstasy of the Son is reflected on the face of the Mother, and the tenderness of the Mother is reflected on the face of the Son. Each is giving and receiving at the same time, and they are miraculously joined in this exchange. In a way, it is the relationship between the island of the Cité and the cathedral itself. The human and the divine exist side by side, the one participating in the nature of the other. The Cité unites the solemnity of Notre Dame with the delicate coquetry of the Sainte Chapelle, even as the coronation group unites the benediction of the Christ with the adoration of the Virgin. The Son is extending to his Mother a scepter, but it is only a flower, and here again in the carved stone an object unites the material world and eternity. A flower from northern France for the Virgin of Israel to hold when she becomes Queen of Heaven, under the respectful gaze of the vast company in the *voussoirs* overhead: kings of Judea and France, angels and saints and prophets.

The progression shows the progression of a race. Our Lady is crowned by her Son and reigns over her cathedral, as the cathedral dominates Paris, as Paris reigns over France. The slopes of all the hills of Paris lead to Notre Dame. The students from the mountain of Sainte Geneviève walk inevitably toward the Seine and the Cité and Notre Dame. Even the artists from Montmartre and Montparnasse, from the north and the south, follow the inclination of their slopes. By day I am able only to look at the details, such as the coronation of the Virgin in her portal, and, on the pillars and capitals, the carved images of the flowers and leaves of France: roses and lilies and daisies; and the more humble watercress, cabbage and plane tree leaf.

On each new return to Paris, I find myself unwilling to resume contact with the city otherwise than at the center, at the Cité itself. The façade of Notre Dame is neither Romanesque nor Gothic in any pure sense. It is a measured wise Gothic, harmonious and robust at the same time. A colossal façade built by an entire people, with the variety and eternity of that people. A return to France should begin there where its genius appears in its most limpid form, in its consecration to Our Lady. Both the history and the genius of the French are inscribed on the façade. The vagaries of weather have darkened the stone and altered the countenances of the sculptured figures. But not enough to change the gravity of the faces which still, despite the revolutions affecting the very stones of this cathedral, bear the mark of the Christian who knows himself to be a sinner and vulnerable to the world because he is vulnerable to the prince of the world. Even the faces of the Virgin and the Christ in the left portal have, combined with their holiness, the experience of pathos and of life. Only the sculptured figures of Greece might resemble gods.

XV

Jean Cocteau, 1960

It was February 1960, a few days before I was to leave Paris where I had been working for two months. During the fifties, on two occasions, I had had reason to write to Jean Cocteau, first, for permission to translate some of his poems for an anthology, and second, for permission to undertake a more ambitious project—the editing and translating of a group of selected writings I was to call *The Journals of Jean Cocteau.* In the most friendly spirit, Cocteau guided me in his letters, counseled and encouraged me. The ease with which he welcomed me among his large number of correspondents, delighted me, and I responded in a similar tone of friendliness tempered with the strong admiration I have always felt for the man's accomplishments.

When I requested help in the choice of illustrations, Cocteau sent me folder after folder of drawings and photographs, many of which I was able to use. He sent me three drawings as gifts: an early drawing based on *L'Après-midi d'un faune,* a drawing of himself at Oxford, and a drawing of two imaginary profiles, his and mine, separated by an ocean. Once in Paris, a mutual friend of ours, James Lord, brought me a very large drawing Cocteau had inscribed to me: a dog-unicorn with the face of Jean Marais, with a tent in the background and an heraldic inscription in the foreground.

These signs and messages coming at intervals during three or four years, made it possible for me, in that February of 1960, when a New York publisher suggested I do further editing and translating of Cocteau, to write to him with the hope he might be in Paris at that time. I sent the letter to his Paris apartment. Three days later, early in the morning, a woman telephoned me "de la part de Jean Cocteau." He was in Paris just for that day, and would I have lunch with him. I was to come to the apartment at one.

The door was opened by a smiling elderly woman who greeted me with the words: "Vous êtes Wallace Fowlie. Je vous connais." I must have expressed surprise at her knowing me, and she continued with the cordiality of an old friend. "I was the one who mailed all the letters to you, and the photographs and the books. You see, I know you well. M. Cocteau arrived last night from Saint-Jean-Cap-Ferrat, and this morning many many people have come by to see him. The last are with him now, and you will have to wait a few minutes. I will put you in the small parlor." She had been guiding me during this speech of explanation toward *le petit salon*.

It was indeed small, a kind of secret alcove, whose walls were lined with dark red velvet. The window was concealed with the same velvet. Two photographs were on the wall: Rimbaud and Mallarmé. A small blackboard bore the familiar profile Cocteau has drawn so many times. The room had a strange formal air, but the poets' photographs and the chalk profile (of Heurtebise?) put me at ease. Two or three times, during the next ten minutes, Madeleine (I learned later that was the housekeeper's name) opened the door to tell me it would be a few more minutes—and always added: "Il y a eu un monde fou ce matin." She was proud of this fact, proud that the man she served had attracted so many friends and visitors.

Then, at last, Cocteau opened the door and came in quickly, waving a paper in his hand. I had not realized the shortness of his stature and was unprepared for the visible signs of age on his face. Almost before greeting me, he explained the paper, a few lines he had just written, which I was to use as a pass that afternoon to attend the film-showing of *Le Testament d'Orphée*. Eighty-five friends had been invited for that private showing, and I would be the eighty-sixth! I accepted gratefully, but refrained from telling him I would be unable to go that afternoon. Then, with that first message dispatched, his face broke into a smile, and jovially he pressed my arms and shoulders: "Is it really you, in the flesh, after all that correspondence back and forth over the Atlantic?" It was a welcome that would have put anyone at ease.

"I am taking you to lunch just around the corner at Le Grand Véfour."

At that time I did not know it was one of the oldest and most celebrated restaurants in Paris. Cocteau added, as a special inducement, "At my table, my name is on my chair, and Colette's place, similarly marked, is beside mine. We used to eat there together, two faithful inhabitants of the Palais-Royal."

As we left the apartment, I heard Cocteau say to Madeleine he would be back at two-thirty for the next engagement. Madeleine pointed to a blackboard attached to the door, where evidently the day's schedule was written out, and said firmly, "Yes! no later than two-thirty!"

We walked then, at a swift pace, to the Grand Véfour. Cocteau clung to my arm and talked all the way. Our entrance into the restaurant was impressive. Cocteau was surrounded and warmly greeted by the owner, the head waiter, the barman, two or three waiters, the lady cashier. It was a family welcoming him home. I stood aside, but with each new person he introduced me as "mon traducteur américain." No one paid the slightest attention to that. He was the center, and as we slowly walked to the table, to his table, we were flanked by attendants. He checked with the owner on whether he was planning to attend the first showing of *Le Testament d'Orphée*.

At the table we stood for a moment as Cocteau pointed out his name on the brass plaque on the back of his chair. And on the back of my chair, the name of Colette. "We ate here together on so many occasions."

I knew of their long friendship, of the number of years when they were neighbors in the Palais-Royal section of Paris. I remembered how Colette, stricken with severe arthritis during the last years of her life (she died in 1954), spent her days on a divan-bed she called her "raft" (mon radeau) and enjoyed the unannounced frequent visits Cocteau paid her. She used to say to him as he came in: "Assieds-toi sur mes pieds, Jean." As writers, they had almost nothing in common. Colette's clean prose was nourished on things, on their smell and their form. Cocteau's poetry reflected myths and symbols. But in common they had many of the intangible values of life: an inexhaustible curiosity, a kindness of spirit, a profundity of sentiment. Their friendship was so well known that it surprised no one when, at Colette's death, Jean replaced her in the Belgian Academy.

When we were in our places, side by side, and as the maître d'hôtel handed us the large menus, Cocteau pointed out to me a center table and briefed me: "You see, it's an old restaurant. Fragonard died at that table." And then, passing on to a practical problem, asked me if I would choose meat or fish for lunch. "Etes-vous homme à viande ou à poisson?" I chose a *sole* and he *rognons*. The wine waiter approached then, an elderly man who called Cocteau *maître* and whom Cocteau addressed by the familiar *tu*.

[173]

I had noticed he used *tu* in speaking to everyone at the Véfour, from the proprietor to the busboy.

There was considerable discussion about the wine, because of my *sole* and his *rognons*, but finally a half bottle of very light red wine was decided on, especially after I assured the two men I would drink very little wine. The elderly *sommelier* went off. Abruptly, Cocteau exclaimed we could not begin with the main dish, and, calling back the maître d'hôtel, he ordered "six huîtres pour Jean Cocteau et six huîtres pour Wallace Fowlie." I had already noticed his tendency to speak of himself in the third person.

When the two plates of oysters reached us, the wine problem again became critical. I was aware that Cocteau enjoyed inflating the dilemma, and he was aware that I was aware. The wine steward was called back, and with the appropriate gesture and tone of voice, Cocteau explained we could not drink red wine with oysters. I imagined that a half-bottle of white wine would eventually be ordered. But that was too predictable. Cocteau had been looking around at the other tables of which only three or four were occupied, at some distance from ours. He said, "Don't you see on those other tables large bottles of white wine already opened? Go over to one of them and ask for a small glass of white wine for Jean Cocteau and a small glass for his guest Wallace Fowlie."

The wine steward was as dumbfounded as I was. At the moment he could not assemble an answer, and Cocteau repeated his request and assured the old man that the clients would be happy to supply him with two glasses of their wine!

"Maître," began the wine waiter, "I know the state of your health, and I know it is unwise for you to have two kinds of wine at a meal. I have chosen for you a red wine so light that it can be drunk appropriately with oysters."

A tactful solution. Cocteau was visibly relieved. The steward and myself were even more relieved.

"You are thinking I am poor," he said to me.

"That is impossible," I replied. "What about your book royalties and films and plays?"

"All of that is so carefully recorded that I have to pay taxes of sixty-three percent on my income. I am able to live thanks to the generosity of my good friend and benefactress Mme Weisweiller. Most of the year I live in her villa in Saint-Jean-Cap-Ferrat, Santo-Sospir."

I had known of Cocteau's various addresses: the Paris apartment, the house at Milly-la-Forêt, near Paris, and Mme Weisweiller's residence in the Alpes Maritimes. I asked him about the housekeeper I had just met. Madeleine had served him for several years. She was housekeeper, secretary and guardian for him. She knew how to discourage the tiresome visitors and keep the schedule of appointments when Cocteau was in Paris. That sturdy Burgundian woman was servant and friend in her devotion and steadfastness. The Paris apartment was so small she had to organize it carefully. Cocteau took his breakfast in the kitchen, and it was there he visited with his friends who had the habit of passing by in the morning. The small red parlor, where I had waited, was kept for more formal visitors. Madeleine called it "le salon des académiciens." "The next time," he said, "you will sit down in the kitchen." He had no way of knowing and neither did I, that this was the only visit I would ever have with him.

"What are you working on now?" he asked me.

"I am translating two plays of Claudel."

"Don't bother with Claudel," was his swift answer. "Work on Jean Cocteau."

I smiled, but he did not, and he finished his thought by saying, "Cocteau will last longer than Claudel."

I asked him what his relationship with Claudel had been.

"Very intermittent, but always cordial. I called on him when I was making the rounds of the Académiciens, and I asked him if he would vote for me. He took my two hands in his, and said, 'Yes, Jean, with all my heart. But tell me one thing—why, in heaven's name, do you want to be a member of the Académie Française?' I told Claudel that such a move was so unexpected that it was in keeping with my entire life."

Then I thanked Cocteau for the "pass" he had written out and given me to see the private first showing of *Le Testament d'Orphée*. I had read about the film. Already the literary weeklies were running articles and documentations on it. The topic was, of course, close to Cocteau's heart, and he spoke of it at some length. He began by saying I would see Mme Weisweiller in the film, in a scene shot in the garden of her villa at Saint-Jean-Cap-Ferrat. He had no subsidy for this film and had decided to use his friends for the various parts: actors, actresses, artists who gave him their time and talent. This meant he had to wait until something brought them to the south, to the region near Saint-Jean and the two centers where most of the film was made: Les Baux-de-Provence and Villefranche. It was the culminating film of his career, the synthesis of his legends and themes.

Cocteau spoke, not rapidly, but steadily, and without transition from topic to topic. I no longer remember how he shifted from *Le Testament d'Orphée* to Mauriac. But Mauriac's name came up, and he spoke of the man and of his behavior at the première of *Bacchus*. I had seen a performance of *Bacchus* a few years previously, and I had collected the articles and reviews of the Mauriac-Cocteau quarrel, the open letters and the discussions of the letters. The problems involved were not really on religion and morals. They represented a clash of temperaments. Cocteau felt this, and I listened attentively to his analysis of Mauriac. In one of his typical aphoristic flashes, he recapitulated the problem by saying: "You see, François Mauriac is the type of man who fundamentally does not like people. You and I do . . . ."

The dispute had been so public and so strenuous that Cocteau believed a definitive break had been reached between him and Mauriac. Thus, at a subsequent large gathering, Cocteau was surprised when Mauriac sat down beside him and affably asked, "Alors, mon petit Jean, comment vas-tu?" "But I thought you had insulted me by your behavior at *Bacchus* and in print afterwards," was Cocteau's reply. "No, no, that was our literary side," said Mauriac, "the histrionics of the profession." "It was serious for me, however," said Cocteau, "and I had no intention of deceiving my public."

I was familiar with several of these stories that Cocteau related in the third person, but he often expressed a more personal attitude than he had on the printed page. He spoke fervently of Igor Stravinsky. In the middle part of their careers the two friends had been estranged, and their recent reconciliation had meant a great deal to Cocteau. Many years had gone by since Cocteau had written so movingly of *Le Sacre du printemps* and hailed it as a turning point in contemporary music.

I initiated a discussion about Jacques Maritain. Ever since the time of the two famous letters in 1926, both Maritain and Cocteau had remained faithful to their friendship. Cocteau's return to his faith in 1926, which he owed in part to Maritain, was expressed years later in the chapels he decorated. I had imagined, and I was right in this, that Cocteau's feelings for Maritain were as affectionate and loyal as ever. And so I told him of Maritain's fears he might not be able to spend the last years of his life in France. I suggested he take up this problem with André Malraux.

"Why just Malraux?" was his reaction. "I will telephone De Gaulle, who admires Maritain and knows his work."

It was half-past two, and I stood up as I reminded Cocteau that he had promised Madeleine to be back at the apartment at this time.

"But I want you to have another memory of Jean Cocteau in Paris. Tomorrow Mme Weisweiller and I go to Saint-Moritz. I have to go there periodically to build up my red corpuscles. For this trip I am having a woolen jacket made. Come with me to the store while I have a fitting. That will give us further time together."

Outside of the apartment, Mme Weisweiller's chauffeur put us into the automobile and we soon drove up to Dior's. At the end of the store was a counter for men: ties, handkerchiefs, etc. We went there. When Cocteau's name was announced, three tailors appeared. The beige-colored jacket was tried on, and Cocteau indicated changes in every detail. As I watched him convince the tailors that he was right to ask for this and that change, I remembered his long career in the theater where he assumed responsibility for costumes as well as settings and mise-en-scène.

As we walked back through the main part of the store, it was apparent that Cocteau's presence had been signaled to everyone. We walked through the gauntlet. Our farewell on the sidewalk was brief. He took out from his pocket a small gift, which he gave to me, and said that we would meet again at the end of the afternoon at *Le Testament d'Orphée*. "Orphée" was the last word I heard him say.

XVI

Paris, February 1966   Edouard Dermit
Paris, March-April 1966

In February 1966 I made my nineteenth trip to France, and the reasons for going there were the same as they were on the first trip in 1928: to use French as my daily language, and to become acquainted with what was new and significant in the Paris literary scene. In 1928 when I lived in Montparnasse, I read faithfully the sixteenth-century poets for my course with Professor Chamard at the Sorbonne, and I was unaware of the surrealist activities going on exactly at that time at Le Dome and La Coupole, La Rotonde and Le Select, which I passed every day. Since that time, whenever I teach the poems of Du Bellay, Ronsard and Maurice Scève, I think of that impressive figure of white-bearded Chamard, carefully enunciating his course in the Amphithéâtre Richelieu. And when I try to teach the theories of André Breton and the poems of Robert Desnos, I recall my ignorance and innocence of 1928 when I was living in close proximity to those young men, not very much older than myself, who were actively formulating and demonstrating a literary movement that has held my attention ever since 1947 when Dean McKeon at the University of Chicago asked me to prepare a public course of lectures and gave me exactly two minutes in which to choose the subject. I blurted out "surrealism" because I was most ignorant of that aspect of the twentieth century!

During my visits to Paris in the thirties, Jacques Maritain was the name that seemed uppermost in the literary scene to which I was especially drawn. For a documentation on my thesis on Ernest Psichari, I met Maritain and his wife, Raïssa, and attended several of the Sunday evening gatherings in Meudon. In that salon there were discussions of Thomism, of painting (especially the work of Chagall, Rouault and Severini), and of literature. A few of the literary figures I studied then had some connection or other with Maritain and the Meudon group: Cocteau (before he had left the group after only a brief moment of allegiance) and Julien Green (who did not attend the gatherings but whose writings appeared significant to the philosopher).

On my return to Paris after the war, in the fall of 1948, there was considerable discussion about Claudel's play *Partage de midi*, and its première scheduled for December. Barrault had finally secured Claudel's permission, and the text was to appear in print. Articles, interviews, the production itself, and the publication: all of that seemed to attract more attention than anything else that fall and early winter. Two of the original four actors were playing *Partage de midi* the week of my arrival in 1966: Barrault and Edwige Feuillère. Eighteen years, during which time the play had become almost as well known as *L'Annonce faite à Marie!*

The spotlight, momentarily at least, in 1966, was on Boris Vian, whose works were being republished and reevaluated. Early in my visit I met one of my former students from Colorado to whom I would have recommended Vian if he had not already begun work on a thesis on Sartre's political views!

In the fifties, I remember buying a curious book by Vian, but signed by Vernon Sullivan: *J'irai cracher sur vos tombes*. A slightly pornographic volume that brought fame to Vian. Before his death, in 1959, at the age of 39, he had played many roles in the colony of Paris artists: engineer, trumpet player, writer, pataphysician. He helped to found and promote Le Tabou on the rue Dauphine, a bistrot originally, and ultimately an existentialist club with Sartre, Juliette Gréco and others.

Boris Vian was an authority on Jazz. His admiration for Jarry and Queneau explained his joining Le Collège de Pataphysique in 1951. Jacques Prévert speaks of him in a poem:

> Il jouait à la vie et avait
> Toujours des bontés pour elle.

Young people today reading his two books, *L'Automne à Pékin* and *L'Ecume des jours*, recognize in them their own reactions to the spirit of the day, to the particular brand of humor and sadness which is theirs.

These readers are perhaps already leaving the period of *le roman nouveau* and Robbe-Grillet and discovering that Boris Vian appeals more directly to them.

In Paris I have always been eager to learn what the current literary fashion is, to read the reviews of the newest books, to see the displays in the bookstore windows. In 1966 I felt some of that eagerness, but it was mingled with the sadness that comes from the rapid change in such phenomena. Somewhat distrustful of the blatantly announced successes, I was more interested in seeing the new evolution in established writers, new reevaluations of books and authors that already had a history.

Julien Green's third volume of his autobiography had just come out and was being reviewed. It was called *Terre lointaine* and relates the year 1920, when at the age of twenty he went to America for the first time and attended the University of Virginia. The book is largely about his irresistible attraction to the male students, to their physical beauty and casualness. A courageous book that gives a principal clue to *Moïra* and *Sud*. I had encountered Green only twice: once in Princeton (my only visit to Princeton) on the invitation of Maurice Coindreau. That most amiable man drove Green and myself around the countryside, showed us the campus of the university, gave us lunch in an inn, and introduced us to his friends the Casadesus. I remember nothing of our conversation save the relative silence of Julien Green. Coindreau and I did most of the talking.

Green's career, from the early novel *Mont-Cinère* to *Terre lointaine* had been one of the six or seven literary careers of twentieth-century writers I had followed the most assiduously, with the most continuous interest and sympathy, and with the conviction that here was an authentic writer. In my thinking about him, he has always been associated in my mind with two others of those six or seven writers: with Gide, on the one hand, always so eager to attack the religious beliefs of Green and encourage him to follow the bent of his nature; and with Jacques Maritain, on the other hand, a steadfast friend through all the personal dramas of Green, who helped to sustain him in his religious beliefs. Green's life had maintained a midway course between the tempter-friend, who in 1966 had been dead for fifteen years, and the wise counselor-friend, who was still living at the age of eighty-three.

Jacques' niece, Eveline Garnier, told me her uncle was coming up from Toulouse where he lived with the Petits Frères de Jésus, and was spending the first week of March in Paris. Almost all the elements of my first visits to Paris in the thirties were still present, and I constantly had the impression that nothing had changed and that I was continuing to study the careers and the books of thirty years earlier!

Jacques had probably forgotten by then that he was my godfather. During the war years when I was teaching at Yale, I often went to New York to visit him and Raïssa and Véra in their apartment at 30 Fifth Avenue. One evening he asked me about the circumstances of my conversion. In the course of the discussion I told him of my baptism in the French church at Bennington, Eglise du Sacré Coeur. The priest had prepared me with a short series of instructions in the catechism. He finally set a date, a Saturday afternoon, after confessions. When I appeared in the sacristy, he realized he had made no plans for godparents. He called in a young woman who had just made her confession and told her she was to be my godmother. I did not even know her name. This woman, whom the priest scolded after the baptism, because she did not know the creed by heart, was my only sponsor. I had no godfather. Maritain was moved by the story and offered to be my godfather. I was proud indeed to send his name to the priest in Bennington. He was the godfather of so many friends, and of children of his friends, who had come to him for a word of advice and encouragement, that he certainly could not remember us all. "Je serai votre parrain!" As he said this, Véra and Raïssa both clapped their hands in approval. The little scene came back into my mind the evening when Eveline told me her uncle would be in Paris March 6th.

But the place of honor in this Maritain-Psichari-thesis cycle was occupied by my oldest and most faithful friend of all, Henriette Psichari, who the year before, celebrated her 80th birthday. In her advanced years, her face resembled portraits of her grandfather Ernest Renan. She was still working at the Education Nationale, 29, rue d'Ulm, and was still living at 22, rue Beautreillis. On countless nights after spending the evening with Henriette, I walked back to my hotel on the rue Cassette, a thirty-minute walk, across the Pont Sully, on the edge of the Ile-Saint-Louis, and then along the boulevard Saint-Germain to the rue du Four. Even tired, I always cherished that walk because my mind would be so filled with thoughts and emotions that I needed the physical exertion and the peacefulness of midnight (all would be peaceful until I reached the Cinéma Danton just before Saint-Germain-des-Prés, and from then on I would be in the swirl of Paris night life crowding the streets and sidewalks) to put them into some order, or simply to rehearse and savor them.

[181]

When I first met Henriette, she was planning to write a book on her brother Ernest. On our second meeting, she had written the book. From then on, she was the friend who every two years had been engaged in writing a new book and who read to me the chapters just finished. On our first evening together in February 1966, after our simple supper (*jambon et salade, endives braisées, yogourt, banane*), she produced the inevitable manuscript. "What is the subject?" I asked. "L'ère des conversions," was the answer, and again the circle seemed to be completed, because the opening pages were on the conversion of Ernest Psichari, with references to all the other celebrated conversions of that time: Maritain, Cocteau, Jacob, Sachs.

On the evenings when no reading was done, Henriette's son Olivier Revault d'Allonnes was present, at either rue de Beautreillis or in his own apartment, 22, rue Saint-Paul, close by, where he lived with his wife, Claude, and three of his four sons. Olivier is one of the really liberated spirits I have had the privilege of knowing: open-minded, generous, and perspicacious at the same time. He teaches esthetics at the Sorbonne, and is editor of *La Revue d'esthétique*. When he asked me, on our first reunion in 1966, to do an article for the magazine, I said I would if he would correct my French. He replied that I used to correct his French when he was a *lycéen* and when I had to read his *dissertations* on *Le Cid*.

The changes were many that spring when I was living in the Hôtel Paris-Dinard, 29, rue Cassette. Communications were immediate between France and America, between New York and Paris. A garish looking "Drugstore" occupied the corner of the boulevard Saint Germain and the rue de Rennes. The weekly *Express* was imitating *Time*. De Gaulle disapproved of the war in Vietnam, and Johnson seemed determined to build up the war. The criticism of one country by the other was more flagrant, more facile, more journalistic than ever before. The tone of violence, however, had shifted from France to America. The scorn now started at home, in New York and Chicago, and was levelled on French culture, not only on the political views of the Fifth Republic, but on the so-called decline of the arts in Paris, on the shortsightedness of the French in housing for families, in housing for schools, in French avarice, in the pompousness implicit in the phrase rampant everywhere: *le prestige de la France*. The intelligent Frenchman—and there were many on the Quai d'Orsay and in the Hôtel Matignon—should know that no really great country has to keep shouting to its inhabitants and to other countries that it is great. When De Gaulle spoke of the role of France, his eloquence was moving. But in the speech of less great orators, the sense of nobility was lost, and all one heard was a strident nationalism.

I arrived that winter full of questions. It has always been hard for me to remember that the Frenchman will answer your question whether he knows the answer or not. Cautiously I try the same question on two or three friends, and receive two or three different answers. There is no lull in a French conversation because there is no hesitation. The joy of speaking is always present, and the skill in organizing an answer is a verbal accomplishment. The clarity and the assertiveness of speech cover up ignorance. I never hear a Frenchman say: "je ne sais pas." The verb *savoir* is not conjugated in the negative.

When his name occurred in a conversation that winter, Pavel Tchelitchew was very much on my mind. I realized that since his death I had missed knowing he was on this earth. Twenty years earlier when we met frequently in New York, he helped me to reach some sense of myself. He was gentle and strong at the same time. One day he commented at length on my book of essays *La Pureté dans l'art*, and said he approved of everything in it save my excessive use of the word *God*. "N'employez pas si souvent le nom de Dieu, car chaque fois que ce nom est dit, il faut qu'il soit mis en lumière. Il faut qu'il arrive comme un éblouissement sur la page. Vous diminuez son importance en disant 'Dieu' si souvent."

A litany of places and of people associated with those places kept returning to my mind as I walked along the boulevard Raspail one day in the sunlight. I had moved too fast through too many places the previous nine months: July, in Los Angeles, where I saw garishness, hugeness, speed, smog, ugliness and exaggerated beauty. August, at the Huntington-Hartford Foundation, in Pacific Palisades, where the hours passed slowly in that California canyon. I remembered best from that place the creatures of God's creation: racoons, deer, rattlesnakes, the mare and her colt, the families of quail, the thrushes in my garden. I remembered the sweet smell of the eucalyptus trees, the gnarled shapes of the oaks, the huge sycamores. I wandered about indulging in sight and smell. In September, in Ezra Stiles College at Yale, I made a joyous rediscovery of New Haven. There I met and talked with old friends: Catherine Coffin, Bill and Margaret Wimsatt, Paul Weiss, Henri Peyre and his new wife Lois, Georges May . . . . And I thought constantly of my New Haven friends who had died: Jess Clark, Mabel Lafarge, Father Riggs, Andy Morehouse, Marguerite Peyre, Victoria Weiss. I was reminded of the good things at Yale, of how contented and stimulated I had been there, but also I was reminded of all

I would not have experienced if I had not left. I am from many places. That has been my fate. I refuse to acknowledge regret. Everything has counted for the good. Hindrances and disappointments help, too.

In September, in the train taking me from New York to North Carolina, I remembered the feeling of having seen too many faces during the summer, too many old friends. I can carry the past only if I can put it in a sentence. The lightness of a book is all my life should weigh. Just a bit heavier than the ashes this body of mine will make . . . . The wars of that year, the riots and the hurricanes told me the power of disorder, but I knew that the power of order is more prevalent, and that the universe is moving toward God, toward what his priest Teilhard called Omega.

The rue Cassette where I lived was so close to Saint-Germain-des-Prés that I passed through it at least once or twice a day. It was always crowded. The new Drugstore Saint Germain was doing a flourishing business. Lipp's sign *complet* was always on the door. The parked autos filled every possible space. All the tables were taken at the Flore and the Deux Magots. And yet, and yet, it was not the same. The golden age was over: the age of Sartre and Beauvoir, of the singer Juliette Gréco and the songs of Boris Vian and Jacques Prévert. The atmosphere of the *âge d'or* had been really created by the young people, soon after the war, who crowded into Saint Germain, and who were eager to find ways of living the moral and philosophical problems of the day. They came from Paris and the provinces to a kind of rendezvous under the most beautiful tower in the world: that of the twelfth-century Eglise de Saint Germain. Everything favored discussion and that relaxation that comes only from freedom of speech. Gallimard's publishing house was close by and Plon's not far away. Those young people were aware of the immediate ancestors of the celebrities they could see nightly: of Apollinaire and André Salmon and Léon-Paul Fargue who had frequented the Flore (his father had fired the ceramics that line the walls of Lipp), of Gide who had preferred Les Deux Magots.

The reasons in 1966 for spending the evenings at Saint Germain no longer had the validity they had through the fifties. Sartre and Simone de Beauvoir originally chose the Flore because it was heated and they could work there. If those young people surrounding Sartre in the cafés during the day and in the *caves* during the long evening hours were not writers themselves, they read serious books: *La Nausée* of Sartre, *L'Etranger* of Camus, and the American novelists. Their thoughts and their attitudes and their poverty were in the songs of Léo Ferré ("Tous ces poètes de deux sous et leur teint blême") and in the poems of Prévert ("O, Barbara, quelle connerie la guerre!") But in 1966, the moment of the existentialists of Saint Germain belonged to history. Such sentences as *l'existence précède l'essence* and *l'enfer, c'est les autres,* are now to be found in textbooks. *Les beatniks* and *les minets* and *les vé-vé* appeared less aggressive, less pessimistic, less interesting. Histrionics had replaced philosophy. American and English varieties had infiltrated, and prices had gone up so high that the real seekers, the real youthful philosophers had fled. The French youths who turned up then at night in the 6th *arrondissement* of Saint Germain probably came from the wealthy 16th *arrondissement.* They mingled with the American youth, who were also more affluent than in former years.

I learned there was a history of existentialist Saint Germain, written by Boris Vian, the best qualified to be its historian, and which had been believed lost. It had come to light and was to be published that summer. The myths, the personalities and the poses would be revealed by the man who perhaps best incarnated all the aspects of Saint Germain: the cafés, the church, le Tabou, the natives, the tourists, those assimilated with the natives, the *caves* (believed by some to have been invented by Jean Cocteau, who, at any rate, became with his film *Orphée,* the cinematographer of Saint Germain), Juliette Gréco, who claimed to have been an existentialist from birth.

In the states a teacher of French literature, and in Paris a reader who questions in order to understand better, in order to teach better, I have always been conscious of leading the strange life of one participating in two cities, two countries, two attitudes, two civilizations. It is hard not to "take over" French attitudes and views and assimilate them. To be, in a word, more French than American. This would be wrong and obnoxious. At one time I had to struggle against it deliberately. Now there is no need to struggle, because I am happy to be what I am: an American whose intellectual interests center on the study of French literature. The artifice of using a foreign language in America has to be made into an art, a performing art without its ever altering one's basic personality formed by all the indigenous influences at work on each individual.

Living in France is the cure to the danger, even if the act of living there brings necessarily considerable sadness. It is a sadness that comes from all our painful approximations to speaking, thinking, feeling like the French. How much better it is to acknowledge the differences, to accept them for self-illumination and for the illumination of the French! My best students—some of them were there in France in 1966—were tempted to adopt the traits and attitudes that appealed to them. I saw them being tempted, and then I saw the sadness that came to them from knowing there was something wrong or impossible from such a transaction. All Americans have to adjust to America, but that adjustment is carried on from birth, day by day, without its ever appearing to be an adjustment. The adjustment to the study of French, and even to living in France, is of another kind. It is a conscious appropriation of values and knowledge and experiences that will help to situate an American with respect to his own country and heritage.

On March 22, I had my first encounter with Edouard Dermit. He had already sent me photographs for the book I had written on Cocteau, and we had exchanged letters. His invitation to take lunch with him brought me back, after six years, to the small apartment, 36, rue de Montpensier, in the Palais-Royal. Every detail of my visit with Cocteau, in 1960, was present in me. The housekeeper (not Madeleine, but a younger woman whom Dermit called Simone) showed me into the small salon, decorated in the same red velvet. When he entered, he appeared of course older than in his film roles—Paul in *Les Enfants terribles,* and Cégeste in *Orphée* and *Le Testament d'Orphée*—but I would easily have recognized him. Direct, simple, attentive, and seemingly eager to talk about Jean, he made the meeting memorable for me. First, he showed me, with the pride of a young boy showing his prize toys, photographs of the fresco paintings he did in the new chapel at Fréjus. He copied exactly all the drawings left by Cocteau for this work, and while he was thus engaged, he remained alone for almost a year.

Then he showed me the bedroom of the apartment, which I had not seen on the other visit. Innumerable pictures on the walls, several of which showed Dermit, and posters and mementos. A large rosary hung beside the bed. There was a recent photograph of Dermit and the son of Raymond Rouleau, in a scene from the unsuccessful film *Thomas l'imposteur.* As he talked about this detail and that, I began marvelling at how this man had participated in Cocteau's life, at how he had learned so much of what is in reality literary history. He was already besieged by people writing books and theses, by those preparing exhibits and memorials. Dermit is a painter by vocation, but has done nothing since finishing the frescoes of Fréjus.

He took me to a nearby restaurant (not Le Grand Véfour). He greeted the proprietors and those in charge, with simplicity but with the precision of a man who knows who he is, and who knows that others know who he is. Our table conversation, lasting more than two hours, was illuminating. In great detail, he spoke of Jean's last hours and of his death. Dermit believes Cocteau knew he was dying. He had lost all sensation in his arms and legs. Dermit kept massaging them but to no avail. Finally, when the end came, he said good-bye, and then seemed, without sadness, to turn within himself and focus all his attention on what was coming, on death itself. He quite deliberately shut out the living and concentrated his curiosity on the next event . . . . Dermit spoke of Cocteau's presence at Milly, of feeling he is being guided by him, being protected by him. He is fully aware of all he owes to Cocteau and of all he can do now to preserve his memory.

The days were cold during the month of March, and yet almost every day, I could see the leaves grow on the small chestnut tree in the tiny garden under my window of the Paris-Dinard. Their development was like a valiant fight against the elements. The sap must have been moving through the trunk and the branches, to open those fresh green leaves. The season would change, and I would soon be away from here, at the other end of France, in the Midi. Strangely enough, with the knowledge that I was going to Saint-Paul, I had been mentally preferring the small Provençal town to Paris, elaborating subconsciously on the advantages of being in a house of my own, over the prison of my hotel room. How easily one finds reasons to do what one wants to do! I kept examining the reasons as they formed in me, and tried to sort out the specious from the valid ones. Paris that year had been very much the past, the past in terms of strong ardent friendships: Henriette Psichari, Eveline Garnier, Jim Kennedy, Alice Coléno, Olivier Revault d'Allonnes. In each of those cases, the past was so rigid that I had not been able to dissociate it from the present. That winter, more than in the past, each of those friends had involved me in his or her family or immediate group of friends, and I had missed some of the closeness of feeling, some of the intimacy of confidence that had once made our relationship more meaningful, more exciting. The fault may well have been mine. The fault may have been in the length of absence, in the heaviness of age. Friendship needs constant improvisation and spontaneity. Let us leave to family relationships the heaviness of routine and habit!

It was not sadness I was trying to describe, it was not a sense of dis-

appointment I was accusing, but rather a sense of settledness, of permanence in sentiment. There was no need to win over, to justify myself, to
explore some unexplored thought. I was depressed by the impossible exertion it would take to know the younger members of those groups I had been
seeing, and who might, under different circumstances, offer me the excitement of discovery and conquest which friendship, in my terms, demands.

Tempestuous, exciting, demoralizing—by what other words could I
describe my friendship with Jim Kennedy, which goes back to my years at
Yale? The brilliance of his mind, his inexhaustible curiosity, the warmth of
his heart, have always dazzled me. With Bill Munn, whose temperament
and tastes are close to my own, Jim has built up a business of consultation
and financial advice, in the penthouse of the New York Times Building,
rue de Caumartin. In 1966 there was a third member: a German lad of
24, Günter, who had spent four years in the Foreign Legion. Günter was an
expert photographer and fast becoming a financial expert. His use of
English was miraculous, and his use of French too. When the four of us
were together, linguistic questions popped up at every moment, in the
midst of our ponderous deliberations concerning the *mores* of the day, the
characteristics of the French and the destiny of France. Jim ruled over us
all, with his candor, his knowledge, and the extraordinary gentleness of his
strength.

One evening in April I was saying good-bye to Gary Woodle, a student
from Colorado (we had just looked at Picasso's memorial figure to Apollinaire in the garden of Saint-Germain-des-Prés, and had admired the moon
over the tower of the church), when he said to me: "I feel you are closing a
chapter of your life—the Paris chapter of March 1966—and tomorrow
when you fly to Nice, a new, carefully planned, carefully organized chapter,
will begin. It will be a new page, a new notebook."

A bit startled by the accuracy of his comment, I blurted out some re-
joinder about his need to discipline his life and stop wasting his time at the
bar Seine or *Old Navy*. He offered to do this, provided I would begin wasting some time in one of those dives he frequented. We both joked, a bit
uneasily, about the proposed plan for self-renewal, and then separated, he
to go back to the *bar Seine*, and I to go back to my room at the Paris-Dinard
and plot out some of the new month's work. His remarks caught me unprepared. Is that the picture I give to friends and students: of a highly organized, disciplined life?

It is a sense of shame, I suppose, that forces me to hide as much as
possible the pattern of my ridiculously departmentalized and timed exis-

[188]

tence. Everything in me admires the opposite kind of life: spontaneous, free, ill-organized, or organized around the impulse of the moment, the life that is perpetual improvisation for the charm and seductiveness of the passing moment. I admire the man who can fall asleep when he is tired, who can eat when he is hungry, and play when he wants exercise and relaxation, and read a book for the enjoyment of reading. I admire the man who is guided by his instincts and bodily needs, who enjoys easy relationships that are not demanding. Perhaps I admire this man because I do not know him, outside of fiction and films. I think of him as the type of man whose desires and whose life are brief . . . .

XVII

Saint-Paul-de-Vence, April 1966   Nice: Atlantic Hôtel
Jean-Marie Le Clézio   Santo Sospir   *Les Paravents*   *fleur
de la Pentecôte*   La Résidence, 1970   Atlantic Hôtel, 1975

When I saw Nice from the airplane, I wanted to be going there rather than to Saint-Paul. All the practical matters of running a small house were still preoccupying me: food to buy and where to buy it, the *butagaz* and how to light it. Saint-Paul has the charm of a town to be visited but not to be lived in. My house (Les Terrasses) was fortunately outside the town, on the road to Vence, high above the road, with a magnificent view. I watched the white doves in the air above the famous hotel La Colombe d'Or, and down below, in the valley, a flock of lambs grazing.

Holy Week, and the tourists were all there, Germans and French, English and American. Things quieted down about 7:00 P.M. I took my evening meal, about 8:00, in La Résidence. Excellent food, well served, in an attractive dining room. Just the *pensionnaires* and myself were there. The owner, who is the mayor of Saint-Paul, Marius Issert, welcomed me because I knew Dr. Alain Lesage, in whose house I was living. Cold and rain made me uncomfortable, and I kept thinking of Nice and the luxury of a hotel, and the proximity of movie houses, bookstores and newspapers, and the American Express on the Promenade des Anglais. My first telephone call in Les Terrasses came from Jean Ferrero, ebullient with new projects for film-making, and who urged me to go to Nice.

La Fondation Maeght at Saint-Paul, high on a hill outside the town, is an impressive structure designed by Sert, in a setting of rare beauty for the

presentation of the works of art in the collection: Giacometti in particular
—who creates his own world wherever a few of his statues are put together
—Miró, Kandinsky, Braque. Giacometti and Braque seemed to be the best
represented. But countless others were there too: Chagall, Picasso, Rouault,
Pollock, Calder.

After three hours spent in Nice on Wednesday of Holy Week, I found
myself discarding reason after reason for staying in Saint-Paul longer than
the month of April. The attractiveness of the city was overwhelming: even
its crowdedness and noise were acceptable. As I walked along the familiar
streets, avenue Jean Médecin, Dubouchage, Victor Hugo, Pastorelli, and
saw again the *points de repère* of four years earlier—Le grand café de
Lyon, the Scotch Tea Room, the Prisunic, the newspaper center near the
Place Masséna—my mind was made up. The Atlantic Hôtel, with The New
Bar, where Gilles Daziano and I used to chat in the evenings of April 1962,
had the best kind of room for my needs.

Holy Saturday was spent for the most part inside my little house of Les
Terrasses. Rain and cold outside, and inside, even greater cold except for
a few feet immediately in front of the small movable heater. I dispatched
all too quickly the writing I had planned to do. Then I invented chores to
fill the hours until dinner at La Résidence, in front of the big open fire,
with the attention of two or three of the waiters. The brother of the owner
of La Résidence kept coming in, looking for things to do, calling out to the
waiters about various small duties they had already performed. Whenever
he felt too keenly the uselessness of his entrances, he went to the fireplace
and poked the logs, usually with disastrous results. I enjoyed the scattered
bits of conversation with the waiters, and at times felt that they, like myself, would prefer a more continuous dialogue.

That Holy Saturday I missed a familiar church because the square-
shaped church at Saint-Paul was still strange to me. I had been thinking
of those pages of Renan when he describes the bells of all the churches in
France going to Rome on Good Friday and returning on Holy Saturday, in
order to ring out the Easter message on Sunday.

At high mass, Easter Sunday, I followed not only the mass itself, but
a microcosm of French traditions and habits. In the first place, the mass
was sung in Latin, as if the two priests in charge, the celebrant and an
older priest who sang the mass and directed the singing of the hymns and
gave out various orders during the service, were determined not to accept
the Church's injunction to say mass in the vernacular. The celebrant was
dignified and reserved in his gold vestments. He gave the sermon, which

was excellent in form and content, strong rhetoric and almost without any of the pious clichés I dread hearing in sermons. The many duties of the other priest, who was, I imagined, the curate, made him appear almost comical at times. The church became filled soon after the beginning of the mass. The front rows were occupied by the children of the parish, whom the priest was constantly prompting and admonishing to speak up or to sing louder. The side pews, resembling tribunals, were occupied by prosperous bourgeois families who sat conspicuously apart from the others and seemed to feel themselves apart. They were different in their dress and behavior. They looked down upon the congregation, quite literally from their raised position in the church, and perhaps symbolically in the distinction of their class. At the other end of the social pattern were the simple white-haired women of the people, dressed in black, intent on their prayers and devotions, and a few young men, poorly dressed, workers obviously, who were there also for religious reasons, and who made their pascal communion reverently and unostentatiously. Against the back wall stood the industrialist from Paris and Roubaix who had befriended me at La Résidence. He and I were, I think, the only representatives of La Résidence and La Colombe d'Or. He was that admirable type of Frenchman—cultivated, refined in manner and bearing, concerned about matters of the mind and the spirit, who is reasonable and magnanimous in his thoughts and actions. He lent me Jacques Borel's Goncourt prize novel, *L'Adoration*, as a kind of testimonial to my interest in French literature, at the end of our first conversation.

At Saint-Paul I visited frequently with Jacques and June Guicharnaud, who were staying at La Colombe d'Or. They were my link with my life at home, with the university world, with literature and especially its professional aspects. It was good to know them better, since our meeting at Yale in September. They told me of the impressive array of celebrities who lived at or visited La Colombe: Prévert, François Périer, Anouilh and his family, Simone Signoret. And I told them about my struggles with the butagaz heater, and about the pleasure I had each evening at La Résidence: an hour spent reading or writing close to the open fire in the dining room, and then the gastronomic delights of the dinner.

As I grew accustomed to my house in Saint-Paul and the waiters and owners of La Résidence, I thought less and less about my life in Paris, about my apartment in Durham, and students and friends there and elsewhere. Oh! it was all there, intact in my memory, and the arrival of a letter was all that was needed for the resurrection of some other life to take place.

[192]

A walk through a city park is more of an adventure, more of a stimulation for me, than a walk in the countryside. The vagaries of mankind have to impinge upon nature for me to find it interesting or even attractive. As I would walk along the road leading from Saint-Paul past the Fondation Maeght, I imagined the heightened sense of attentiveness I would have experienced if I had been walking along La Promenade des Anglais or l'avenue Jean Médecin in Nice.

So, after sixteen days in Saint-Paul, I went to the Atlantic Hôtel in Nice, in search of an atmosphere more in keeping with my nature and habits. The hotel is a *palace*, but not pretentious. I had a good room, *au 4e*, with a view of the sky and mountains. A long table to work on, good lighting, a comfortable bed with table, light and telephone within reach. The large bathroom was closed off from the room. Breakfast in bed was always a treat, and the hot bath before it. The New Bar downstairs was in excellent taste, better than the hotel itself. Outside, in every direction a huge choice of restaurants, snacks, bars, cafés, countless movie houses. The Scotch Tea House was still near the garden by the Promenade des Anglais, and served meals as well as the coffee I liked so much and the scones . . . .

How different I am from the French! My attention is almost totally fixed on words and phrases, on intonations I hear, on grammar I wonder about. I am concentrated, when I am speaking or when I am listening, on precisely those matters the French do not have to heed. As I walk about, I find myself rehearsing the names of objects, or making mental notes to find the French word for some object I cannot name. One day, in Saint-Paul, I picked a wild flower I had noticed growing everywhere, especially on walls. Its color was a light rose, similar to the rose Picasso used for his *saltimbanques*. I had seen the sister of the two men who run La Résidence working one day in her garden, and asked her the name of my flower. She confessed she did not know the real name, but told me people at Saint-Paul call it *la fleur de la Pentecôte*, because it blooms usually at Pentecost.

Nice is, first, a big city, and I wanted that for its animation. And then Nice is a very special kind of city, half-French, half-Italian. Perhaps the presence of the sun and the sea makes the people more amiable. The various groups of foreigners who are there seem contented and more at ease than they might be elsewhere. Perhaps it is because the French in Nice are really Italian, and don't force any particular standards of living or customs on anyone.

Gilles Daziano invited me to his mother's home (L'Oliveraie on the Chemin des Pins) to meet the American contralto Marie Powers. I remembered her dramatic performances of the Menotti operas, *The Medium* and *The Consul*. An exuberant woman who spoke uninterruptedly about her career, her associations with Toscanini, with Lawrence Olivier and Vivian Leigh, and others. Meeting her brought back memories of Chandler Cowles and Katty, and their two sons, Christopher and Matthew. (Chandler was producer of the Menotti operas.) And then a stream of memories connected with Bennington, because it was there I introduced Chandler to Katty.

I had met Henri Giordan four years earlier in Nice and looked forward to seeing him again. He lived twenty-five kilometers away, in Coaraze, and came to Nice on the days he taught two courses in comparative literature at the faculté des lettres. When he entered the Atlantic— I was waiting for him downstairs—I was amazed at how little he had changed: the same slight build, the same quiet voice with the slight Midi accent, the classical Latin features, more Italian than French, the same seriousness of thought with the intermittent flashes of humor. But after an hour of talk, I realized he had changed in being more sure of himself, more aware of the wiles of the world, more determined to make his way, with the knowledge that he had something to offer. I had remembered that he had skipped the *agréga-tion* to become immediately a candidate for the doctorate. Soon after we separated in May 1962, he went to Italy where he spent two years writing his complementary dissertation on "Romain Rolland et l'Italie." This thesis had been defended and had just appeared in print. Then a third year, at Nice, with no job. In 1965 he was appointed *chargé de cours* and was teaching for the first time.

Henri Giordan was for me an example of the French intellectual, sound in his methods of research, fully aware of human frailty as well as of human goodness, erudite in his special field of study—Bernanos, in Henri's case— a believer in the real values, and distrustful of human motives . . . . All this seemed apparent to me as he spoke of the difficulty in documentation he had, especially in preparing the second volume of Bernanos in the Pléiade edition, of which he was editor. There were problems with the Bernanos family, and with the priest at Saint Jacques-du-Haut-Pas in Paris, who was in charge of the letters and manuscripts.

I dined one evening in early May in my favorite Nice restaurant, La Poularde, with Odette Bornand who, four years earlier, had introduced me to the restaurant. On certain days all of Nice seems to be a movie set, and all of its colorful inhabitants in costume, ready to play *les figurants* in some film. That evening, at the table next to ours, Albert Finney sat down with a group of friends. I did not recognize him at first, but when he began to eat, it was then I saw "Tom Jones." His casualness of manner and the way he ate—with fingers, fists and avidity, brought me back to that extraordinary scene in the film. The Festival de Cannes was to begin in three days. The studio of La Victorine, in Nice, is used more and more by American producers as well as French. The histrionic part of me reacts with delight to the encounters and spectacles in Nice. Everyone around me is either playing a role or soliciting a role to play.

Day by day, class by class, as I have tried to teach French literature to American students at home—to classes of girls at Bennington, to classes of boys at Yale, to my mixed classes at Duke—I have composed for myself, certainly more than for my students, a picture of France, an understanding of the French, notions concerning the power and originality of certain texts, conclusions concerning the prevalence of certain ideas. I dwell upon these matters not only in the classroom but during many of the hours when I am alone. In France, when I am at a considerable distance from my students and my classroom, it is impossible for me to determine which process has been the stronger in my life: the process by which I have studied objectively French writers and tried to teach them, or the far more subtle process by which France has fashioned me, has permeated all of my thought and my reactions, and made me into a strange being neither French nor American, but something half-way between.

Whenever I felt momentary disappointment or irritation in Paris or Saint-Paul or Nice, I knew it was because the France I was touching and hearing did not correspond exactly to the France I have created in myself. My France is the country of my vision that has been developed through the years by my study of French books, by my dreams about them, by the sound of the French language which I listen to as reverently as I would a cantata of Bach, and which I try to imitate. My France is a land I have created out of the mind of Valéry and certain pages of Proust, out of a sonnet of Mallarmé and an essay of Montaigne.

Sometimes it is the beauty of a single work that is able to radiate an effulgence within me. All my basic traits were formed in and by New England: its people, its climate, its churches, by the city of Boston, by the history of Concord and the writers who once lived there, by the ruggedness of the Maine coast, by Harvard where I studied, by Yale where I taught, and by Bennington where I led my fullest life in terms of the arts, by my schooling in Brookline, by my long association with Austin Warren, who has the purest Yankee spirit I have known . . . . And yet, and yet, there is another story to my life, another version, which began at the age of twelve with my first French lessons, which every year since then has overshadowed the first, or merged with it so closely that one now is indistinguishable from the other.

Throughout my years of teaching, the most difficult kind of student to help has been the gifted writer who chafes under the strictures of the classroom, under the assignments of papers to write, and examinations to prepare, who believes he does not want to be a critic, and who is certain he wants to be a creative writer. When the student—and this is true for Bennington and Yale and Duke—does turn out a good critical essay, he or she will worry that if an equal amount of consistent diligent effort had gone into creative composition, that would be more to the point. The complaints are all real and justified: one writes to please a teacher; by analyzing a novel, one kills it or kills the enjoyment of it; graduate school means endless meticulous erudition and a still more dramatic need to please the professors. Where is there a congenial stimulating community where literature is discussed? Does any college, any university provide this?

When the questions come straight at me, I try to answer . . . . It is true, Shakespeare never took graduate courses. But James Joyce did, and Samuel Beckett did. If you do go to graduate school and teach afterwards, there is no absolute rule saying you will have to become a scholar in the traditional sense. Robert Penn Warren did not, Howard Nemerov did not, and these men, Mr. Warren at Yale, and Mr. Nemerov at Washington University, continued teaching and writing. The writing of course papers should not preclude other kinds of writing. You say you are drained of time and energy for real writing, when you are really making excuses for laziness. There is no such thing as a literary community, not even in such a congenial atmosphere as Bennington or Harvard Square or Saint Germain-des-Prés. The writer is a lonely man. He has to be. It is better for him not to talk about his writing or about the writing of his contemporaries. If you knew them, you would be sickened by the so-called literary groups in Greenwich Village or San Francisco or Paris or London. To be a writer means precisely to avoid such groups and to learn to live deeply within oneself. It means contemplating and understanding your own life, no matter how limited and monotonous and prosaic it seems to have been. It means reading a book, not for pleasure in the ordinary sense, but for learning more about mankind outside of your own life and in a language that enobles the human spirit. It means being grateful for every pain in your body, for every lack in your life, for every bruise a friend or a foe gives you, for every heartache and every disappointment in love. You are a writer, and it is out of such experiences as these that you will write your books.

During my fourth week in Nice two encounters occurred, of literary importance to me. No, that is not right. I said "literary" because of their obvious relationship with literature, with my courses, and even with the writing I was engaged in at that moment. Their importance was more personal and more sentimental than the word "literary" would imply.

The first of these encounters was with Jean-Marie Le Clézio and his young wife. I had written to him, principally because of Nice, because I was rediscovering Nice through his book *Le Déluge,* and because I was using his themes in the conclusion of my book on violence. He answered me promptly, and by correspondence we arranged to meet at my hotel. In the course of our conversation, much of which was about his relationship with Nice, he dwelt on the solitude of his life there, on even the ostracism he felt his appearance accounted for. He seemed neither Latin nor *méridional,* and he accentuated this in dressing like a young American and in behaving like a timid young American. I kept feeling that his timidity, rather than his physical appearance, explained his ostracism. His wife was a Polish girl, extremely attentive to every remark about her husband's work. She too was an intellectual and was preparing a dissertation in comparative literature, but at the Sorbonne rather than at Nice. Le Clézio still planned to write his thesis on Lautréamont.

At the beginning of our conversation, in The New Bar, where all three of us took fruit juices, Le Clézio said he had read an article by me on Michaux. I said he must be mistaken because I could not remember any such article. He kept coming back to this, and when he said it had appeared in *Quarterly Review of Literature,* I gave in, but still believed he confused me with someone else. After the first difficult moments, I enjoyed talking with these two young people. Le Clézio's timidity lessened, and his wife's, which had been a mild shyness, appropriated, I suppose, to resemble her husband's, disappeared completely.

The year before, they had gone to the United States, rented an auto and driven from coast to coast. Arizona pleased them the most. Le Clézio's first book, *Le Procès-Verbal,* was published by Atheneum but attracted little attention. I was glad to hear *Le Déluge* would be translated by Richard Howard. To fulfill his military service, Le Clézio was going to Bangkok for two years to teach French!

As the minutes passed, a curious experience took place for me. I began confusing Jean-Marie Le Clézio, seated opposite me on one of the low red divans of The New Bar, with his character François Besson in *Le Déluge*. Autobiography is so strong in the novel that I began to realize the confusion did not matter.

The second of those "literary" encounters was an evening visit to the villa Santo Sospir, home of Mme Francine Weisweiller, in Saint-Jean-Cap-Ferrat. The day before, Edouard Dermit had called me and identified himself by the name "Doudou." In Paris he had promised I would meet Mme Weisweiller and see the Cocteau decorations. Her chauffeur picked me up at nine-thirty. That was the time agreed upon, and I had imagined, with my American sense of dinner hours, that it was an after-dinner invitation. But no! I had been invited for dinner without knowing it. I sat at the right of Mme Weisweiller and watched the small group eat a far more delicious dinner than I had just eaten at my hotel at seven-thirty! Doudou had met me at the door and introduced me to Mme Weisweiller and to his fiancée and to another lady who had been Cocteau's nurse during his last illness.

All the coversation was about "Jean." Doudou had beautifully prepared this visit because from the start Mme Weisweiller accepted me as a friend of Cocteau and she therefore knew the details that would interest me. Doudou was present almost every minute. The other two ladies were fairly silent and disappeared after dinner. All the walls and every ceiling had been decorated by Cocteau. All the figures of his repertory are there at Santo Sospir, and Cocteau's writing often accompanies the figures. The ceiling over the stairway going down to Jean's bedroom has a flash of red. Since his death no one has slept in his bed. Between his bedroom and Dermit's is a large bathroom. I went into every corner and examined each depiction of Narcissus and the unicorn and Orpheus. Outside, in the garden leading into the atelier where the three of them used to work in peace—Jean and Doudou and Francine—I watched the flashing of Saint-Jean-Cap-Ferrat's lighthouse, as Mme Weisweiller picked me a rose, and Doudou picked me an hibiscus, in memory of *Le Testament d'Orphée*.

I could tell from the Paris newspapers that the brief series of performances at Barrault's Odéon of Genet's *Les Paravents* was over. From all accounts of the unprejudiced reviewers, the production was extraordinarily fine. The interference of a small segment of the public at a few of the performances did little harm. So, the April–May performances of *Les Paravents* in 1966 became part of theater history in France. The scurrilous diatribe of Gabriel Marcel (*Nouvelles littéraires*) had been dissipated by serious articles of several far more qualified critics. In Nice I was sorry to have missed seeing the play. As I read the reviews, I remembered my readings of the text when it first appeared in print. The reviews stressed the quality of the production, the acting, the courage of Barrault in putting on such a long difficult play, the dramatic intensity of some of the scenes, but they did not emphasize the total value of the text as text, in its relationship to all the work of Jean Genet. Underneath their praise I sensed their reservations about the text, and I recalled my own sense of disappointment with it, and tried to explain to myself the reasons for my disappointment.

Has it to do with what Genet has become in French literature? He is certainly no longer the *poète maudit*. He was that at the beginning, with greater reason than the nineteenth-century *maudits*. His existence had been more wretched than theirs, his mind probably more profound, and the themes of his writing more bold. One after the other, his early books accentuated his position of *auteur maudit*. And few critics dared to write about him. I learned about the existence of Genet in an early brilliant article by Eleanor Clark in *Partisan Review*. For ten years, culminating with the *Saint Genet* of Sartre, and Roger Blin's production of *Les Nègres*, Genet remained the example of an artist offending the public who ostracized him. The power of literature was renewed for me when I first read *Miracle de la rose*, with its intensity of a tragic existence combined with its rich metaphorical language. When a few illustrious personnages in France pleaded Genet's cause, a change took place which I suppose was inevitable. The *poète maudit* became accepted and classified. The 600-page treatise of Sartre made Genet into an existentialist who could be studied as one studies the passion of Phèdre.

The very society that had called Jean Genet a criminal now calls him a writer, a man of letters, and although, if I understand correctly, he does not accept invitations to be lionized, and continues to live in secret and apart from society, something has happened to his writing in such a work as *Les Paravents*. Oh! there are evidences in it of the freshness and power of the first books, of *Pompes funèbres* and *Journal d'un voleur*. All the plays seem to me inferior to the novels, and it is perhaps because of the constricting demands of playwriting, of the knowledge that a public will be present. The prisoner-novelist wrote because he needed to, because he suffered and had to find some way to express his suffering. The playwright is not the same kind of sufferer. He is a professional, and that is the difference. Rimbaud, fortunately, stopped writing before becoming a professional man of letters. But Genet, at twenty, was much more the *maudit* than Rimbaud at twenty. His major books were written thirty years ago before the experience of evil became something of a literary experience. The greatest threat to a pure artist is the power that society has to assimilate him and make him into one of its ornaments.

In the history of Genet's life, society accepted him as the *maudit* and encouraged him to continue writing about his revolt. The final sign of encouragement was the Blin production of *Les Paravents*, in the state-subsidized theater of the Odéon, with such actors as Barrault, Maria Casarès and Madeleine Renaud. It was a curious twist to the history of the *poètes maudits*: one of them, and the most authentic, writing for the bourgeois public of a national theater.

Jean Ferrero, my most faithful correspondent of Nice, drove me one evening along *la grande corniche* to points outside the city from which we had spectacular views of Villefranche, Eze, Saint-Jean-Cap-Ferrat. Along the walls bordering the road I noticed the wildflower, called in Saint-Paul *la fleur de la Pentecôte*. When I asked Jean what he called it, he replied without hesitation, "*la valériane.*" That is the name of a medicinal plant, and I wondered if he was right.

A few days later Harry Moore invited me to accompany him on a long auto trip to Le Lavandou. Between Fréjus and Le Lavandou there are three villas in which Richard Aldington lived at various times, and Harry, who is writing a biography of Aldington, wanted to photograph the villas. Thanks to an intelligent chauffeur, Ange Raimondi, and his 1966 Mercedes, we found two of the villas. Raimondi, who had been chauffeur for Bess and Harry Truman and for Jack Warner, was so well informed that I asked him if he knew the name of the flower that was still blooming in profusion. Without hesitation he replied that it is called *lilas sauvage*. That gave me three names: *fleur de la Pentecôte, valériane, lilas sauvage*. My next move was to pick one of the flowers and ask a pharmacist in Nice if he knew the name!

On the auto trip we stopped at Fréjus, which I had never seen, and passed through other towns I remembered from other visits: Saint Raphaël, Saint-Tropez, Théoule, la Napoule. I wanted this time to see the Hôtel du Cap, at Antibes, in memory of Fitzgerald and the scenes in *Tender Is the Night*, one of my favorite books. Harry was more than willing, and Ange drove us up to the hotel, a majestic building, with a garden that goes down to Eden Rock and the sea. In the novel, Fitzgerald has the sea come up to the hotel, a deliberately altered detail. Then in Cannes, we drove past the Majestic, the Carleton, the estate of La Begum, widow of Aga Kahn, who is buried in the garden, according to Ange. (Later, I learned that the name *Ange* is common in Corsica.)

A young Scotsman, James McNab, who teaches French in Virginia, and whom I had met recently after a lecture in Hollins College, wrote me not to fail to visit Le Peillon while I was in Nice. I had asked a few people about it, but no one seemed to know much about it. Then one Sunday in June, Claude and Monique Bontoux, from Romans, called on me and asked me to suggest a trip in their car. We decided on Le Peillon, which turned out to be a tiny village perched on the top of a mountain peak about twenty-five kilometers inland from Nice. A winding narrow road led up to it. The village, a kind of Saint-Paul in miniature, seemed deserted. We literally saw no inhabitants except a man and a woman running a restaurant, who served us coffee. The man told us that Pierre Brasseur had bought a house in Le Peillon and spent part of each year there.

On our way down from the town Claude stopped the car in order to photograph Le Peillon, and I profited from this to pick the flower whose name I was still hunting for. The next day, in Nice, I showed the flower to a pharmacist, who said he did not know the name, and then showed it to a second pharmacist, who recognized it and called it *la saponaire*. The word was in my *Larousse de poche*. Was this really the name?

If alone for dinner, I had the habit of going to L'Arc-en-ciel, a good restaurant for my particular régime. Twice I sat opposite a professor of philosophy from a lycée in Saint-Etienne, who was in Nice doing research on Nietzsche. (Nietzsche once lived and wrote in Nice.) This gentleman, Robert Sabatier (homonym of the poet and novelist I once met at Alain Bosquet's), asked me about "my" research, and I told him of my search for the flower's name, and my relief at the pharmacist's revelation of *la saponaire*. "Don't trust pharmacists," he said. "During the war my mother-in-law used *saponaire* which grows in our garden, in place of soap. It makes water soapy. I don't believe it is the flower you describe. I will send you a specimen from Saint-Etienne next week!" And so, the little saga continued.

Jean-Marie Le Clézio and his wife took dinner with me one night in June at La Poularde. On the whole, a better meeting than the first one. Marcel Normand had reserved a corner table for us, had placed on it three coral-colored roses, and told me proudly that it was the table always occupied in the past by Marcel Pagnol. The Le Clézios arrived promptly. Every twenty minutes or so, Jean-Marie left the table to telephone to Jean-Luc Godard at the Négresco, but never succeeded in finding him in. Jean-Marie was interested in making a film. That time it was he who questioned me: on American painters, on the meaning of "a happening," on black writers in America, on teacher-student relationships. America was the theme of the evening. "I don't understand why anyone comes from America to France," he said, "and particularly to this part of France, when he has such magnificient scenery at home."

They walked back with me to my hotel, and it was then Le Clézio spoke of his interest in teaching, of his beliefs that teaching methods would have to change in France, and appropriate some of the American characteristics. He spoke at length of the French teacher's fear of being *chahuté*, of the deliberate antagonism students show to some teachers. He asked very pointedly whether such conditions prevailed in America. By this time, when we were saying good-bye in front of the Atlantic, Le Clézio's voice and manner had become strong and forceful. A few hours previously, at La Poularde, his wife explained to me he was suffering from liver trouble, *une crise de foie*. "Il est très fragile," she would say, as he left to telephone to Godard.

The last few days in Nice, just a week before my departure for home, I received the first letters about my Rimbaud volumes, just published by the University of Chicago Press. Neal Oxenhandler's letter was the first, in which he recalled my training him to recite *Mémoire*. Austin's letter came the next morning, in which he said the first book on Rimbaud was his favorite book of mine. But out of the goodness of his heart, Austin had said the same thing about three or four other books! Ben Belitt's letter moved me the most, because he, perhaps best, knew all the personal disappointments and struggles that had gone on while I had been trying to write those books. He recalled the early Bennington years when I taught him Rimbaud and urged him to translate Rimbaud, the beginning of a series of remarkable translations he had done: Lorca, Jimenez, Guillén, Neruda. I felt it was worthwhile to have done those Rimbaud books just to have Ben wish me, at the end of his letter, "all the *luxe, calme et volupté* that Nice can give to the guardian of her country's poets." To those testimonials coming from America, I would add a sentence from Jean Ferrero who told me that by dint of writing books, I talked like one: "Tu parles comme un livre à force d'en écrire."

My arrival at Saint-Paul-de-Vence (La Résidence, annexe No. 6) in June 1970 instigated a predictable wave of memories associated with the enchanting spot, with Nice and Provence, with France and French letters, with rooms in which I had lived and their varying degrees of comfort. The first night when I fell asleep instantly, it was not only from the fatigue of twenty-four hours in airplanes and airports—Raleigh-Durham, La Guardia, Kennedy, Lisbon, Barcelona, Côte d'Azur-Nice—it was from the heaviness of crowded memories that would not be quiet and emerge in orderly fashion.

I suppose the upsurge of memory is going on continuously in me but without the clear focus of that first night's vision. The concatenation of events, the relatedness of everything left me marvelling at the unity presiding over a life. Is this unity the result of chance, of returning occurrences that only seem to provide a plan? I wonder . . . .

Fifteen years earlier André Penchinat drove me to Saint-Paul from Nîmes. It was summertime. He had said to me, while showing me his grandfather's leather factory: "What would you like to see in Provence? I will take you anywhere you want to go."

I said, "Let's go to the Matisse chapel in Vence." That was what he wanted: a specific suggestion, and he immediately consulted a road map, restaurants between Nîmes and Vence, and visiting hours of the chapel. He chose a Thursday afternoon for the chapel visit, and Saint-Paul de Vence for lunch. We went to Saint-Paul Thursday at noon and looked at both terrace restaurants, La Colombe d'Or on the left, and La Résidence on the right. A few men were playing *boules* in the small square between the two hotels. The view from La Résidence seemed more striking and we chose it. We chose *poulet de bresse*. (That was the day I learned the name of Bresse.)

My plans for the summer of 1970 included a week at La Résidence—a week of rest and relaxation before a more vigorous life in Nice would begin. In a letter I had mentioned the hotel and the town to one of my first students at Bennington, Jamie Porter Gagarin, in the hope that after thirty years we might meet in France. Her third son, Nicholas, had just published his first novel and graduated from Harvard. But our dates did not coincide. She and her husband had stopped at La Résidence before me, had loved it, and prepared my coming by ordering wine for my first meal. So, I was received almost like a *vedette*, put in a beautiful room in the annex and told by at least four people in the dining room my first evening that the wine had been ordered by Madame Gagarin!

Marius Issert, proprietor of the hotel and mayor of Saint-Paul, greeted me every day. Yves Montand played *pétanque* with Issert and other village celebrities every afternoon on the square. Simone Signoret was often visible. Vanessa Redgrave was talking with her one day. Marguerite and Aimé Maeght's museum was spreading. They were building a small theater at the foundation. I walked there every day just to see the Giacometti statues.

My room was a delight. It had a balcony covered with red roses. The door-window opening on to the balcony looked out on the town to the church tower. I saw it clearly from my bed where I worked early mornings. On the right side of my bed was another window which looked out on the valley in the direction of the sea. No bed I ever slept in gave me such spectacular views as No. 6 of La Résidence. I heard each hour strike in the church tower, and late afternoons I heard the clinking of the *boules*. With the Issert brothers and the waiters my conversation was about *la pétanque* and gastronomy. I was reliving the repertory of all the French dishes I ever knew.

Each day I enjoyed looking at the landscape and the immediate elements of nature I could touch: the tall cypresses, the olive and fig trees, the orchard—oranges, lemons, grapefruit—the wild flower (*fleur de la Pentecôte*), whose rose color still reminded me of Picasso's *saltimbanques*. As I watched the swallows, I thought of Chateaubriand's *martinets*, which he called his only companions at Combourg.

But I had collected into my hands all the nets of my past, and in between my stints of walking, writing and reading, I tightened the nets and saw the past: the early visits to France, my early efforts to understand the French and their ways, my life-long efforts to appropriate French as a second language and express all my thoughts in it, as well as to understand all the texts to which I was drawn—the erratic flow of Montaigne's sentences, the ellipses of Mallarmé, the sexual overtones of Villon and the blatant sexual language of Genet, the resounding periods of Bossuet and the metaphysical probing of Scève, the explosions of Rimbaud and the pure joy in writing that Stendhal demonstrates for me. France had been a love-affair for me, scandalous in a way, fervent and uninterrupted.

With Jamie Porter and Marne-Lloyd Smith and Kathleen Harriman and Honora Kammerer, in their fourth year at Bennington, we read together the entire novel of Proust. It was my fourth year too at the college, and the group had stayed with me all those years. The girls guided themselves and me through Proust. I have been teaching Proust ever since then, every two or three years, and I cringe when I think how bad, how innocuous that first time through must have been.

So, even in that little town of Provence, my Bennington past became present thanks to Jamie Porter's greeting. My Yale past was there too because of the Guicharnauds, and my North Carolina life too was there because of Alain Lesage's house, les Terrasses. The bond that joined so many friends from the past and the present in my consciousness in Saint-Paul was certain texts of French authors I tried to teach falteringly at the beginning of my career and which I was still teaching . . . in 1970.

My eighth visit in May 1975 to the Atlantic Hôtel in Nice was almost like coming home. I had known from correspondence with the hotel that the management had changed, but the management was three or four dark-suited half-invisible men who moved back and forth between the inner office and the outer desk where Louis, the concierge I had known for ten or twelve years, handed me the key to my familiar room 428, which I had always occupied in the past.

I was prepared to find everything the same because of my professed preference for rediscovery over new discoveries and new explorations. Yes, I had returned to Nice as to an old haunt in order to relive old experiences and recultivate old obsessions. So, on that morning of my arrival, I ignored the new management of the Atlantic and chatted with Louis who summarized the essential news for me: the continuing flow of tourists from Australia, Japan and Argentina, and the changes by death of a few of the permanent residents in the hotel I had known. The aged English colonel and his wife had died within a month of one another. Louis and I agreed that this was just as it should have been.

My other English friend, Mr. Clifford Knight, a resident of the hotel

[205]

for well over twenty years, was still there, Louis assured me. I would see him as usual just before noon in the armchair in the vast lobby where every day he waited impatiently for twelve o'clock and lunch. He was eighty-six now, Louis told me, but seemed in good health and still walked straight as a stick. Louis was certain that Monsieur Knight planned to live in the hotel until his death. His wife had died in the hotel a few years prior to my first visit, and Louis felt assured that he would be "in charge" in the event of Mr. Knight's own death, as he had been at the time of Mrs. Knight's death.

With those first words of Louis, everything fell into place for me because he and Mr. Knight knew the hotel best and had been there the longest. Each one for twenty-five years. In 1950 Louis, at the age of fourteen, was engaged as chasseur. And in the same year Mr. Knight took up hotel residence with his wife. Louis was thirty-nine and the head concierge in charge of chasseurs, and Mr. Knight, at eighty-six, a widower, was waiting, with total equanimity, as far as I could tell, for death.

The first two days passed peacefully, perhaps too peacefully. I rediscovered everything: the Florian restaurant around the corner from the Atlantic, where the proprietor and his wife greeted me as if I had been there a week ago rather than two years ago, la Promenade des Anglais, the American Express, the boulevard Victor Hugo still serenely beautiful with its plane trees and elegant façades, the avenue Jean-Médecin with its crowds, stores and sidewalk markets. I remembered how twelve years earlier, when I first came to Nice, it was called "avenue de la Victoire."

Oh! I was enjoying the beauty of it all: the animation of the streets, *Nice-Matin*, the sea, the bathers, the clear morning sky, the flower market, the Place Masséna and the Galerie Lafayette. But was I deluding myself? Was there a twinge of regret in me that I had not gone elsewhere, where all would have been new? Would this regret grow during the next two or three weeks and finally depress me and suppress the pleasure I was finding and indeed had counted on finding in my rediscovery of Nice?

My conversation with Mr. Knight every day between eleven-thirty and noon was approximately the same as I had remembered it from previous visits. We greeted one another by exchanging reading material. He handed me the *Daily Telegraph*, and I handed over to him my copy of *L'Express* or the Simémon volume I had read the night before. The *Daily Telegraph* seemed to me so obnoxiously conservative that I limited my reading to the book reviews and omitted the daily attacks on Harold Wilson and the United States. Mr. Knight and I always exchanged some comments about the hotel, the way it was being run by the new management, and the loss of the former director, M. Rouvier, now heading a large hotel in Marseille. But we agreed that the continuing members of the staff (only the chasseurs had changed) seemed to maintain the Atlantic in its state of well-run hotel.

From the comfortable chairs where we sat, we could see the full sweep of the lobby, wide and airy and sensibly decorated. We could see Louis at the desk and two chasseurs near the front door. From time to time one of the restaurant waiters crossed the lobby from the dining room in order to enter The New Bar. It was often Olivier who each morning at seven-thirty brought me my breakfast tray. He was recognizable, even at some distance, because of his stooped shoulders. On my third day, we watched him cross the lobby carrying a tray into The New Bar, and Mr. Knight turned to me with the words: "Does Olivier still serve your floor in the morning?" I assured him that Olivier still came each morning exactly on the dot of seven-thirty, as he had always done in the past. In fact, Olivier, the first person I saw each morning, was one of the strong signs of the past continuing in the present, one of the agreeable rediscoveries of my former life in Nice. And I had already learned that François would, as in other years, bring the breakfast tray on Olivier's day off.

As the hour of noon approached, Mr. Knight and I relinquished topics touching on the côte d'Azur—the places we enjoyed the most, such as Saint-Jean-Cap-Ferrat and la Turbie, and the various museums, such as La Fondation Maeght—in order to contemplate lunch and what we might possibly be eating for lunch in just a few minutes: he in the large dining room of the hotel, and I in the Florian, around the corner from the hotel on the rue Alphonse Karr.

In one of our first conversations, I asked Mr. Knight if he remembered the shooting of a film in the hotel a few years before—*Nuit américaine* (*Day for Night*)—of Truffaut, which I had seen in the new Plaza theater in Chapel Hill, North Carolina. I had attended the film because I am a fan of Truffaut and had not known that some of the film was shot in "my" Nice hotel. What a delight to see Nice in far-off North Carolina, the façade of the hotel, the lobby, the stairway, a familar blue vase, and Truffaut, who played himself directing a film in the film, sleeping in my bed in room 428! They had given him for the scene in which he has a nightmare an elegant dark blue bed quilt which I had never had in 428 . . . . Mr. Knight grumbled at my question and declared that everyone had been inconvenienced during those days and nights of the shooting. No, he had not seen the film, and didn't believe it was very good. He paid no attention to my comments, geared to praise Truffaut's art and his film made in La Victorine studio in Nice and the Atlantic Hôtel.

As in the past, the first hours of each day were the best, and I decided that I had returned to Nice for them. I got up at six each morning just when the sky was beginning to turn white. I could see a good deal of the sky from my window on the fourth floor. My room was on the back of the hotel and therefore faced Cimiez, the high section of the city, and the huge hotel where Queen Victoria used to stay, and beyond it, the beginning of the lower Alps (les Alpilles). After a hot bath in my very deep tub, I did some bending exercises and jogging in place in front of the open window, as I watched the sky turn blue. Then back to bed with my writing pad and notes for a few hours of writing that absorbs and torments me every morning, wherever I am, in Nice or in Durham, North Carolina.

I tried always to get some bit of writing done or at least started, before Olivier knocked on the door at seven-thirty. As that hour approached each morning, I would begin listening for the knock and the immediate opening of the door. There was no need for Olivier to wait for my "entrez." He knew, after all those years and all those mornings, that I would be propped up in bed writing and clearing away books and papers for the tray to be placed on my lap. Yes, this was one of my favorite rediscoveries in Nice: Olivier's punctuality, his amiable manner, and the delicious café-au-lait and croissants accompanying my copy of *Nice-Matin*.

This year Olivier appeared a bit older to me, and his back a bit more bent over. He seemed pleased I had returned once again to Nice and to room 428. This he mentioned on the first two or three mornings. His polite cheerful manner was unchanged. I had always noticed his freshly ironed white jacket and liked to think that mine was the first room he came to at the beginning of his day. Our conversation was always brief but cordial. I often tried to tell him about the courage to work that his café-au-lait gave me each morning, and he would try to encourage me not to work when on vacation.

It was, I believe, the fourth morning that I varied our exchange of words. Feebly, instinctively, I was doubtless trying to modify the routines of my Nice existence. When the tray was deposited on my lap, and I had checked the items—especially the copy of *Nice-Matin*, and when the smell of strong coffee first reached me, I heard myself say suddenly, without having planned to say it: "Olivier, were you born here in Nice? Have you lived here all your life?"

He had already reached the foot of the bed, and turned to look at me . . .

somewhat quizically. "You don't know who I am, Monsieur?" Olivier's voice had a slight intonation of suspicion and doubt.

"No, I don't. I have never asked you this before, and never asked about you downstairs." Already I was thinking that I should not have varied my usual morning conversation.

Olivier paused on his way out of the room, straightened his back, and articulated very clearly his next words: "I am an illegitimate son of the Russian prince who assassinated Rasputin." My amazement at this revelation blocked my own words, and Olivier eased the moment by reminding me, just before he left the room, that Nice, after the revolution, was an important center for White Russians.

To my shame (because it revealed a doubt), I checked later in the day, with Louis and Mr. Knight, on the veracity of the story, and found that Olivier had not in the least exaggerated the story of his birth. My sense of surprise lasted throughout the day and began effacing my faint disappointment at reliving in Nice only the familiar experiences and encouraging only what was predictable. A slightly new dimension existed for me in the Atlantic Hôtel. Olivier, the most modest of men, was attached to history, and yet would continue to perform his daily tasks, as he had in the past, with total simplicity and ease, as if nothing unusual characterized him or the clients he served.

Conclusion

Each day is one of consciousness and . . . conscience. Each day—the same pattern with an infinite number of variations in the timing of awareness or . . . consciousness. The body, first, becomes aware of the life it holds, of the life it is, perhaps. And then that life, that sense of living, becomes aware that it is centered on conscience. There the complexity begins, as conscience unfolds in flash after flash of relatedness to history, family, morality, the physical universe and all the metaphysical ambitions that plague us. Yes, the third term, for which the other two are preparatory, is the revelation that conscience—daily, inevitable and providential—is God. Not only conscience itself, but the still point in the center of everything and the outstretched arms of the Father.

The daily activity of conscience seems to be the undeclared and often unwaged war against the organized lies of politics—on all levels: friendships, university life, national and international politics. Defeat comes—almost daily—because of our belief that the "structures" of our life, even if contaminated with falseness, have to be maintained. Otherwise, where would we go? whom would we see? what would we do?

We keep asking in various forms the same question. What is this self, this ego that is our reality? Is it a being outside of which we lay siege, or is it a being we inhabit? After all is said, the precept that goes beyond all others in significance, and which we would do well to repeat each day, is "My kingdom is not of this world." Intuitions concerning this truth overwhelm us unpredictably—in the supernatural tranquility of night, in the strong scent of flowering linden trees, in the ochre-rose walls of Roman streets. At such moments as those of beauty or simply of awareness, we ask: does God depend on us to become himself?

There is no arrival in life, no coming to the shore (which is the meaning

[210]

of the verb "to arrive"). In all that we do, in all of those actions we call human, there is a greater element of chance than there is of decision or decisiveness. After a sentimental crisis, such as the death of a close friend, I live with greater negligence. (Montaigne wrote this after the death of La Boétie: "j'ai vécu plus négligemment.") I pay less attention to history, which has never really attracted me because it is so laden with falsehood and dogmatism. I allow my thoughts to wander, without a guide, without a companion. The dispersal of my thoughts shocks me at times. Nothing endures—not even the thought I had this morning.

The mass of thoughts that accumulate through the day and that form by evening a hopeless confusion give over at last to the beauty of the morning. We are saved by the pastoral, by the sun either visible or invisible as it illuminates a tree in the clearing of a forest or on the edge of a city park. A landscape existing before us suddenly exists for us, and the vision we have of it at the beginning of a day strengthens our heart and blots out the nightmares.

For the believer and the nonbeliever, exterior nature does provide a view of life where there is a sense of order and purpose. By occupying a place in nature, he discovers a correspondence between the cosmos and his own human nature. Whenever that correspondence begins to fade, I find myself asking how I can restore a communion with nature. Why do I lose contact with it? Is it because of some original flaw in me? Some primitive alienation? What is the conflict between civilization and man? Is it perhaps the loss of contact with nature? Rightfully nature suspects civilization. The pastoral, of all literary forms, is the one that always brings out our basic conflicts: the spirt of man and his body, spiritual and physical love, altruism and egoism. It is forever the contrast between the idyll (man in nature) and the actual world.

I have always resented my attraction to society and to worldliness in its various forms, and yet I am fascinated by them. The most telling account I know of this complex of resentment and fascination is Gide's *L'Immoraliste*, which I would willingly place among the ten greatest novels. Great not only in the structure and composition of the *récit*, but great especially in the analysis it provides of Michel's malady. He falls ill because of his alienation from the natural instincts of his body. In a word, he has cut himself off from nature. His body, thus subjugated, has become his enemy: "un ennemi nombreux, actif." His cure begins in the African sunlight, in his new vision of natural life. There he begins to throw off the weight of study and science, and discover the old Adam of the first garden in himself.

Later, in Greece and in Sicily, especially in Siracusa, home of Theocritus, his pastoral obsessions develop. All the stages of his experience lead him to his encounter with Ménalque, who indoctrinates him on the secretive and even mystical forces of sensations. Ménalque's principal doctrine is in the hope that every instinct as it unfolds will eradicate all the things it had brought with it. "Que chaque instant emporte tout ce qu'il avait apporté."

The Gidian-Michel as he moved into and through the various landscapes of Africa, Switzerland, Italy, Normandy, sought a correspondence between his character and the landscape. The absence of a correspondence, when that was the case, was always the source of a *malaise*, a malady, a disease, an anxiety—that kind of *angoisse* later studied by Sartre and Camus, and which is always related to the possibility or the impossibility of man's freedom.

Through the years French literature has become a form of nature with which I have established a "correspondence" or perhaps a "connivance." It is a domain, rich, limitless, where my thinking appears to me more free than in other domains, and where I have the impression that my thinking grows in stability. In other regions my thinking is evasive and misguided. It is there clouded with so many misgivings and hesitations that I often find myself raising doubts both metaphysical and physical: am I at the twilight of an evening or is it dawn? is it the end of a life or the beginning? ... At such moments I turn to French poems I have memorized and recite them to channel my thoughts back into a stable mold: passages from *Le Cygne* of Baudelaire, "Andromaque, je pense à vous"; *Mémoire* of Rimbaud, with its violent outbreak, "et lui comme mille anges blancs"; Mallarmé's sonnet on the sun suicide, "Victorieusement fui le suicide beau."

The words of the French writers, the phrases they have created, the images of the poets, the analyses of concepts—all of these have formed a language—and more than a language—by which I have learned to live day by day, year by year. As I rediscover and rehearse them, a strong sensation of light floods me—the diffused summer sunlight at noon—when Pasiphae left the palace to join the bull on the Cretan field.

Index